POSTCARD HISTORY SERIES

Middletown

On the Front Cover: For many years, the crossroads of Main Street and Third Street (Central Avenue) were the center of the community's business section. By the time this postcard was published, the business community was moving eastward along Third Street. (Courtesy of Roger L. Miller.)

On the Back Cover: South School's tall towers became a prominent landmark. Built in 1871 as Union School, the city's first high school was on the third floor, while the younger grades were housed on the two lower floors. The school served well as a refuge during the 1913 flood. (Courtesy of George C. Crout Collection, Middletown Public Library.)

POSTCARD HISTORY SERIES

Middletown

David C. Clendenin and Roger L. Miller

ARCADIA PUBLISHING

ISBN 978-0-7385-8866-7

Published by Arcadia Publishing
Charleston, South Carolina

Printed in the United States of America

Library of Congress Control Number: 2011932826

For all general information contact Arcadia Publishing at:
Telephone 843-853-2070
Fax 843-853-0044
E-mail sales@arcadiapublishing.com
For customer service and orders:
Toll-Free 1-888-313-2665

Visit us on the Internet at www.arcadiapublishing.com

This little book is dedicated in memory of the late George C. Crout, who willingly shared his knowledge and experience and guided us and others interested in the area's history

Contents

ACKNOWLEDGMENTS

For some time, the authors of this book have discussed putting it together and highlighting some of the many postcards that have been produced since the end of the 19th century to the start of the 21st century. These postcards detail the history of Middletown, Ohio, in many ways. The authors' interest in Middletown's history came about because of the activities of the late George C. Crout, who, among other things, was an educator, historian, and writer. His support, help, and encouragement provided the authors the opportunity to learn of Middletown's great past and to hopefully be able to share some of it with future generations. Crout left a wonderful collection pertaining to the area's local history to the Middletown Public Library. The authors have made much use of it.

The postcards used in this book have come from several different places. Unless otherwise noted, all postcards appear courtesy of coauthor David C. Clendenin. Since there are so many of them, his images will not be individually identified. A few have come from the George C. Crout Collection or the Middletown Historical Collection, both of which are held by the Middletown Public Library. Others are from Roger L. Miller's personal collection, while the Middletown Convention and Visitors Bureau published some of the newer ones. Postcards from these collections will be properly identified.

Many people have been involved in the production of this book: identified and unidentified photographers of the images; Doug Bean, director of the Middletown Public Library; and Melissa Basilone and other staff of Arcadia Publishing, who have all made this book possible.

Least of all, we should not forget our wonderful wives, Brenda Clendenin and Penny Miller. They have put up with a lot for this project to be completed. They have typed, read, proofed, and helped rewrite parts of this book.

The authors want to thank all of the people involved—those mentioned here and those who may have been overlooked. We are grateful for your help and want it known that any error in this undertaking is ours.

INTRODUCTION

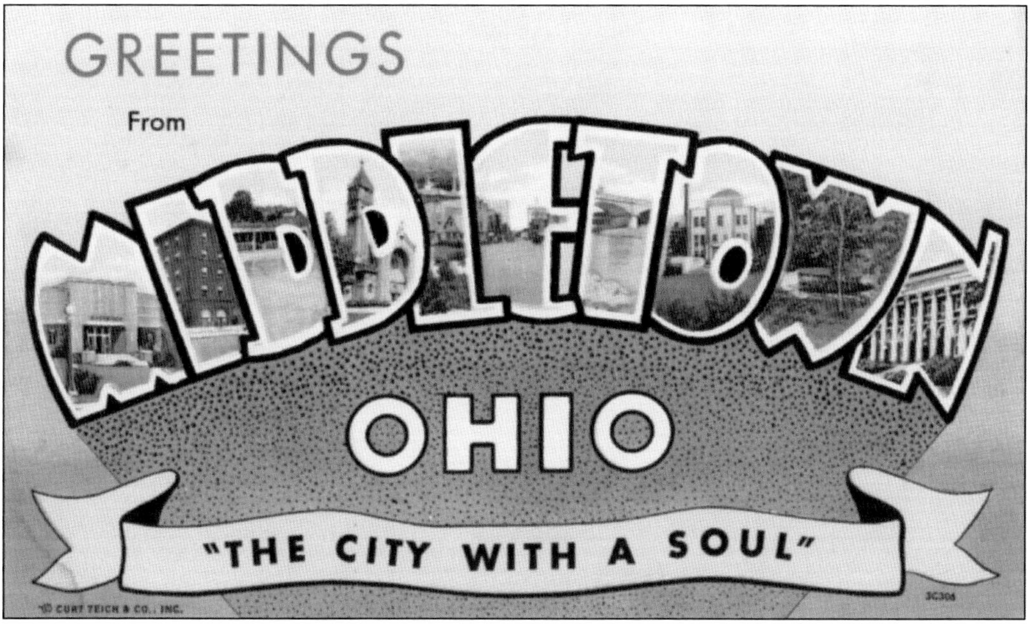

Middletown, Ohio, is "The City With a Soul," according to this c. 1940 postcard. It tells much about Middletown, Ohio. With the help of Middletown's Civic Association, the forerunner of today's branch of the United Way, it became a city with a soul. The Civic Association supported many worthwhile causes. Middletown was an industrial city, but because of its citizens, much else has come to town.

The small pictures, on the postcard, tell a lot about the city. The letter *M* shows the American Rolling Mill Company's Research building. Commonly known as Armco, the company was the first steel manufacturer to have a research section. Opening in 1922, the Hotel Manchester (letter *I*) was an excellent place for travelers to stay at the time, whether on vacation, visiting, or making a business call. Middletown had excellent parks, including Sunset Park (letter *D*), which had a swimming pool. Almost all religious denominations are represented in the city, including St. John the Baptist Catholic Church (letter *D*) and the Episcopal Church of Ascension (letter *L*). There was a very prosperous downtown (letter *E*), with Central Avenue leading west to the bridge (letter *T*) over the Great Miami River. In 1915, when the bridge was opened for traffic, it was the longest concrete viaduct in Ohio. Middletown also had an excellent hospital (letter *O*), and Armco provided a large park—Armco Park (letter *W*)—that anyone could use. Naturally, the largest industry in town was Armco; its office building is seen in the letter *N*. But there is much more to Middletown that can be gleaned from the postcards seen in this book.

One

A Look at Middletown

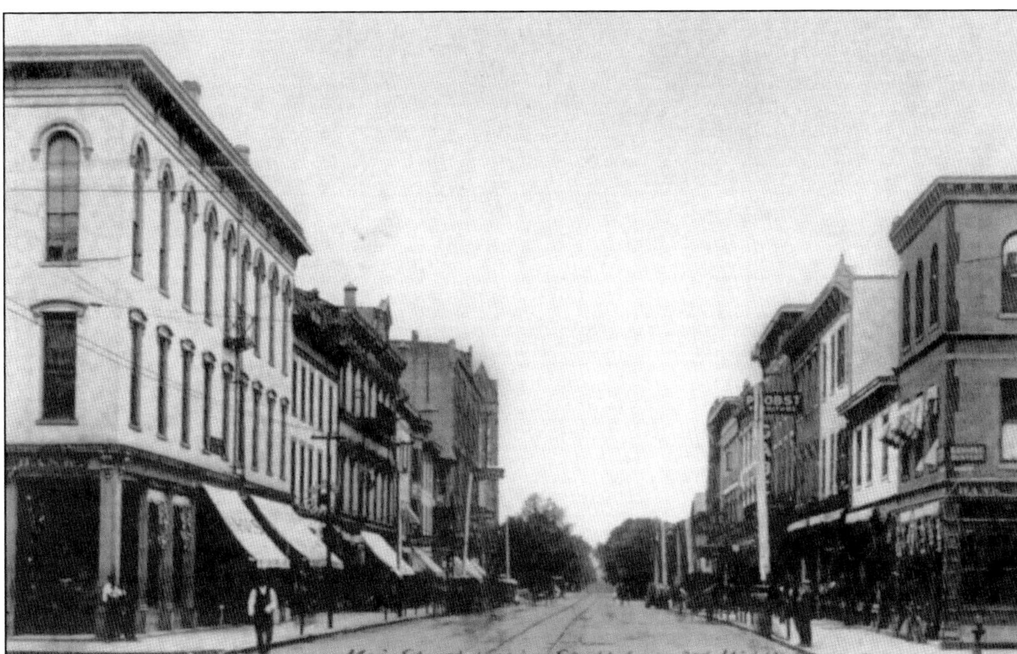

The original plat for Middletown was recorded on November 1, 1802. At that time, the main intersection in the village was the one shown here. The city has grown a lot in its 200-plus years. This corner represents the old downtown business section, which many people can recall. Banks were located on both of the corners seen here.

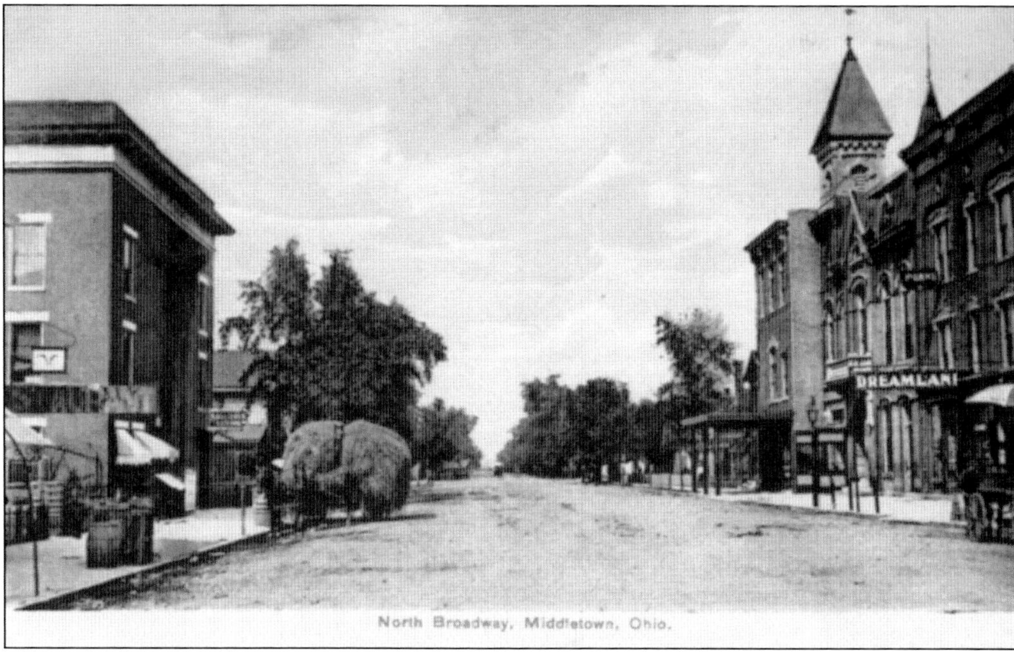

Running parallel to Main Street and a short distance to the east is Broad Street, which was once known as Broadway since it was wide enough to turn a horse and buggy around with ease. The building on the left was the location of the business of A.B. Shetter, who started by selling farm implements. He became one of Middletown's earliest automobile dealers.

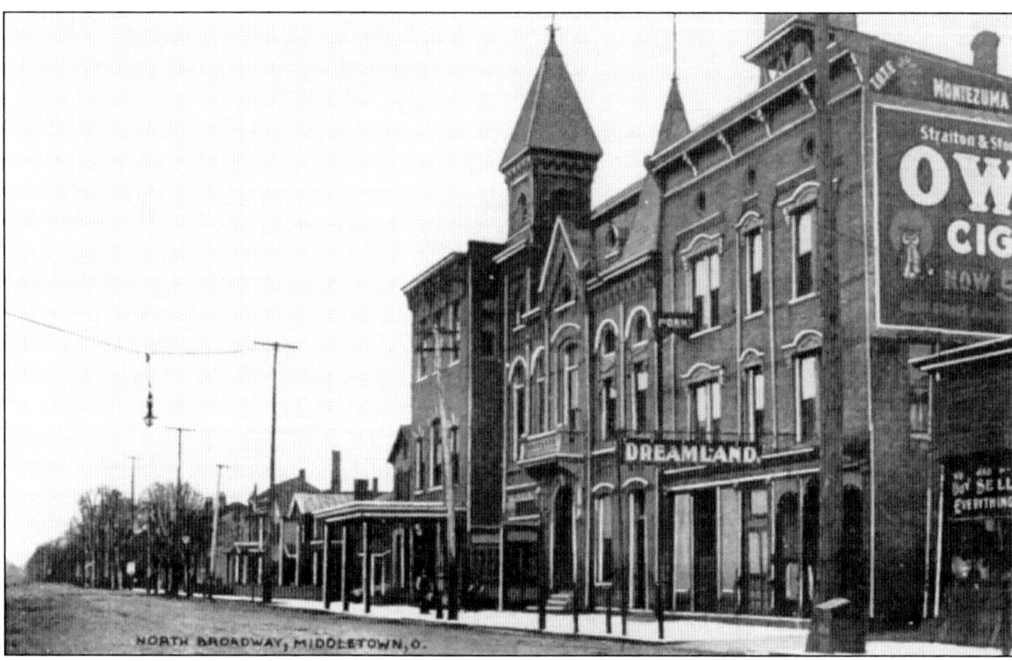

The structure with the tower was the village's first municipal building. Included in it were the mayor's office, the fire department, and the police department.

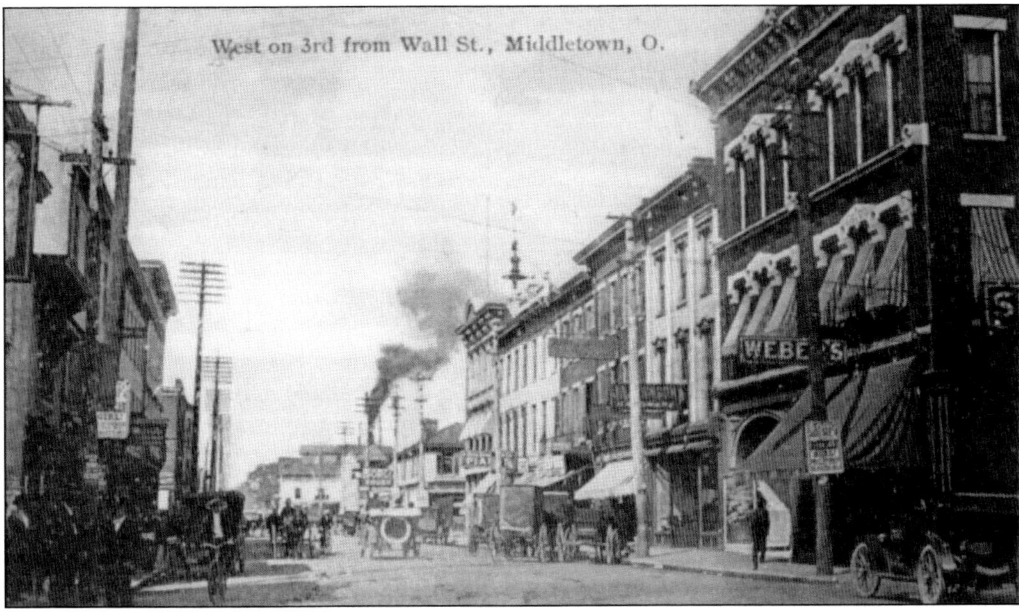

Between Main Street and Broadway on Third Street (Central Avenue) was Wall Street, which was not much more than an alley. This view is looking west from Wall Street toward Main Street and the Great Miami River. This card was postmarked May 18, 1914, with an RPO (Rail Post Office) postmark.

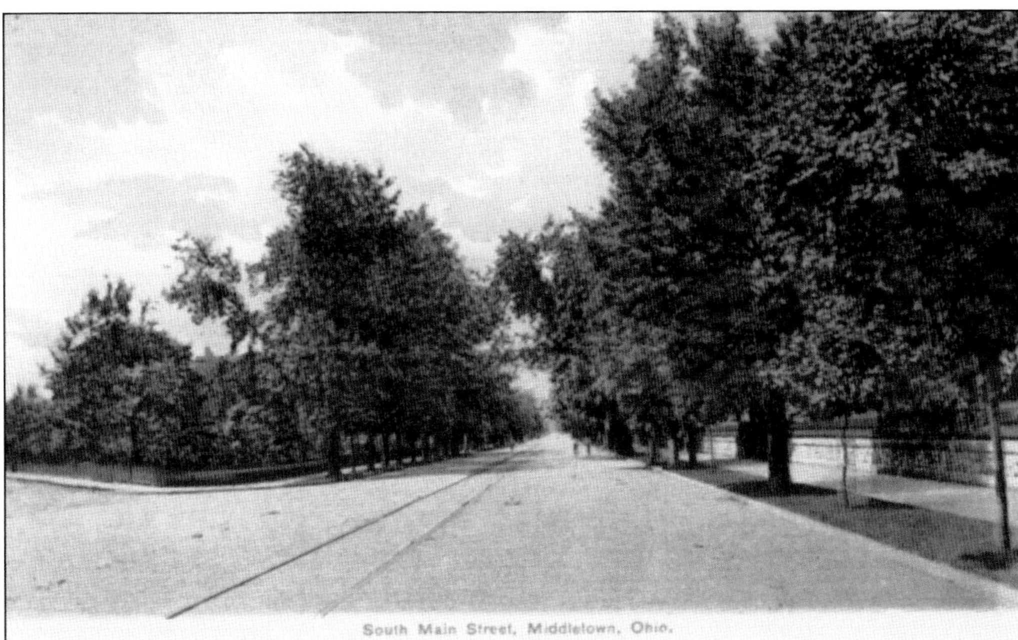

Many of the city's prominent citizens had homes located on South Main Street. In 1897, the electric interurban railroad came to Middletown, providing a new means of transportation to places like Dayton and Hamilton. The street going to the left is Yankee Road.

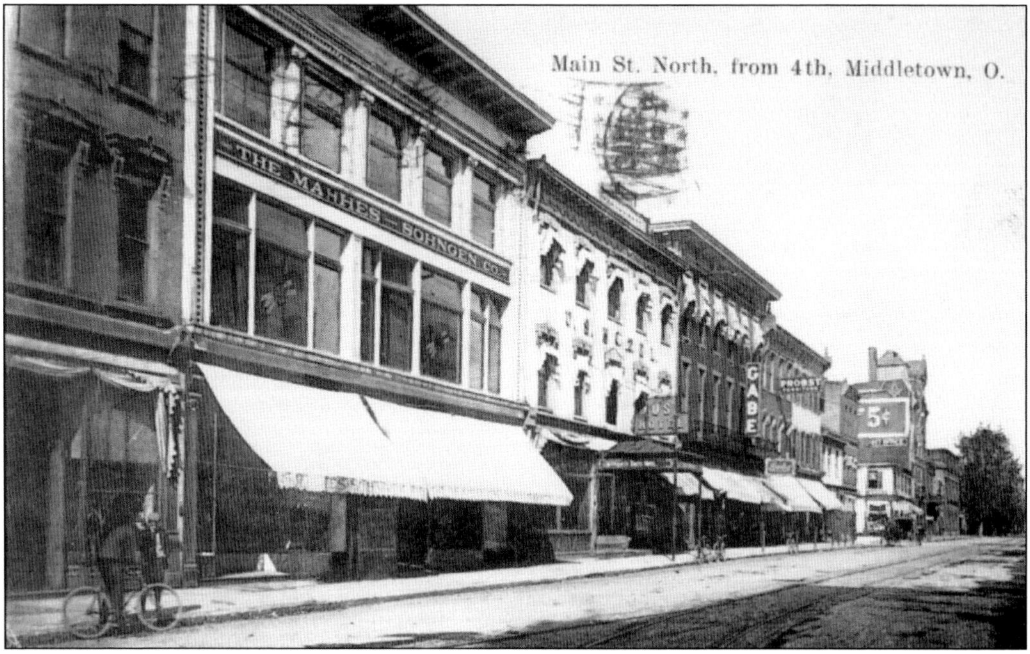

When this postcard was mailed on June 18, 1918, the west side of Main Street was a popular shopping area. The US Hotel was one of several hotels downtown, while the Mathes-Sohngen Company, Gabe, and Probst sold furniture and dry goods.

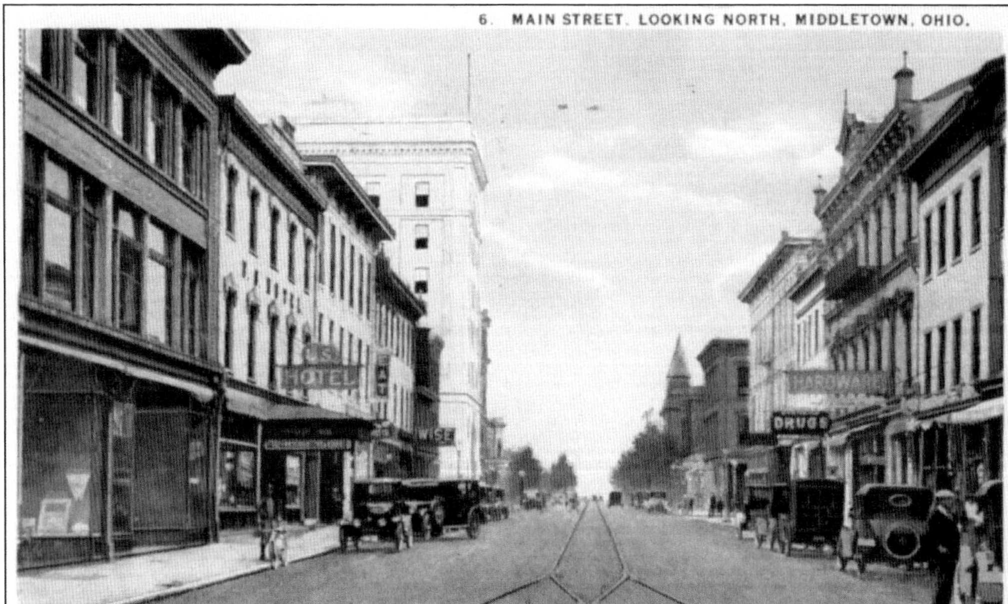

Seven years later, the US Hotel and the Oglesby-Barnitz Bank and Trust Company were still important parts of downtown, but the big change to the area was the building of the First National Bank. Its six floors provided not only a full-service bank but also five floors of offices.

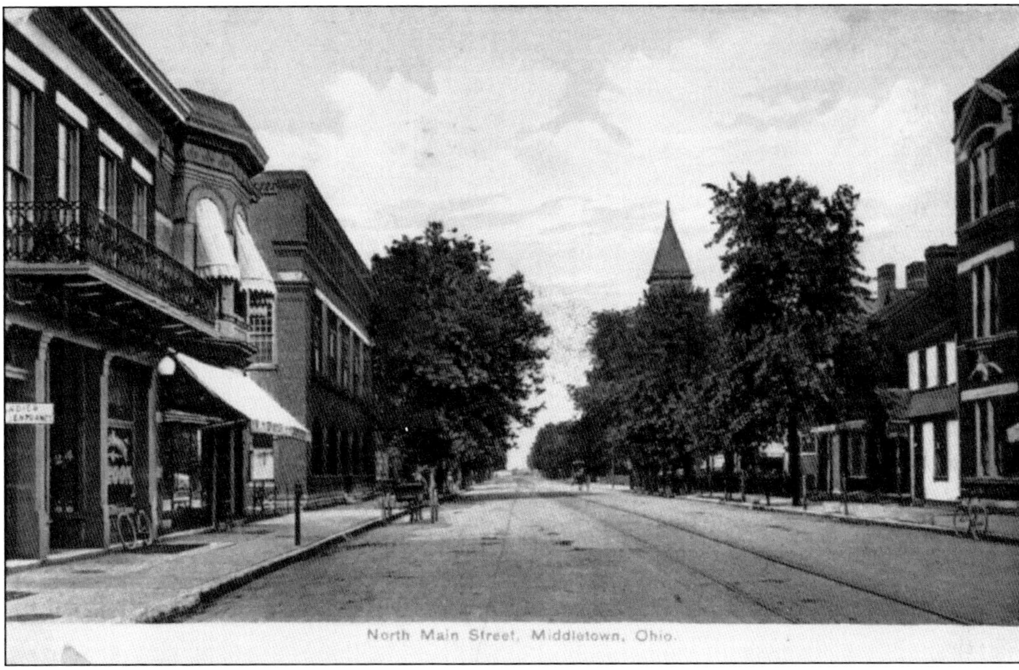

North Main Street started at Third Street. The Tytus Paper Mill is seen on the left. Francis J. Tytus, one of city's early businessmen and industrialists, started it. The electric interurban line passed through downtown on the tracks in the center of the street. North School can be seen in the distance on the right side of the street.

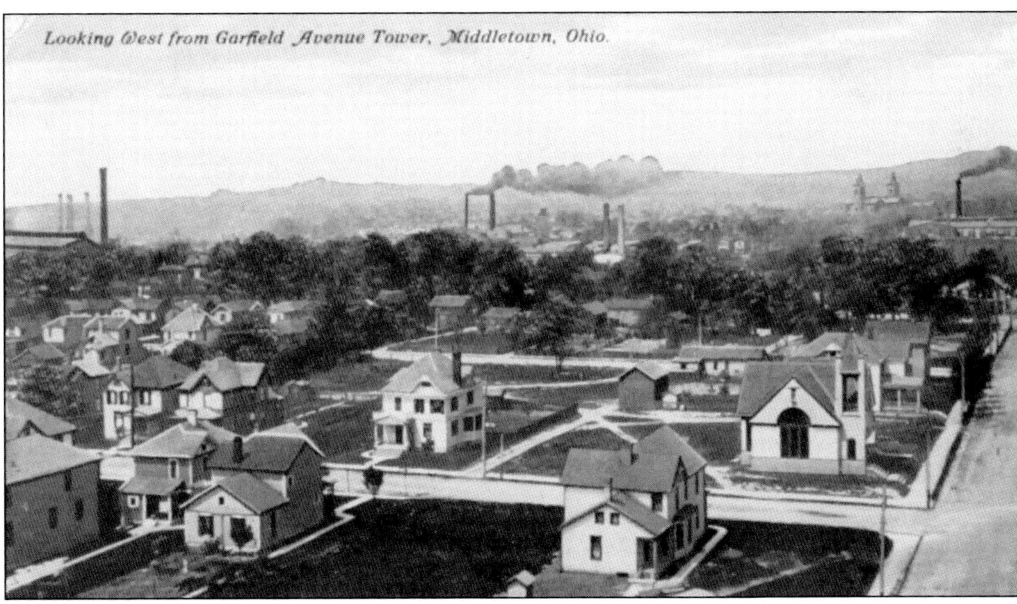

The Garfield Avenue tower was one of two, electric arc-light towers in the city. The little building on the corner was the United Presbyterian Church. On the left is the original American Rolling Mill Company, while several paper mills can be seen in the distance. All were located along the Miami-Erie Canal.

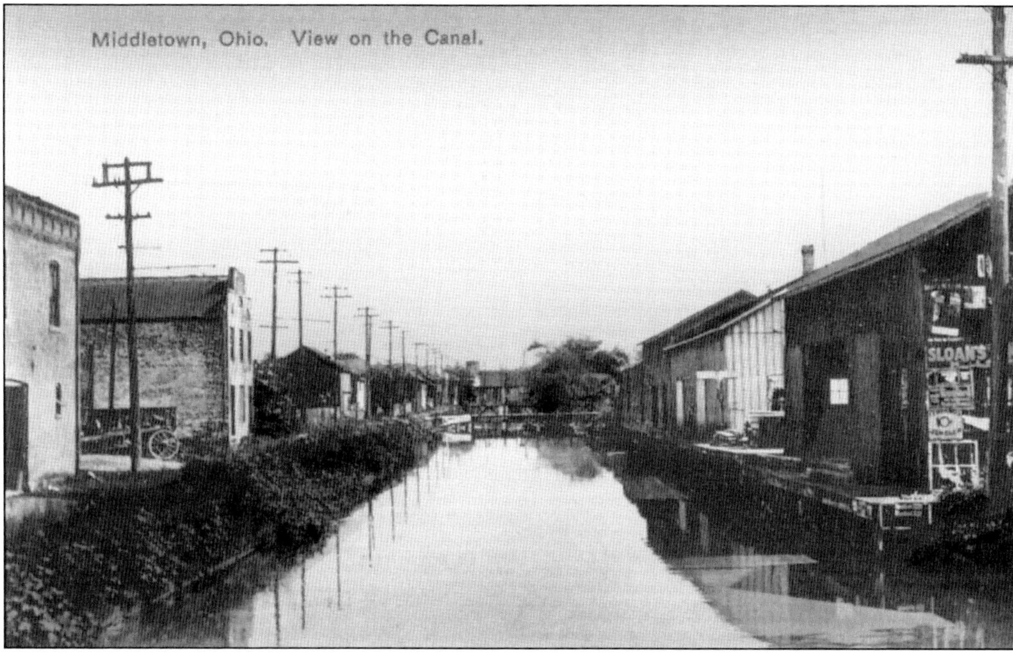

On July 21, 1825, ground breaking for the Miami Canal was held in Middletown. Original plans were to connect Cincinnati and Dayton, but it was later extended to Toledo. It was very important to Middletown's early development. By the early 1900s, when this card was made, the railroads had taken over much of the canal's trade.

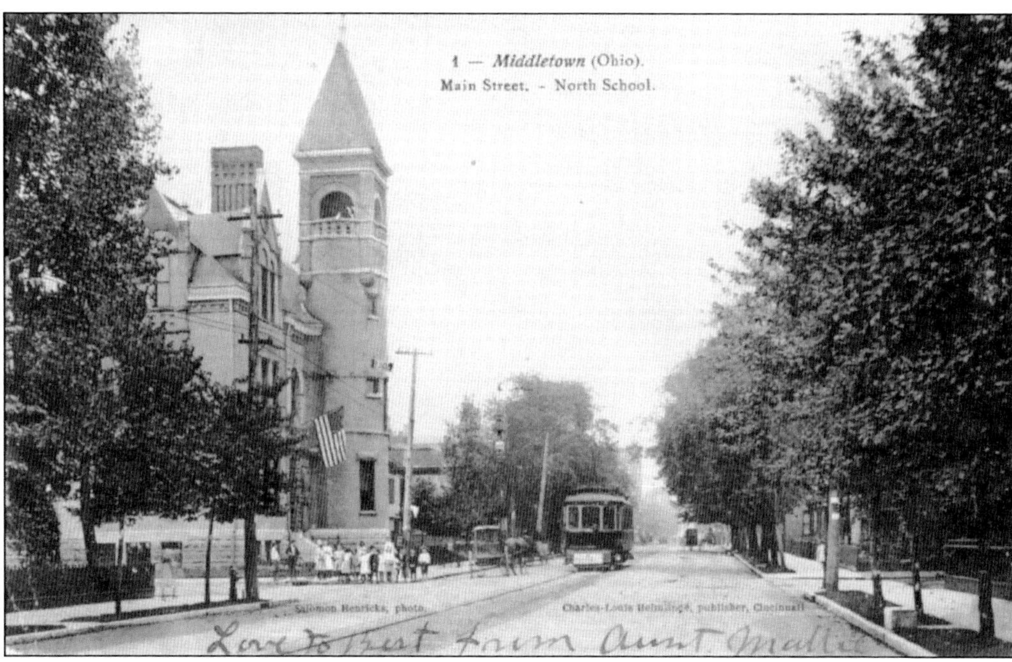

This postcard was postmarked October 28, 1905, and was mailed to Liverpool, England. In this country, it took a penny stamp to mail a card, but this one required two. Opening in 1891, North School was one of four schools in the city. An interurban car is traveling along Main Street.

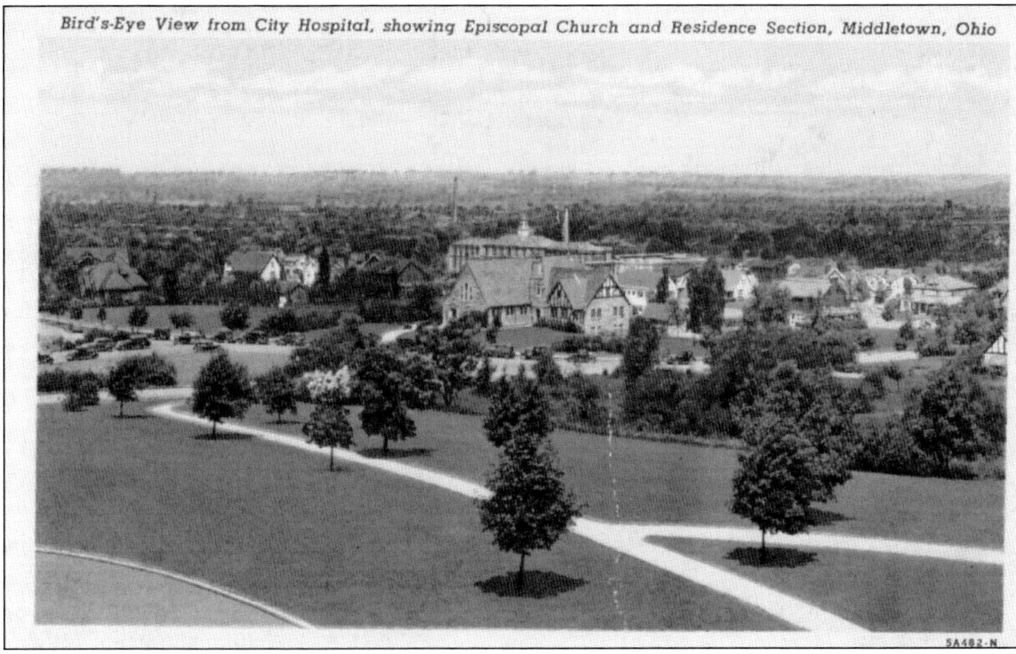

In 1917, Middletown Hospital opened in the east end. It was located on a hill overlooking the city. Several subdivisions, including the Highlands, were later built around the hospital. Constructed in 1929, the Episcopal Church of the Ascension is in the center of this image, which is from the perspective of "hospital hill."

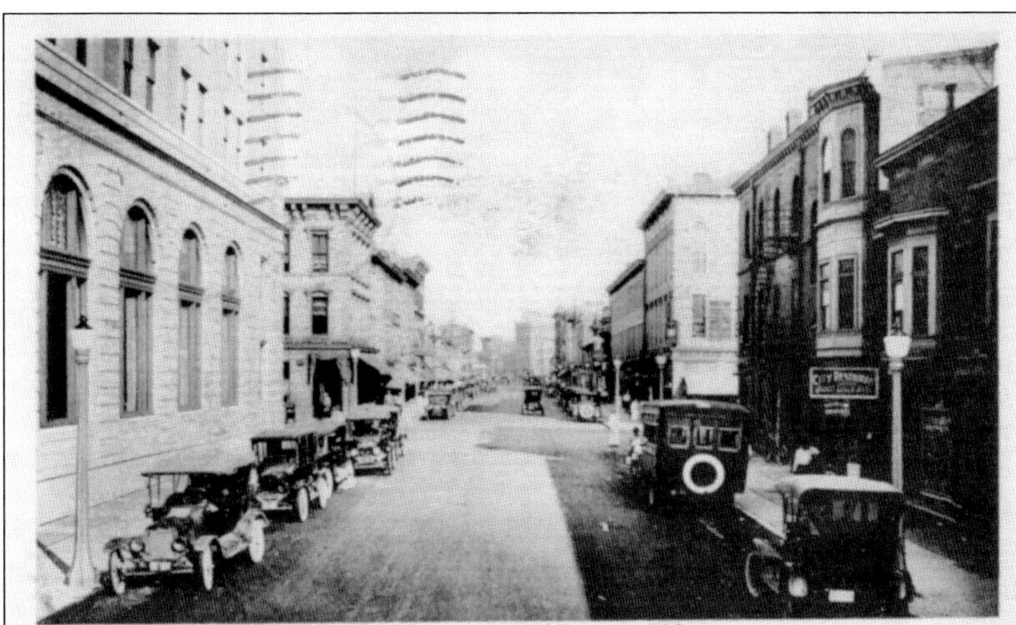

Most of the buildings seen on this card have been replaced with newer ones. One exception is the building on the left, which was built as the First & Merchants National Bank in 1921. The bank has relocated, but the building is often referred to as the First National Bank building. The street is today's Central Avenue.

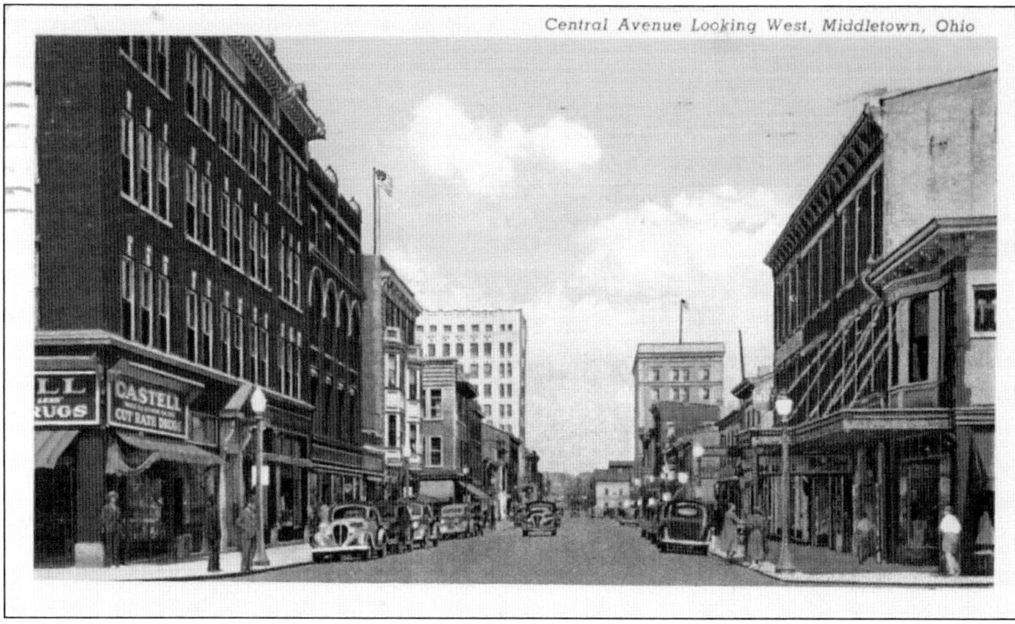

One in a series produced around 1938, this postcard is looking west along Central Avenue from Verity Parkway. During the days of the canal, this was the site of Port Middletown. On the left is the Castell building, which, along with the rest of the block on the south side, was owned by the Sebald family. They made their money in the brewery business. The Gordon Theater is on the right.

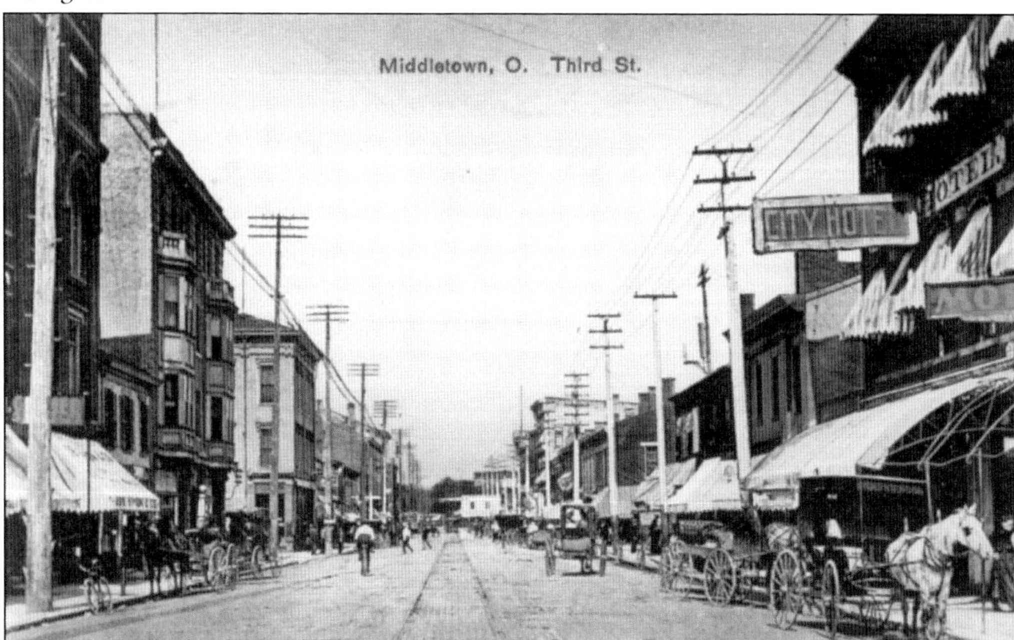

The City Hotel building still stands on Central Avenue. It is one of the oldest buildings in the city. Looking on toward the west, the downtown area is seen as it looked at the turn of the 20th century. The tracks in the center of the street were for a horsecar line that operated between 1879 and 1918.

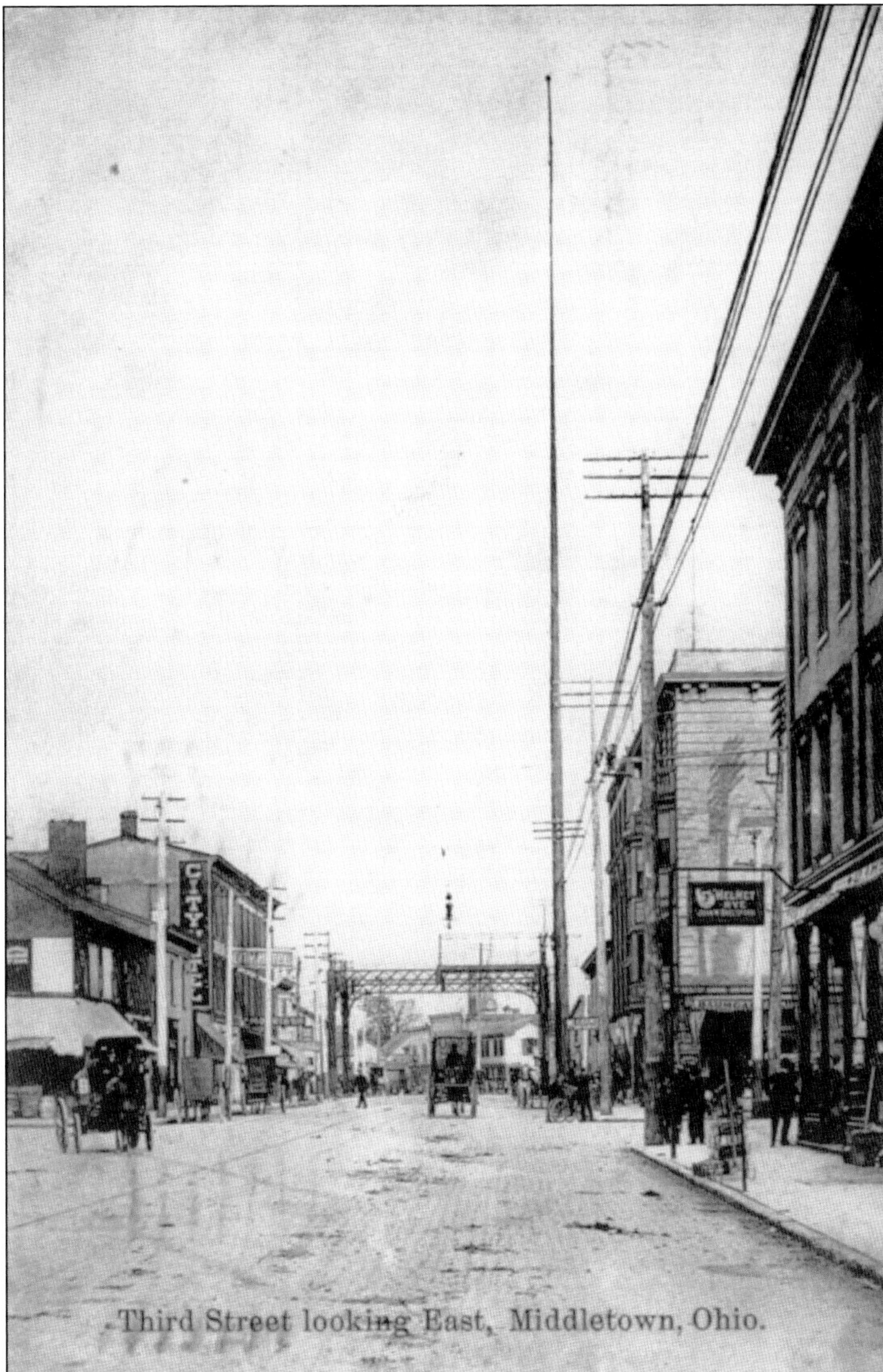

By moving his camera one block west, the photographer was able to take the same scene but from the opposite direction. The sign on City Hotel can still be seen today. In the background is the lift bridge over the Miami-Erie Canal. It was built at the end of the 19th century. The tower carried an arc light that lit up the downtown. It was removed in December 1909.

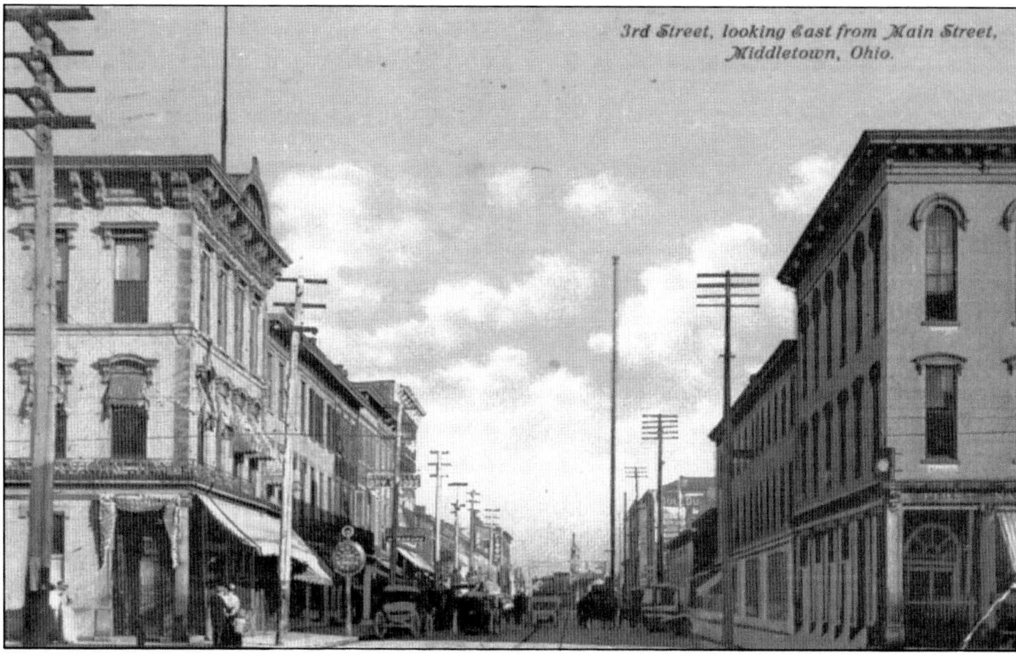

Moving another block to the west and looking east, the photographer captured this scene of Third Street (Central Avenue). All but a few buildings are gone. The buildings on the corners are the First National Bank on the right and Merchants National Bank on the left. Later, they merged together.

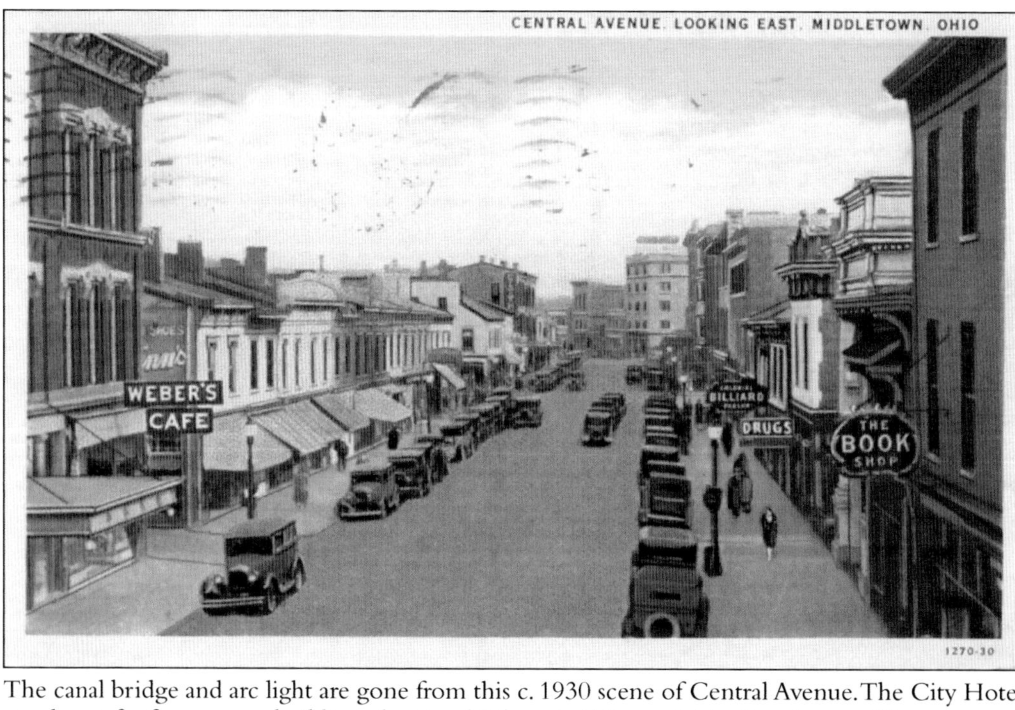

The canal bridge and arc light are gone from this c. 1930 scene of Central Avenue. The City Hotel stands not far from a new building, the Reed-Klopp building, with its five floors of furniture.

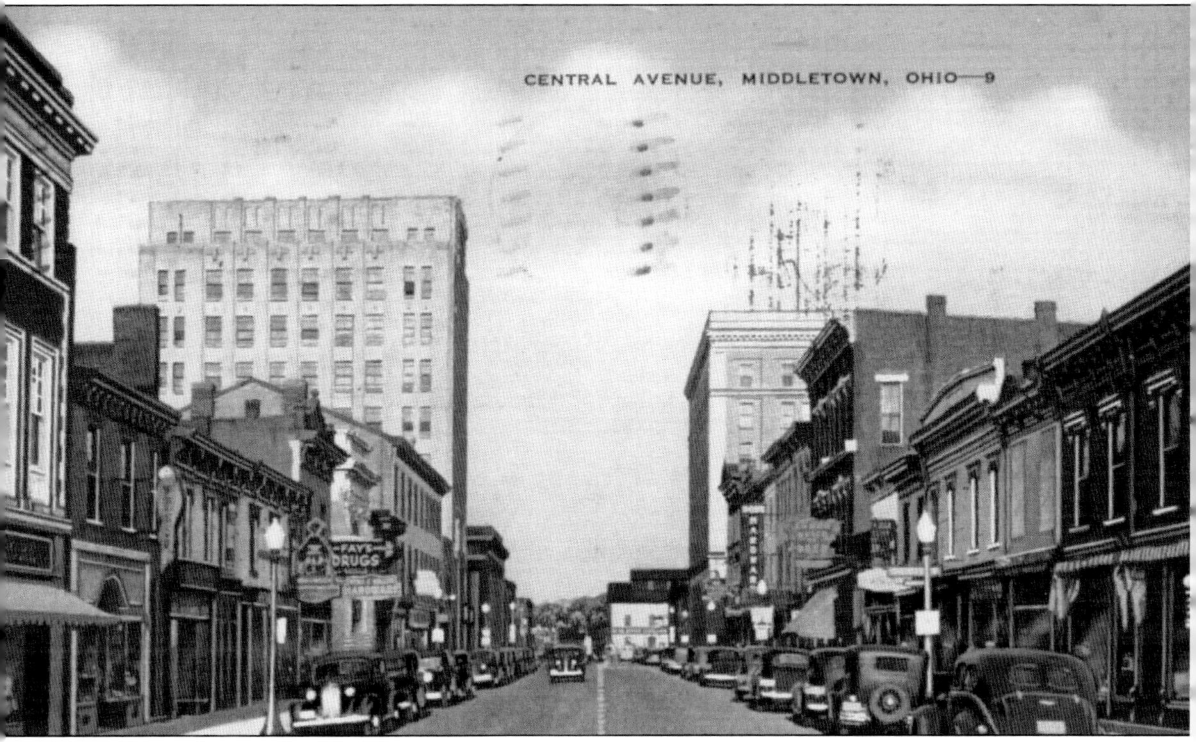

This was postmarked in February 1943, but its scene is several years older than that. It looks west from Broad Street on Central Avenue. The large building on the left was the Middletown Federal Savings and Loan Building, while the First National Bank is on the right. Both buildings still stand and are in use, but both concerns have undergone mergers and have left these sites.

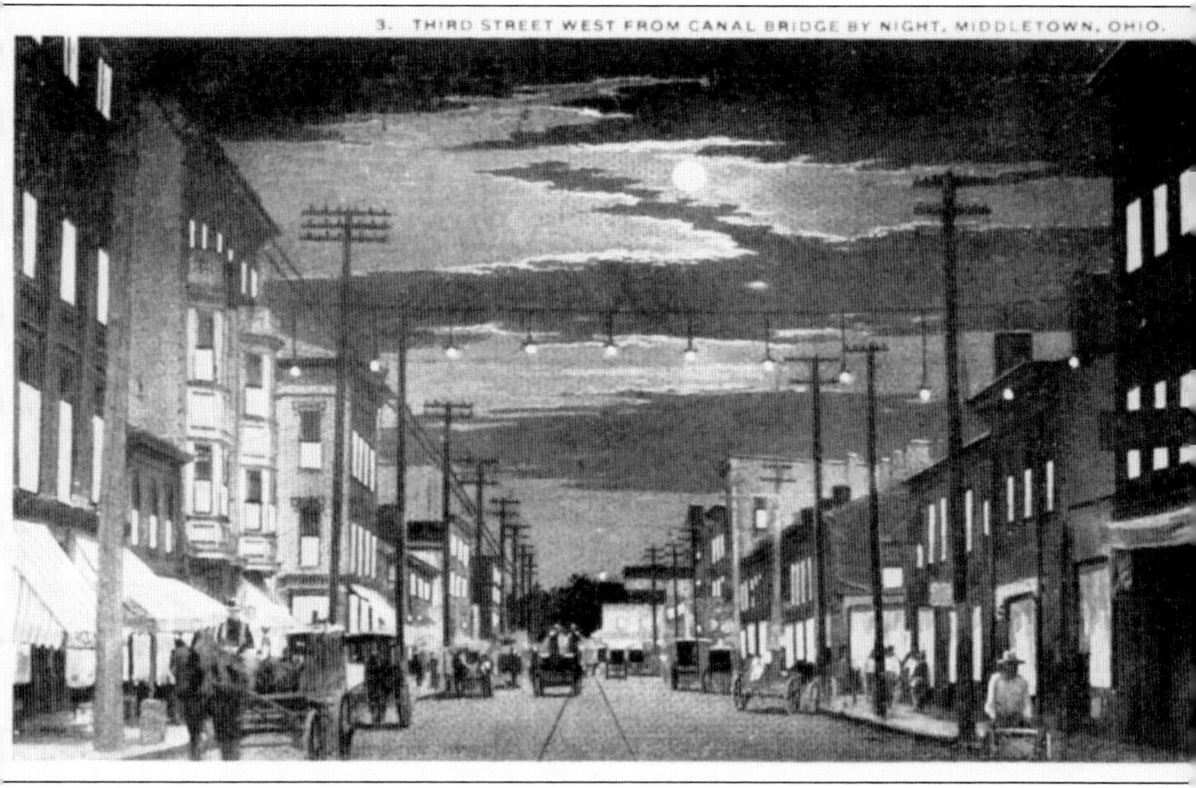

The last Third Street card shows it after dark. Stores were open for shopping into the evening.

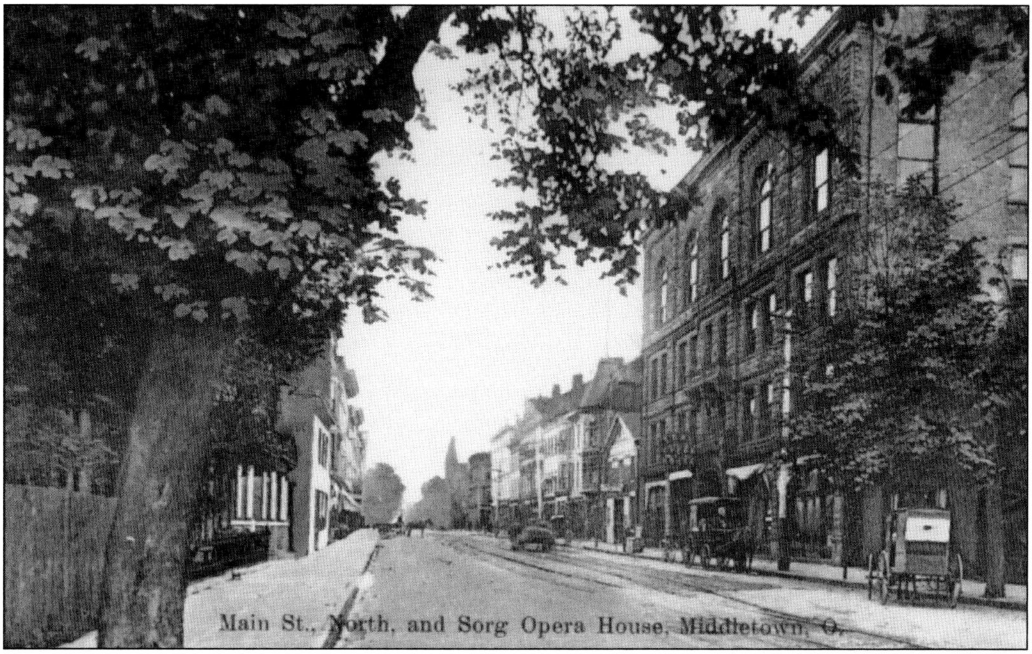

Industrialist Paul J. Sorg built the Sorg Opera House, which is the large building on the right. It opened September 12, 1891, with the play *The Little Tycoon*. Many theatrical troops, as well as other programs, have been presented on the Sorg's stage. Storefronts were located on the street level, while there was office space in the upper floors. The building still stands on Main Street.

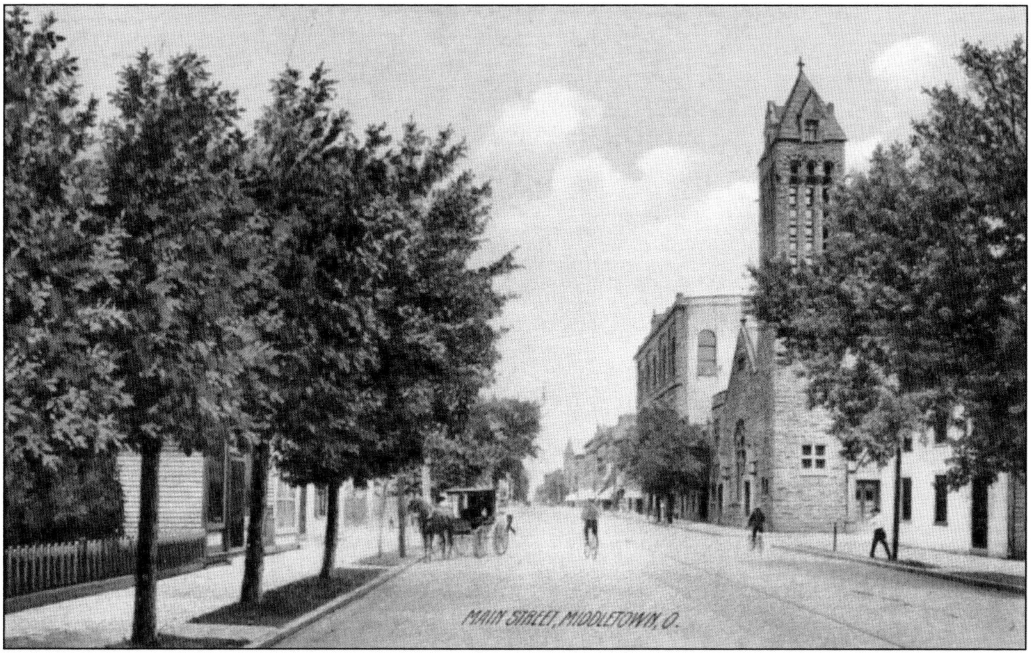

The next two cards are of Main Street looking north from Fourth Street, or today's First Avenue. This one was postmarked in February 1910 and shows the First Presbyterian Church next to the Sorg Opera House. The church was dedicated in January 1892.

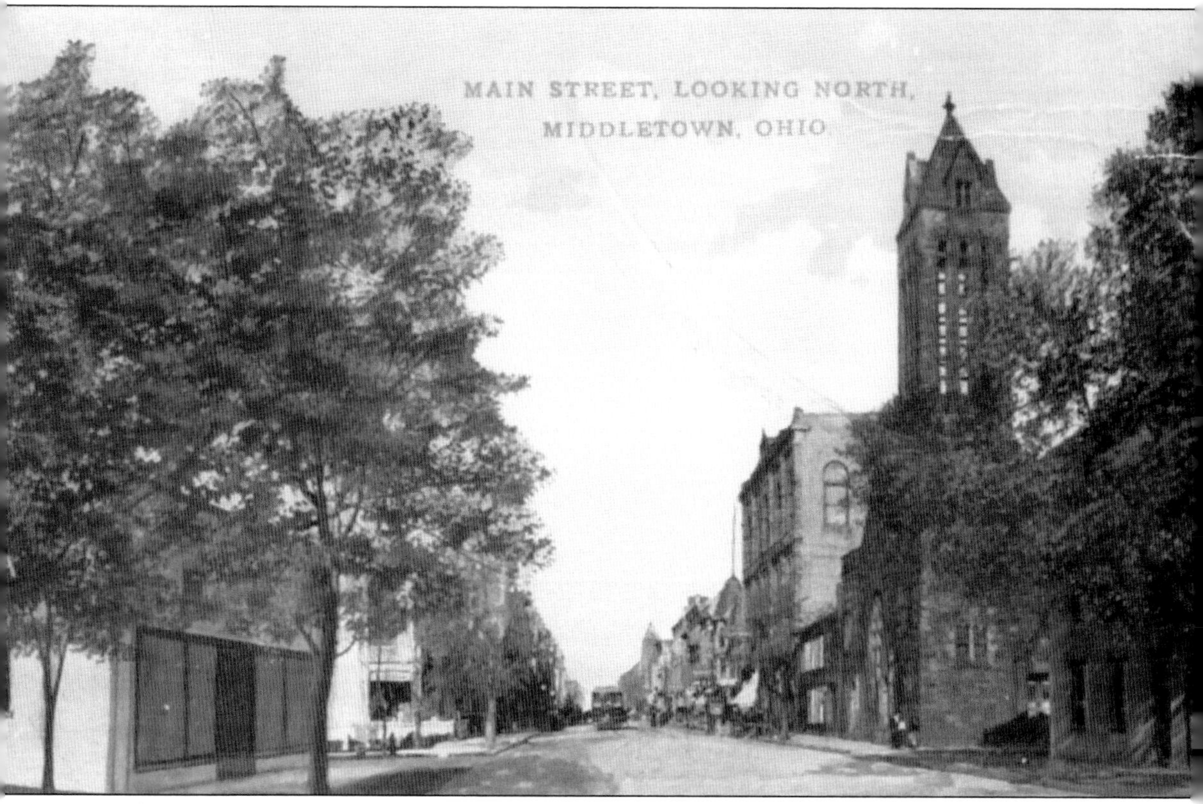

This card was postmarked in August 1911 and shows the same area as the previous one. Note that the building on the left has been added to this tinted card. A building such as this one was never erected on this site. Postcards could be changed without much difficulty.

Two

Industries Come and Go

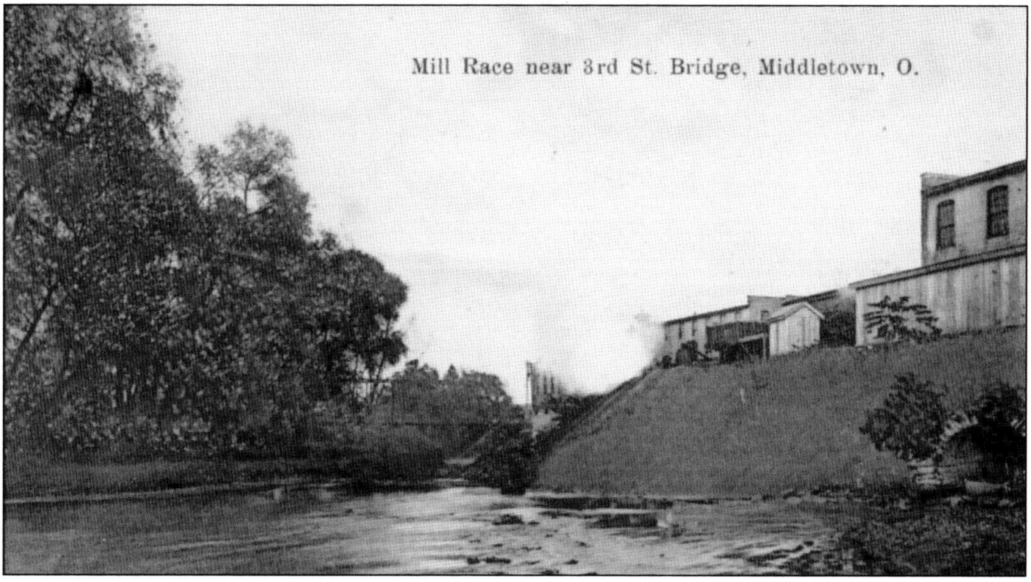

Stephen Vail, who platted Middletown, was fortunate to locate his new town along the Great Miami River. It provided water for transportation and powering many small mills. With the coming of the canal and its locks, larger mills were constructed. In 1851, a hydraulic canal was constructed, providing locations for additional water-powered mills.

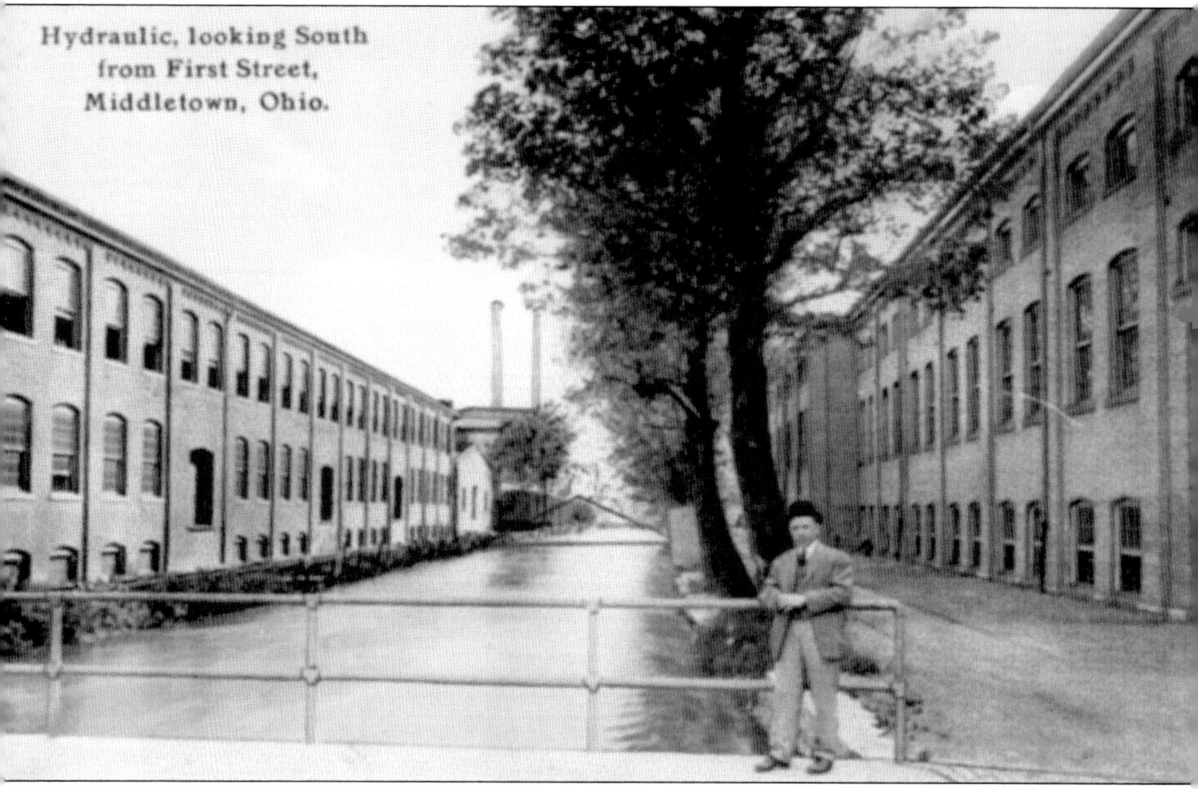

Middletown developed into an industrial city with several tobacco-processing and paper mills. Large amounts of water were needed to manufacture paper. Here, the water passes through two of the paper mills that became part of the Sorg Paper Company. First Street is today's Columbia Avenue.

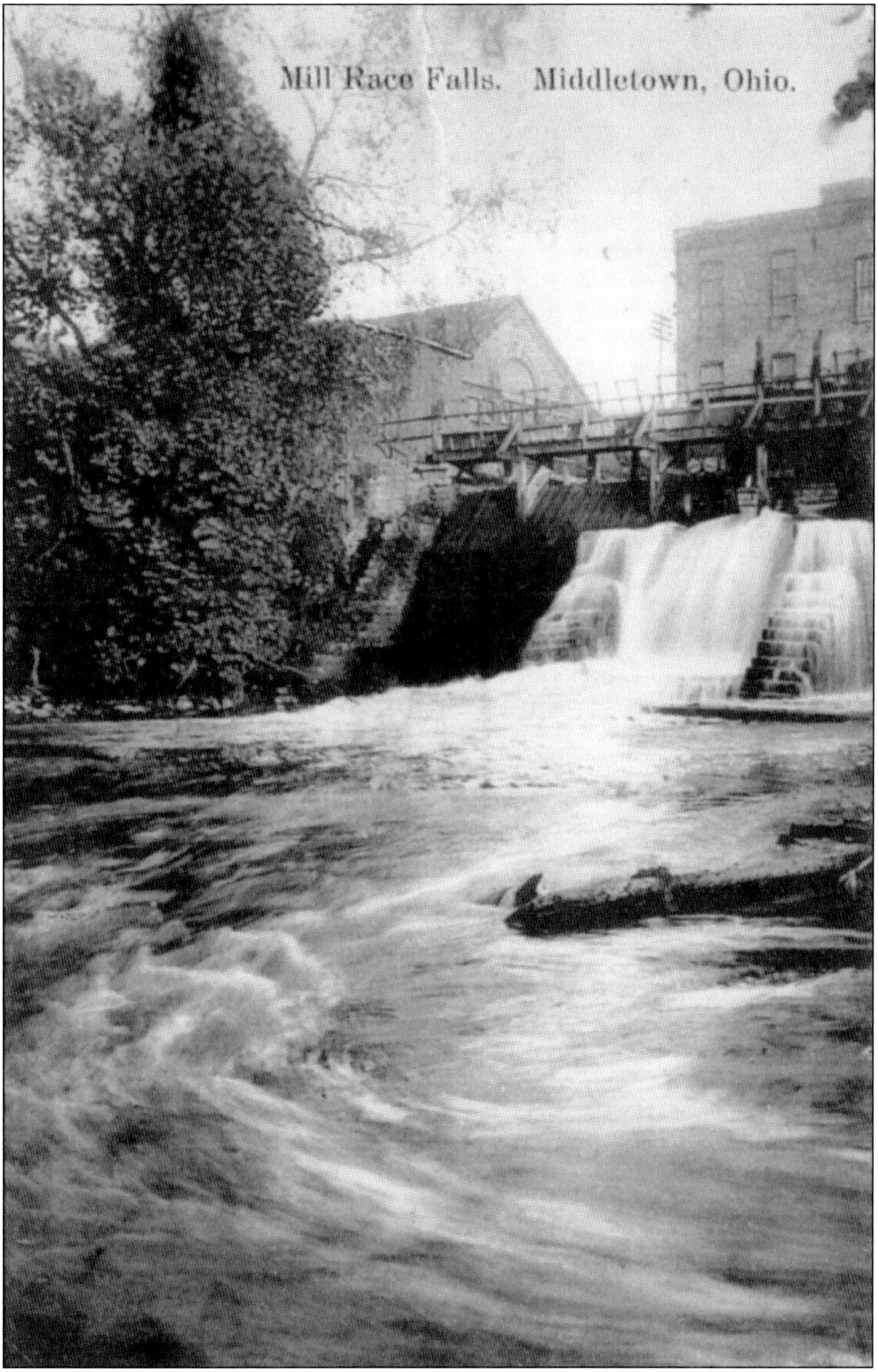

The water is exiting the Sorg Paper mill on its way back to the river. In doing so, it would provide waterpower for additional mills.

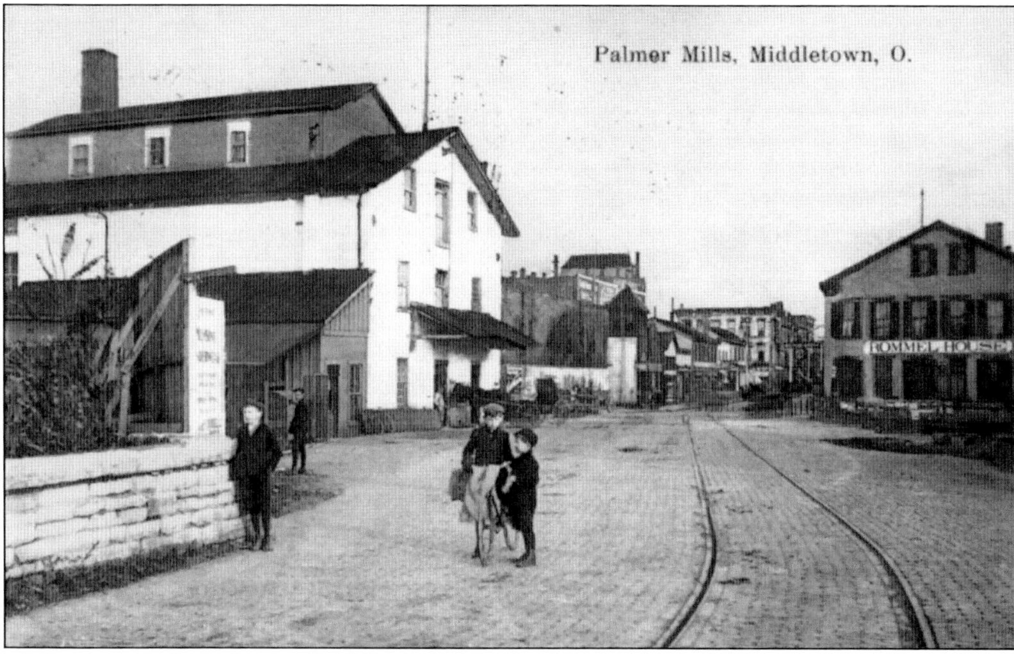

One of those mills was the Palmer Mill, which was located by the Middletown Hydraulic Canal on West Third Street. The mill had been constructed by Joseph Sutphin and John L. Martin, who sold it to Charles B. Palmer. This mill was well known for its "The Crown" and "Our Pride" flour. It was later operated by Frank Diver.

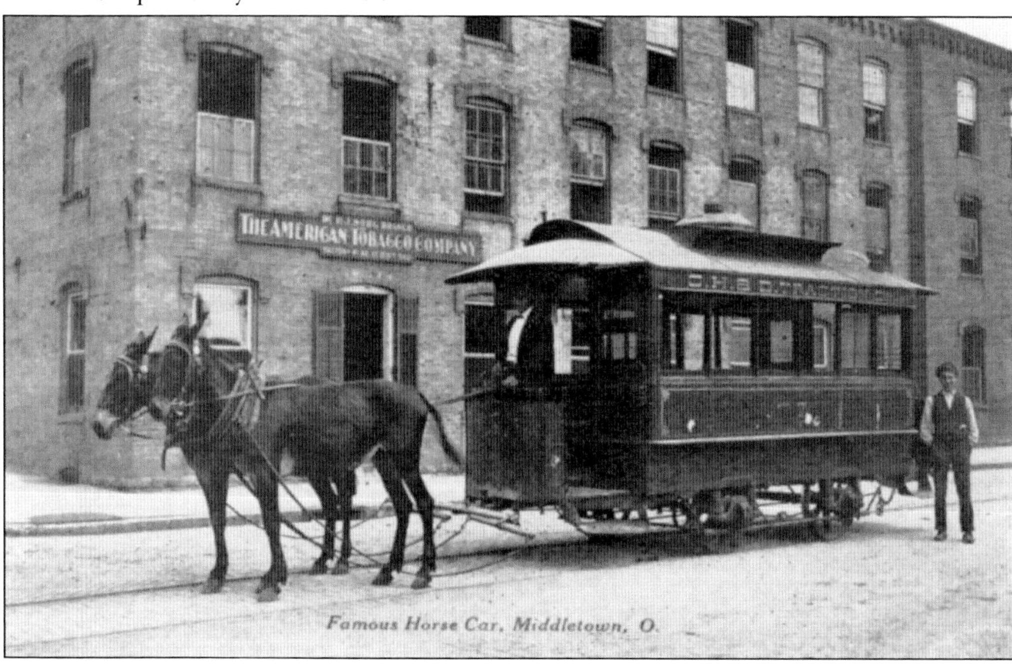

In 1870, Paul J. Sorg came to Middletown and, with others, located a tobacco-processing plant along the Miami-Erie Canal. After leaving that firm, he started another tobacco factory along the railroad tracks in the east end. The Paul J. Sorg Tobacco Company became very successful. Covering a full city block, it remained in operation until 1950.

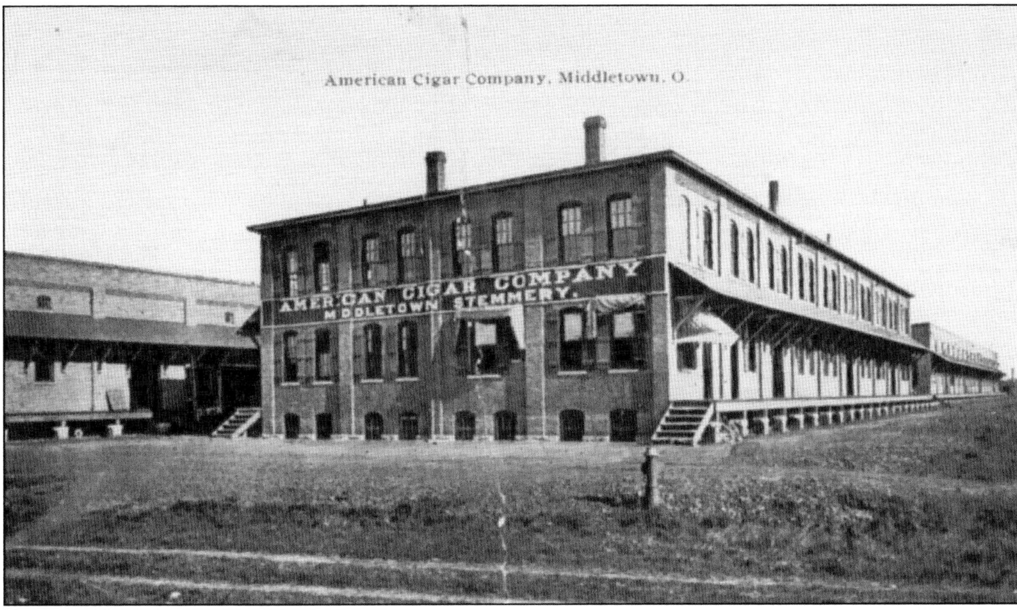

Another tobacco concern to operate a plant in the city was the American Cigar Company. Tobacco was such an important industry that many large warehouses and plants were located in the city.

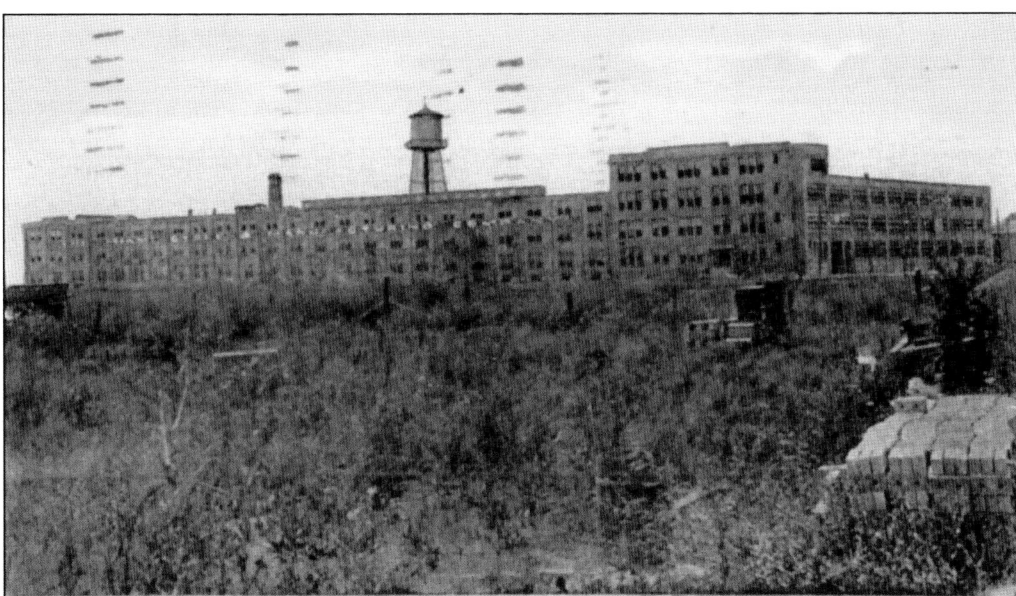

Miami Cycle and Manufacturing Co. made bicycles and motorcycles. During the peak years, 100,000 bicycles and 10,000 motorcycles were manufactured, but after World War I, the company found that the bicycle and motorcycle business had about disappeared. As the Hotel Manchester was being constructed, a need for steel cabinets developed. Miami Cycle provided them, which led to the formation of the Miami Cabinet Company.

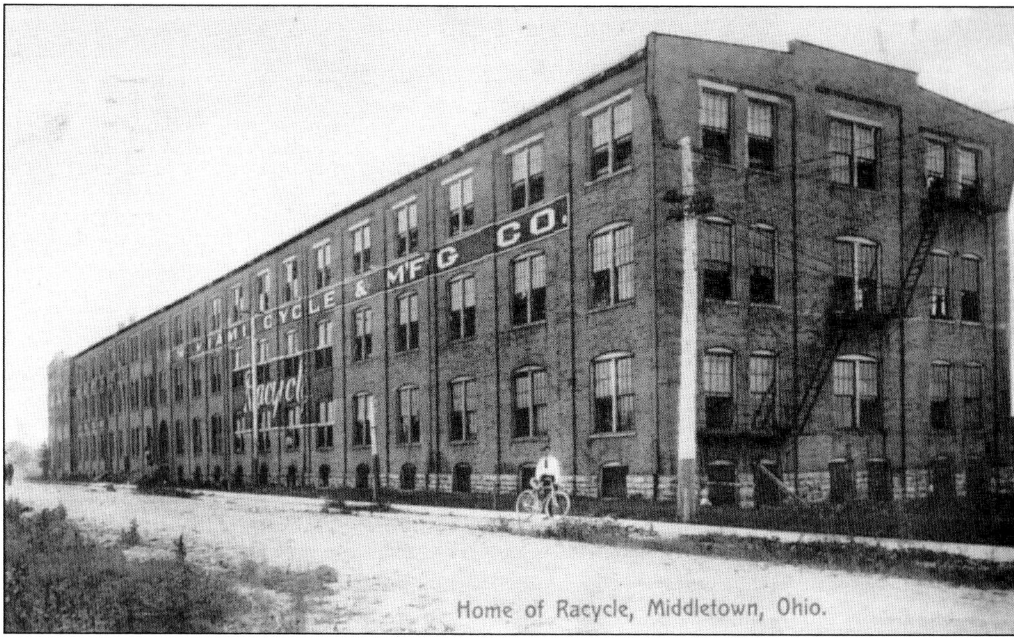

Postmarked September 1, 1912, this card was sent by "M.E.J.," who referred to going to work at this company and that he had "got first at Boston easy." The man who sent this card, Maldwyn E. Jones, was a motorcycle racer and won a race in Boston, Massachusetts, before moving to Middletown. He went to work at Miami Cycle and Manufacturing Co. and raced the company's Flying Merkel motorcycles.

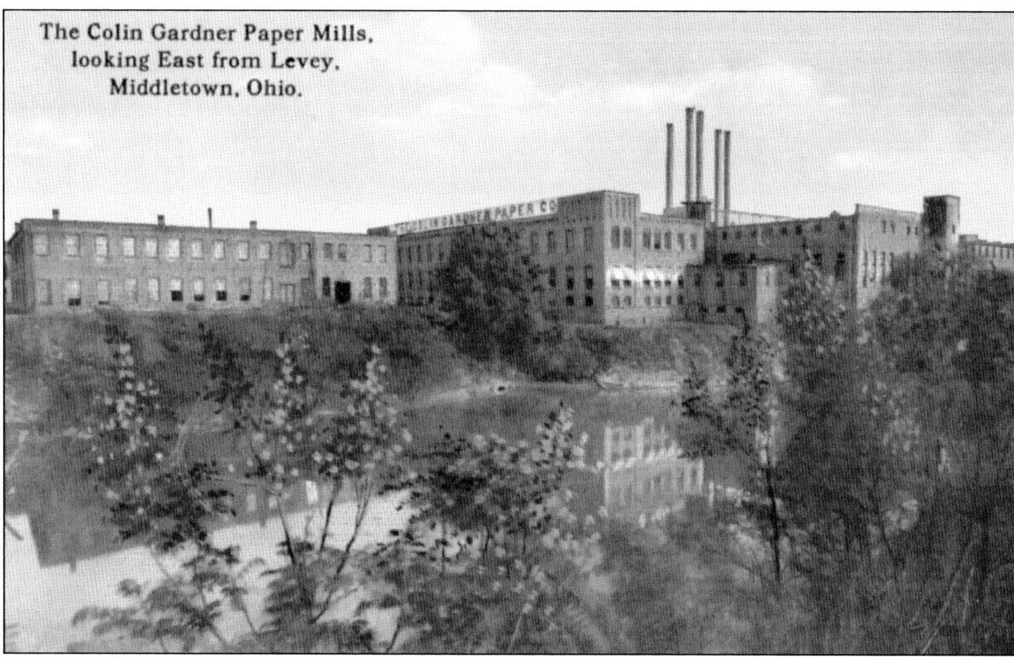

Francis Tytus operated a large paper-manufacturing business. Tytus and his son-in-law Colin Gardner were partners, but after a fire in 1900, Gardner went into business on his own. This mill was located along West Central Avenue at the Middletown Hydraulic Canal.

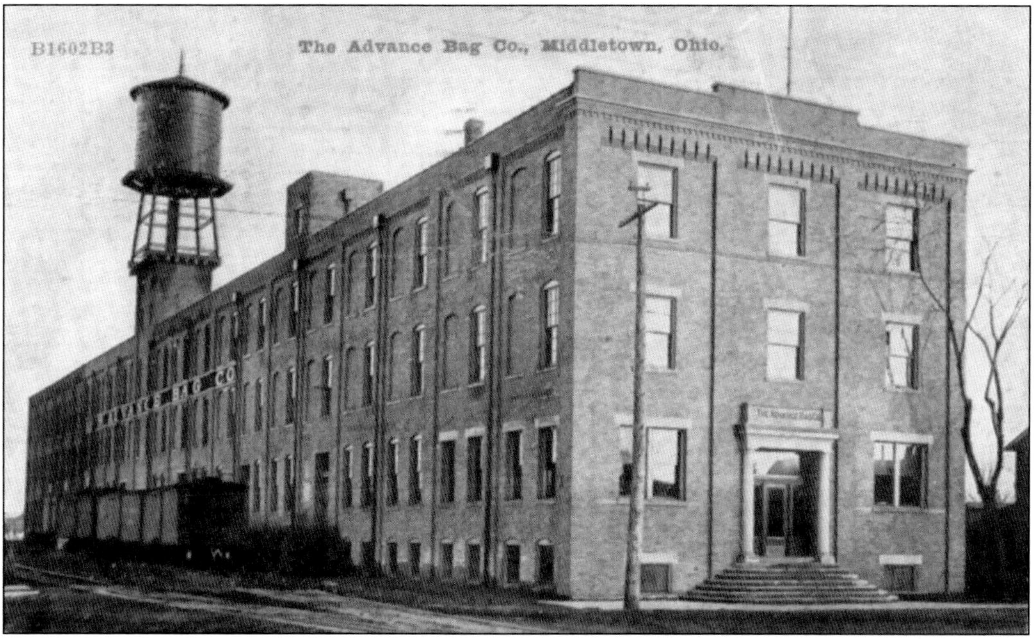

This building once represented the era when Middletown was the largest producer of paper bags in the world. William Webster had received patents for an advanced bag-making machine. In 1889, improvements on his machine led to the formation of the Advance Bag Company. By 1906, the company was producing 800 million paper bags a day on 50 of the improved machines.

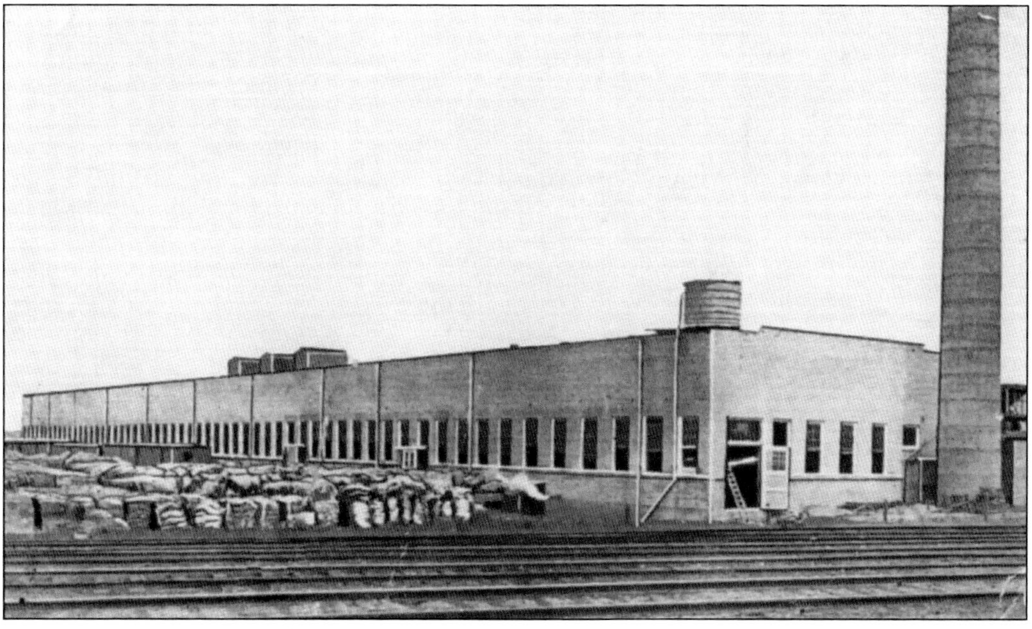

George Harvey had much knowledge and skill in the art of papermaking when he joined Colin Gardner in supervising the construction of the Colin Gardner Paper Company, which went into production in 1901. Five years later, a second mill, known as the Gardner-Harvey Paper Company, was constructed.

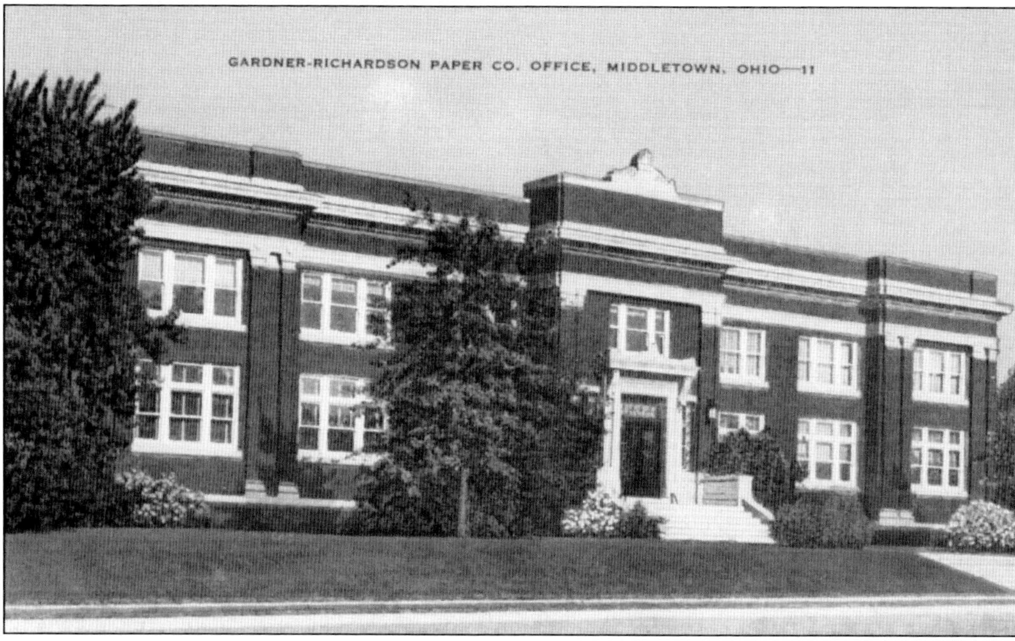

In 1932, the Gardner and Harvey interests purchased the Richardson Company of Lockland, Ohio. The name of the business was changed to Gardner-Richardson Paper Company, and this building on Charles Street became the company's main office.

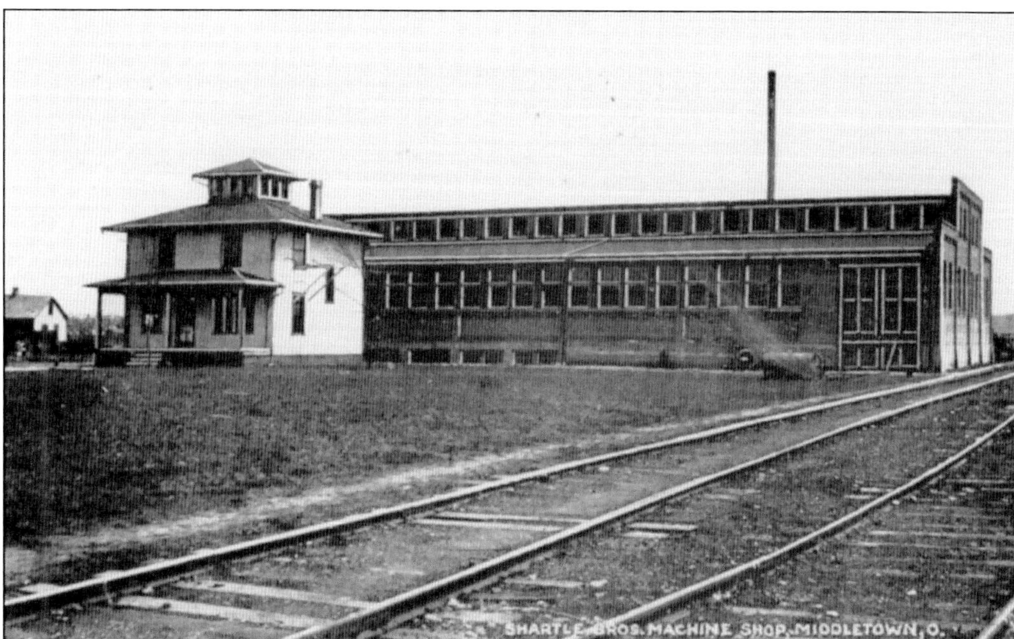

The industrial concerns of Middletown, especially the paper mills, were often in need of new or repaired equipment. Several machine shops operated in the city. Charles Shartle formed one of them, the Shartle Brothers Machine Shop. The company's office was in the house, which was eventually completely surrounded with a new office building. The cupola remained until the building was torn down.

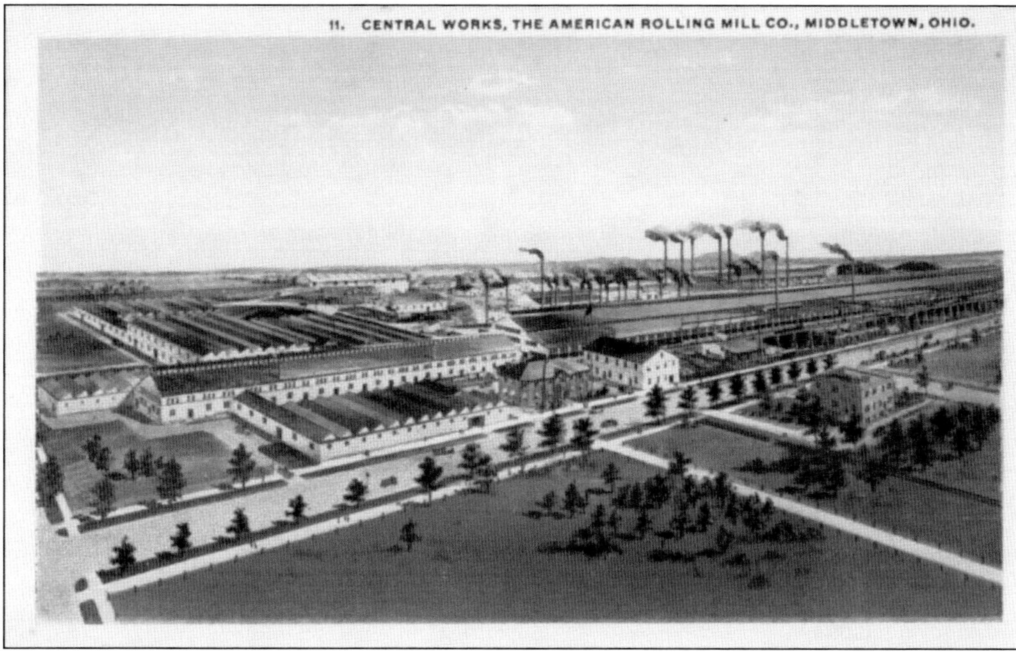

Armco started construction of its first mill in 1900. The new company's idea was to produce steel, starting with pig iron and continuing to a finished product. After 1910, the original factory, shown here, became the company's Central Works.

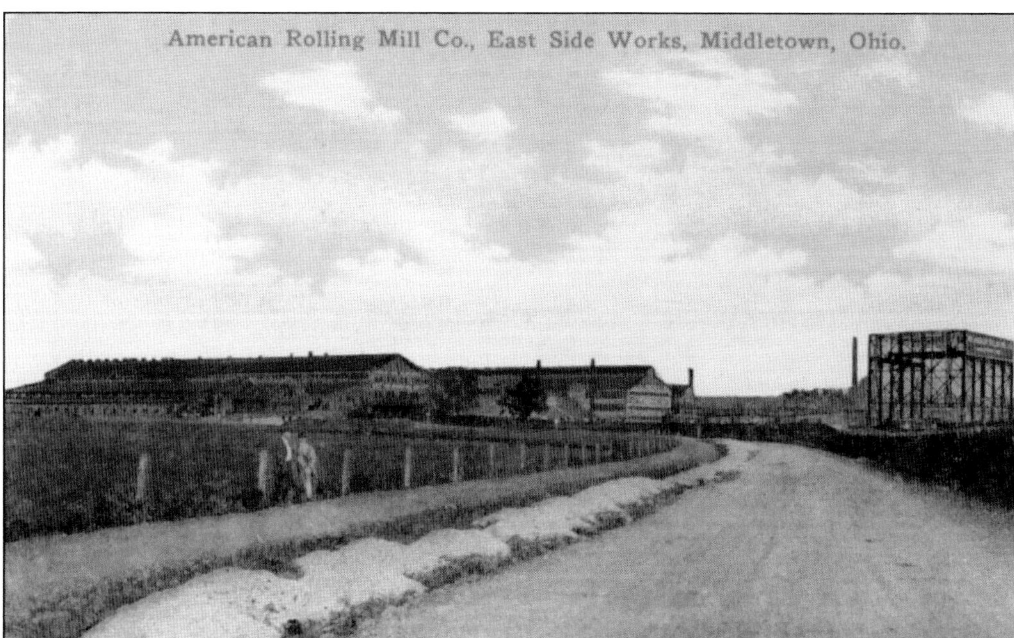

Armco specialized in types of steel that other companies did not want to produce. By 1910, the company had grown so much that it was in need of additional space. On the southeast edge of town, construction was started on a much larger plant that became the company's East Side Works.

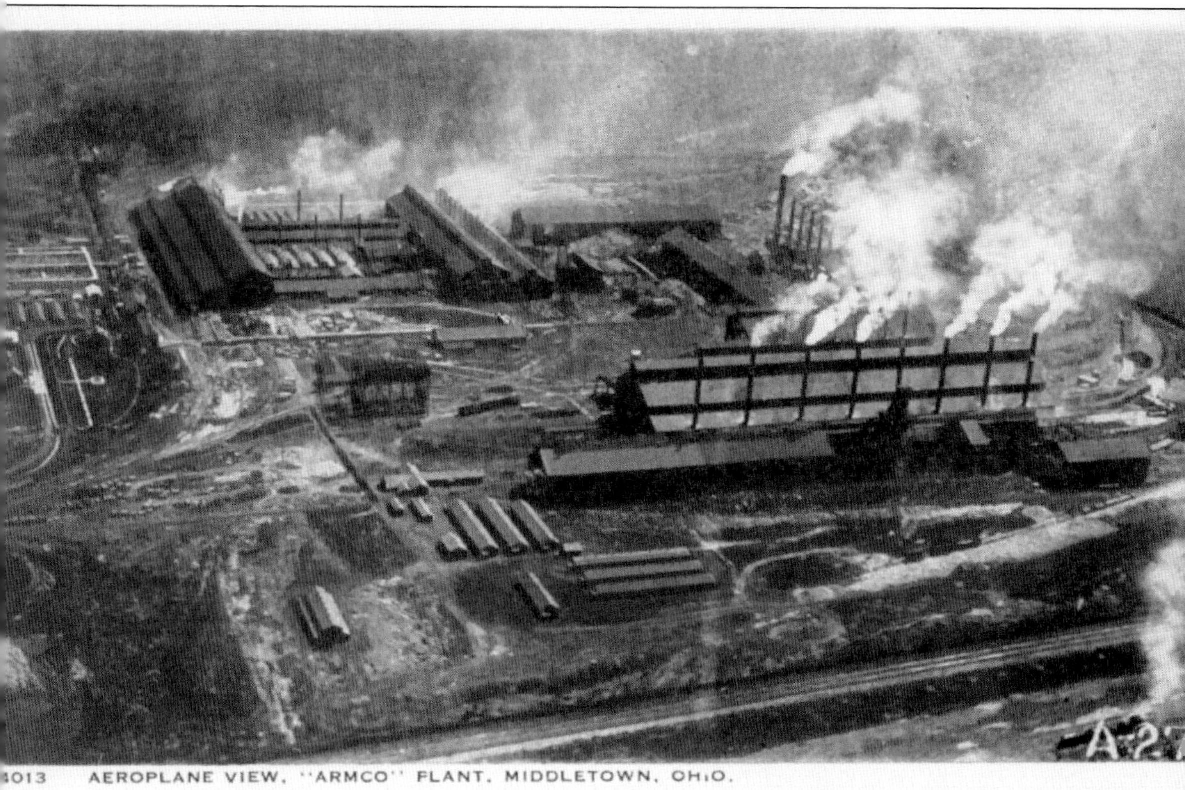

By the mid-1920s, Armco's East Side Works started to grow. The large building just right of center was the No. 1 Open Hearth. Pig iron was brought into the building and converted into steel. Then, it was taken to the other buildings to be rolled, annealed, and further processed.

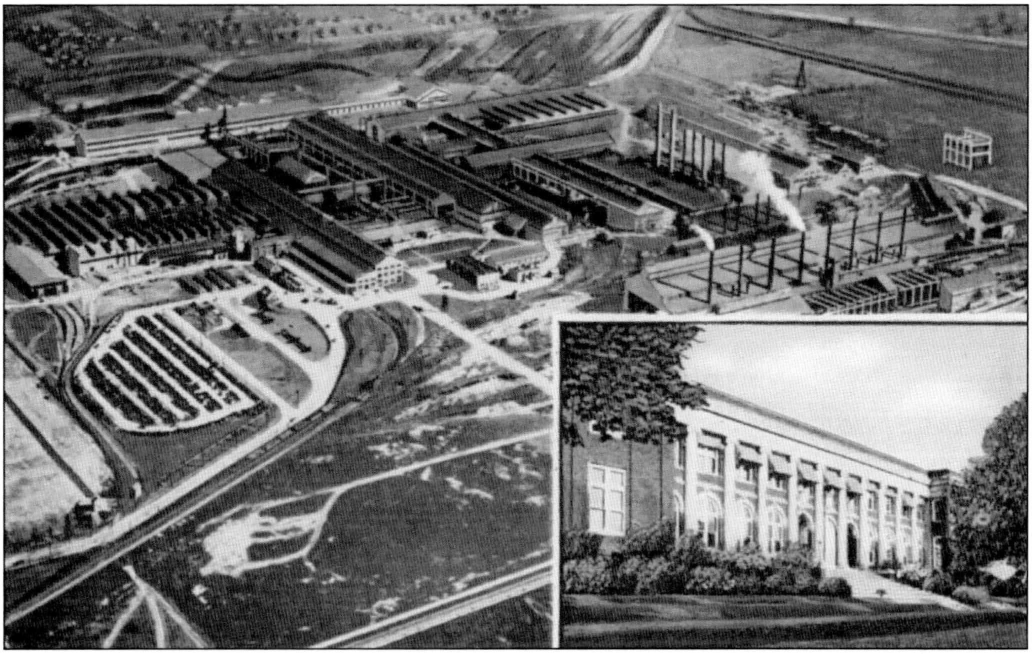

By the late 1930s, Armco's East Side Works had grown a great deal. Among other things, Armco developed the continuous rolling mill (the Hot Strip Mill), and several coating lines were added. During the 1960s and 1970s, this plant was rebuilt and enlarged many times, becoming one of the world's most modern steel plants. It continues to operate as AK Steel's main plant. The inset is Armco's general office, which has recently been torn down.

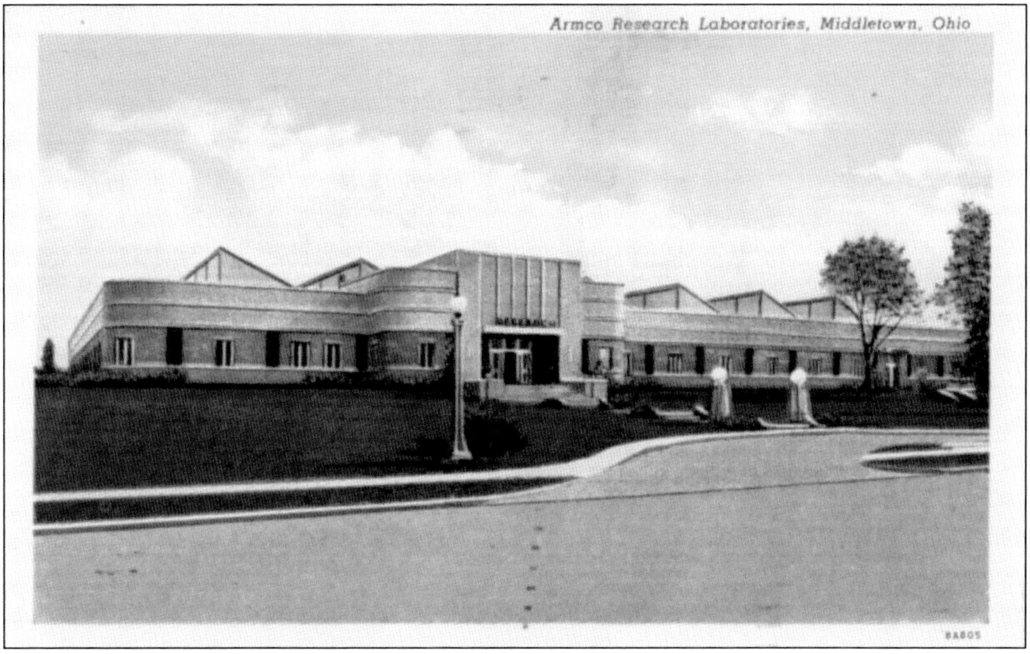

From its start, research played a large part in Armco's production of high-quality steel with unusual properties. The research department was officially established in 1910. Constructed in 1937, the research building is still used by AK Steel.

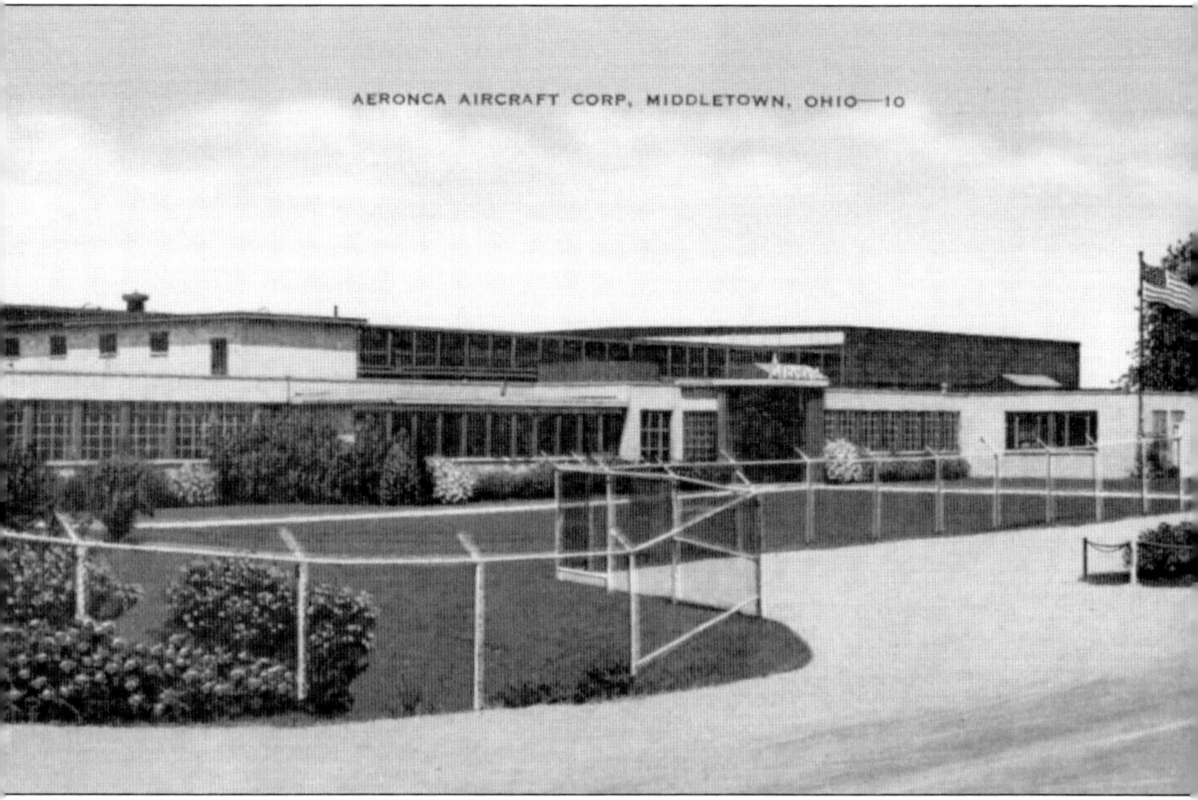

Before moving to Middletown in 1940, Aeronca manufactured small airplanes at Lunken Airport in Cincinnati. It relocated to the local airport and continued to manufacture airplanes. The company manufactured over 17,000 airplanes, most of them in Middletown, before ending aircraft production. Today, as part of Magellan Aerospace, the company continues business as a subcontractor to commercial and military aircraft industries.

Three

The Great Flood of 1913

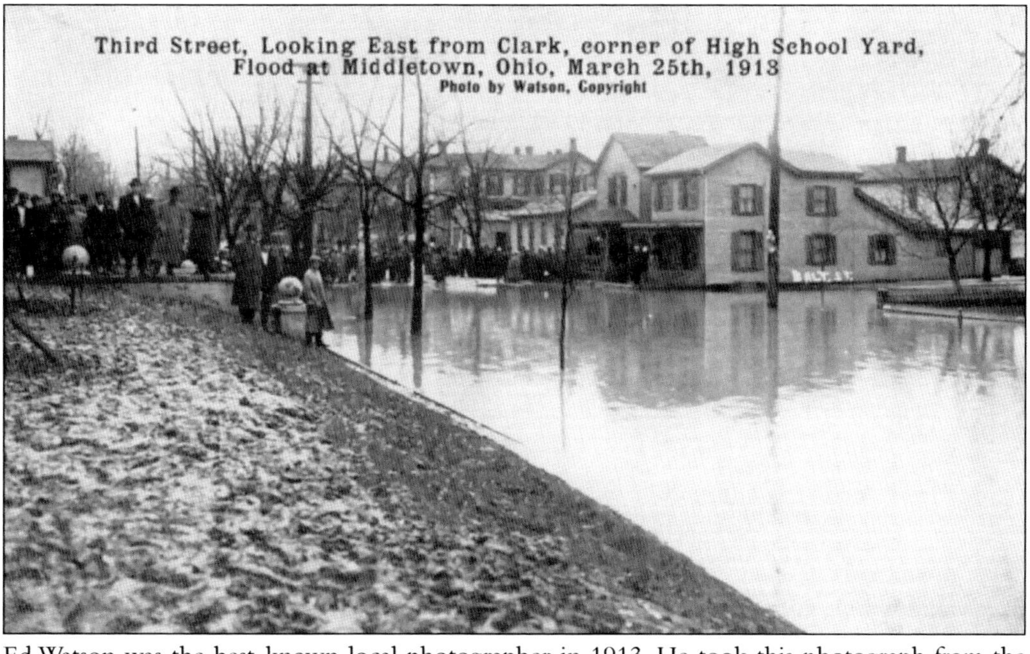

Ed Watson was the best-known local photographer in 1913. He took this photograph from the high school grounds. It was at least half a mile from the river, but the water of the river and Miami-Erie Canal combined into one body that filled the street just past the school.

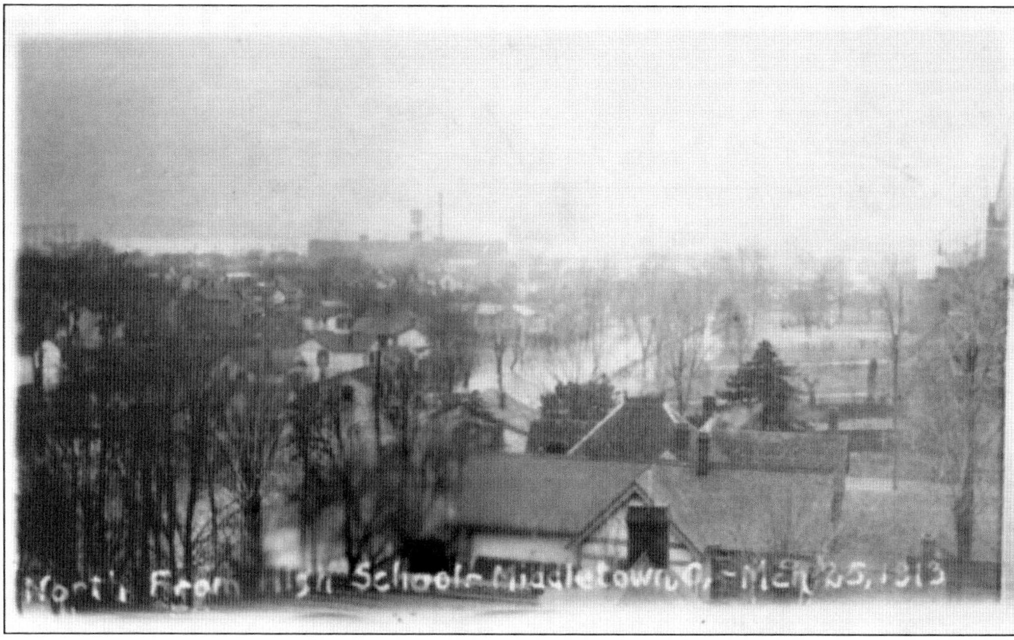

Like most cities and villages that were located in the Miami River Valley, Middletown was extensively damaged by the March 1913 flood. This photograph was taken looking north from the then new (1909) high school, which was located on today's Central Avenue.

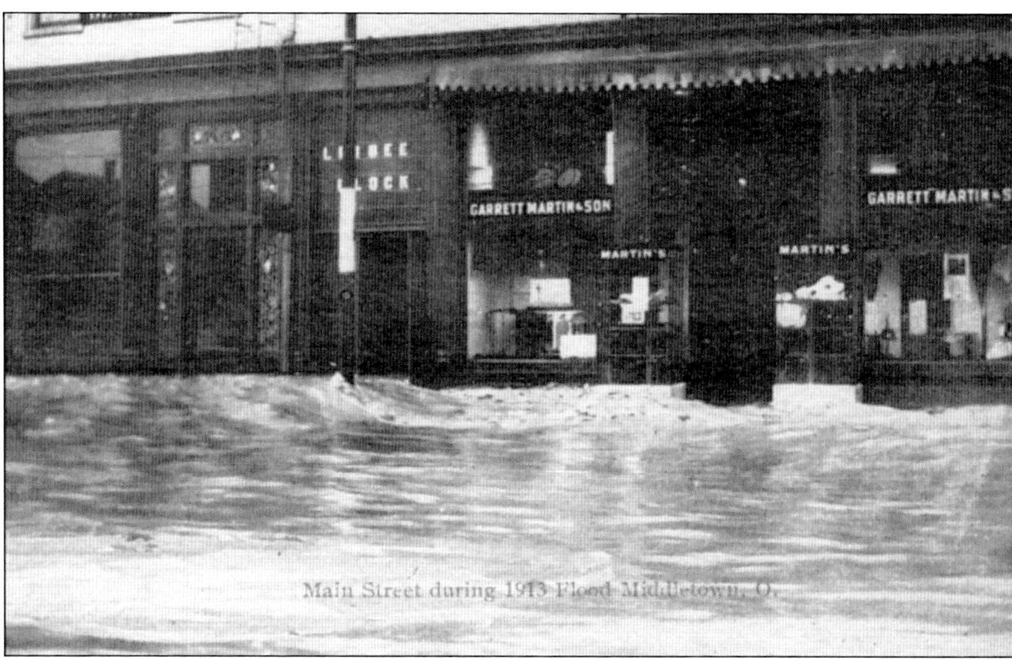

All of the merchants downtown were in the flooded area of the city. The Leibee Building was a large structure with storefronts on Third and Main Streets. Garrett Martin & Son sold clothes from one of the storefronts.

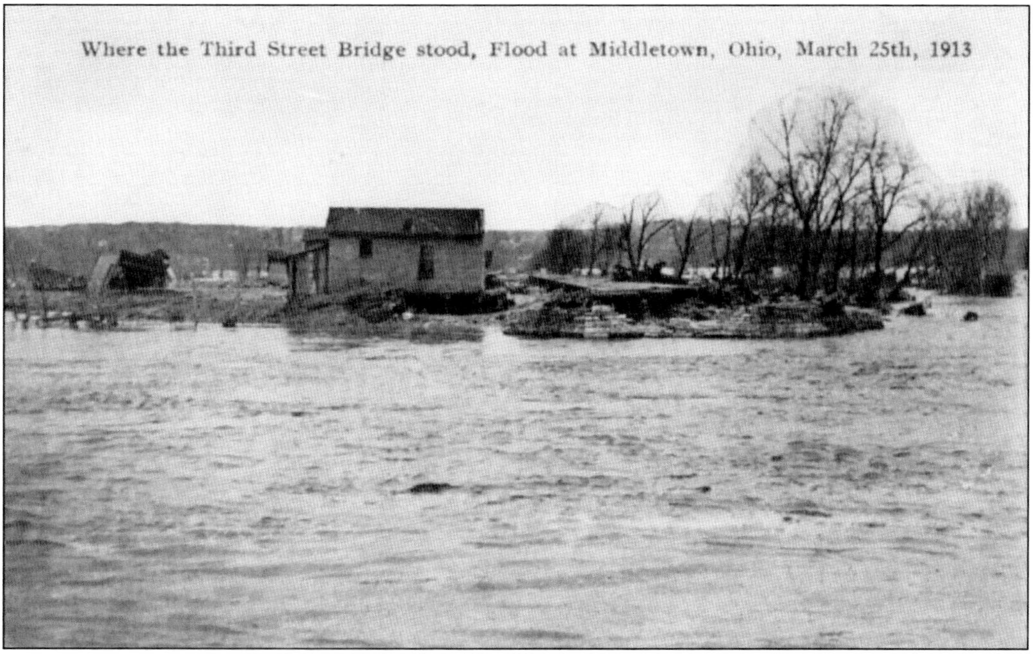

The bridges crossing the river at Middletown were destroyed by the flood. This has been identified as the location of the Third Street Bridge, which was on the main road that went through West Middletown to Gratis. If what is indicated on this card is true, where is the West Middletown hill? Or where are the mills along the river looking east?

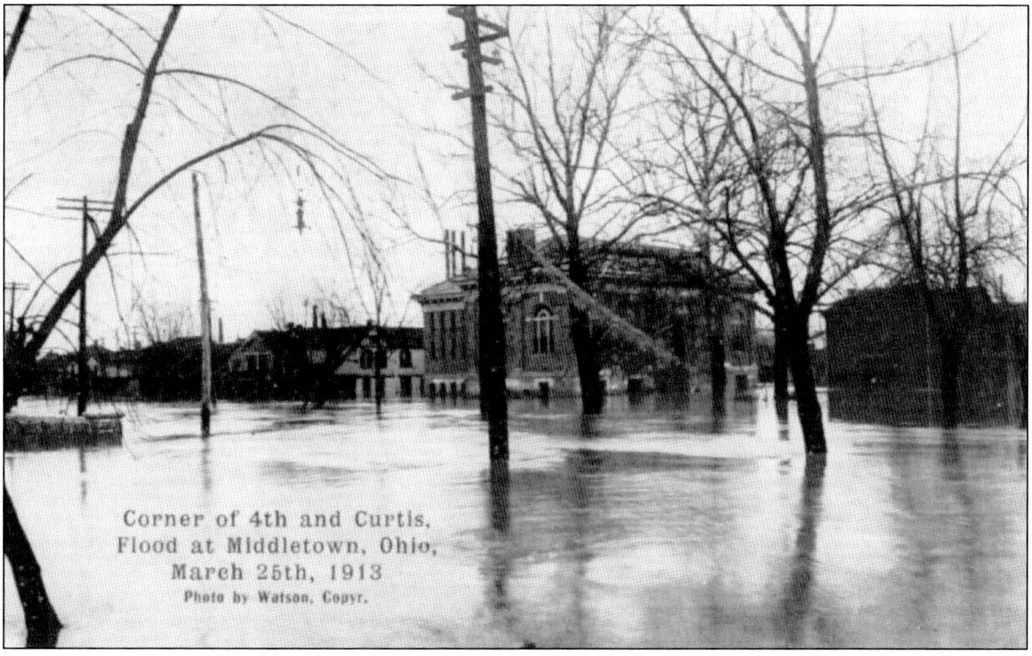

Another Watson photograph shows the public library that had opened that January. Since it sat up high, it received little damage. It continued in use until January 1983, when it was closed and a new, much larger library opened.

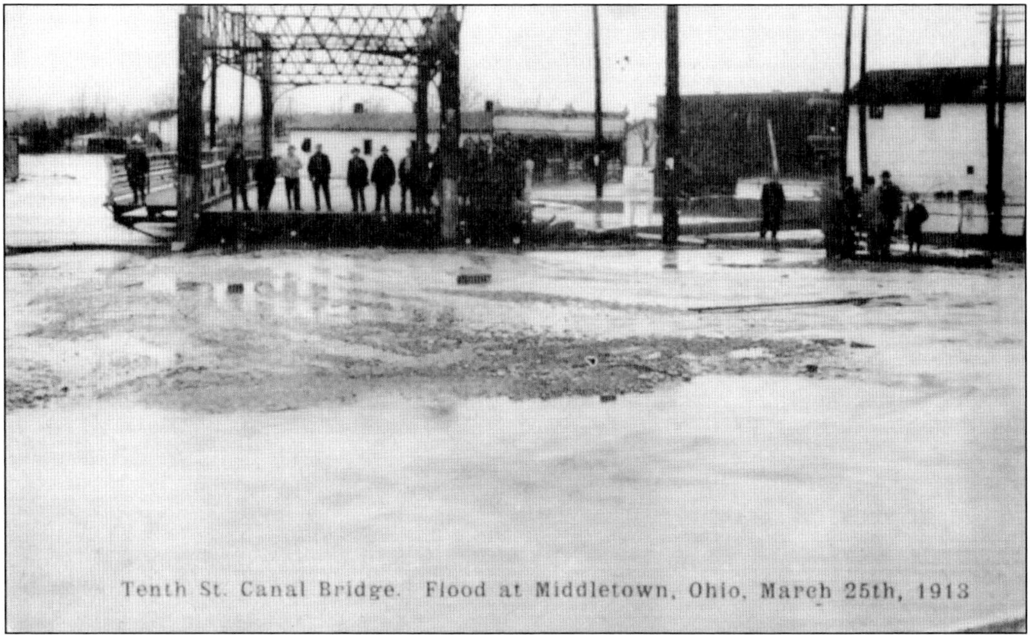

Today, Tenth Street is Yankee Road, while the canal is Verity Parkway. Armco's photographer, Thomas Portsmouth, took this photograph.

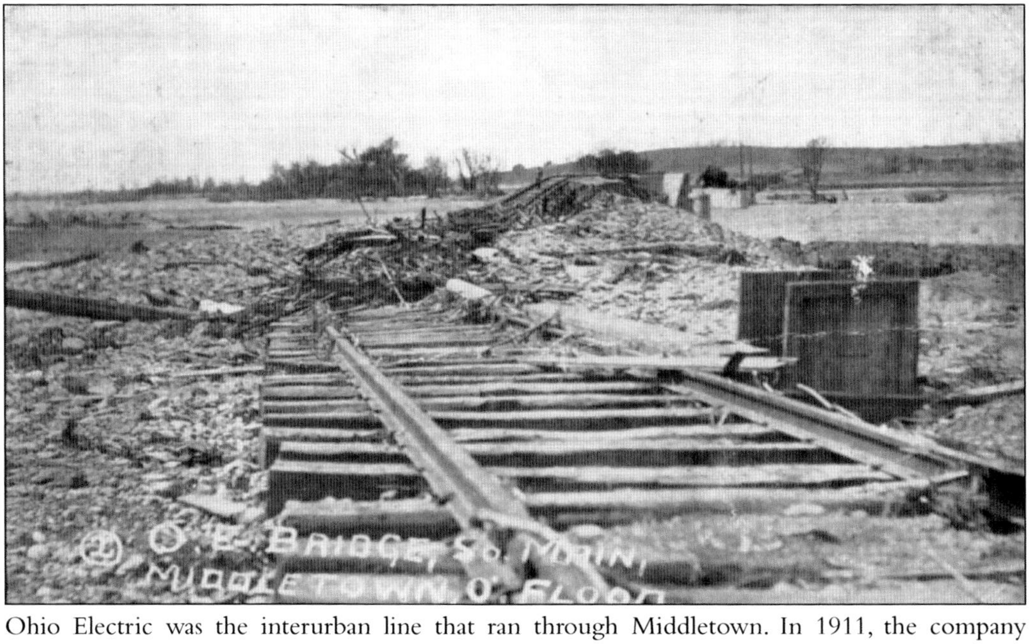

Ohio Electric was the interurban line that ran through Middletown. In 1911, the company constructed a bridge over the Great Miami River that allowed the line to bypass Engle's Corner. The flood took the new bridge out, and it was replaced with a temporary wood trestle that remained until the end of service.

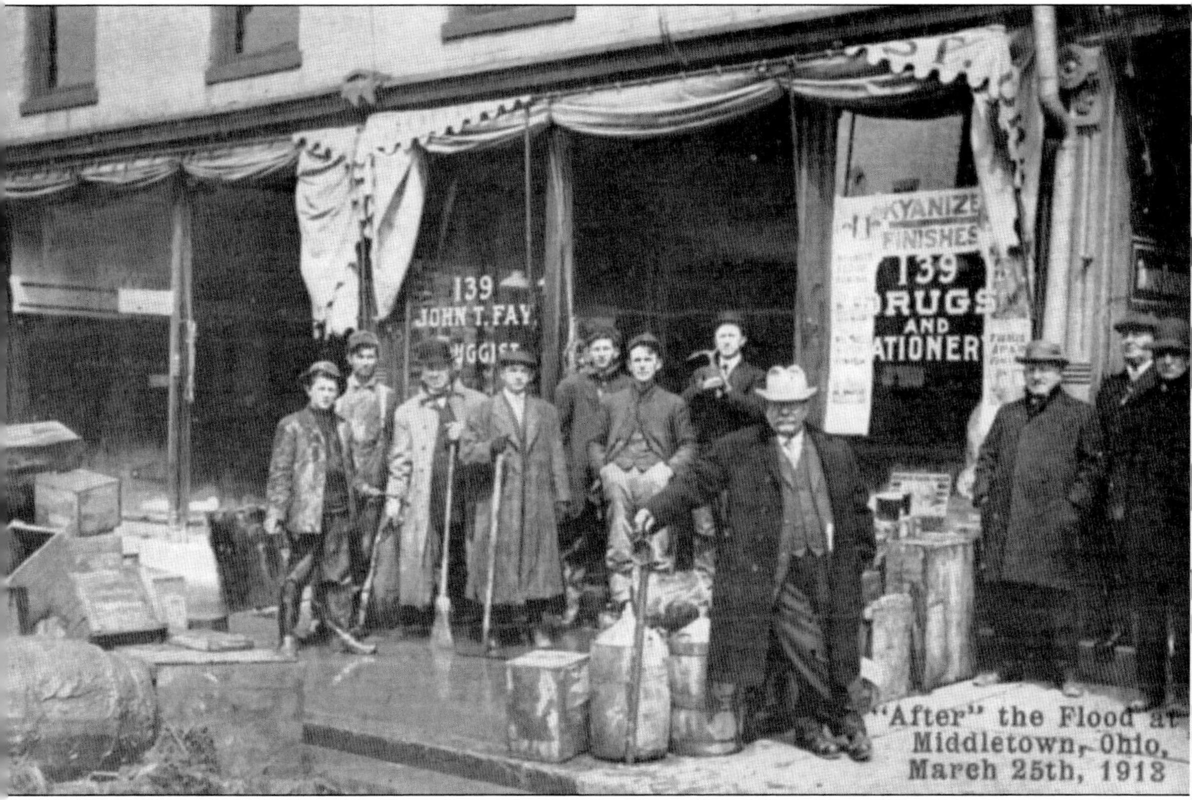

John T. Fay was a druggist located on Third Street. Like all the merchants on the street, his store received a lot of damage. The third man from the right is George "Broomise" Lafayette.

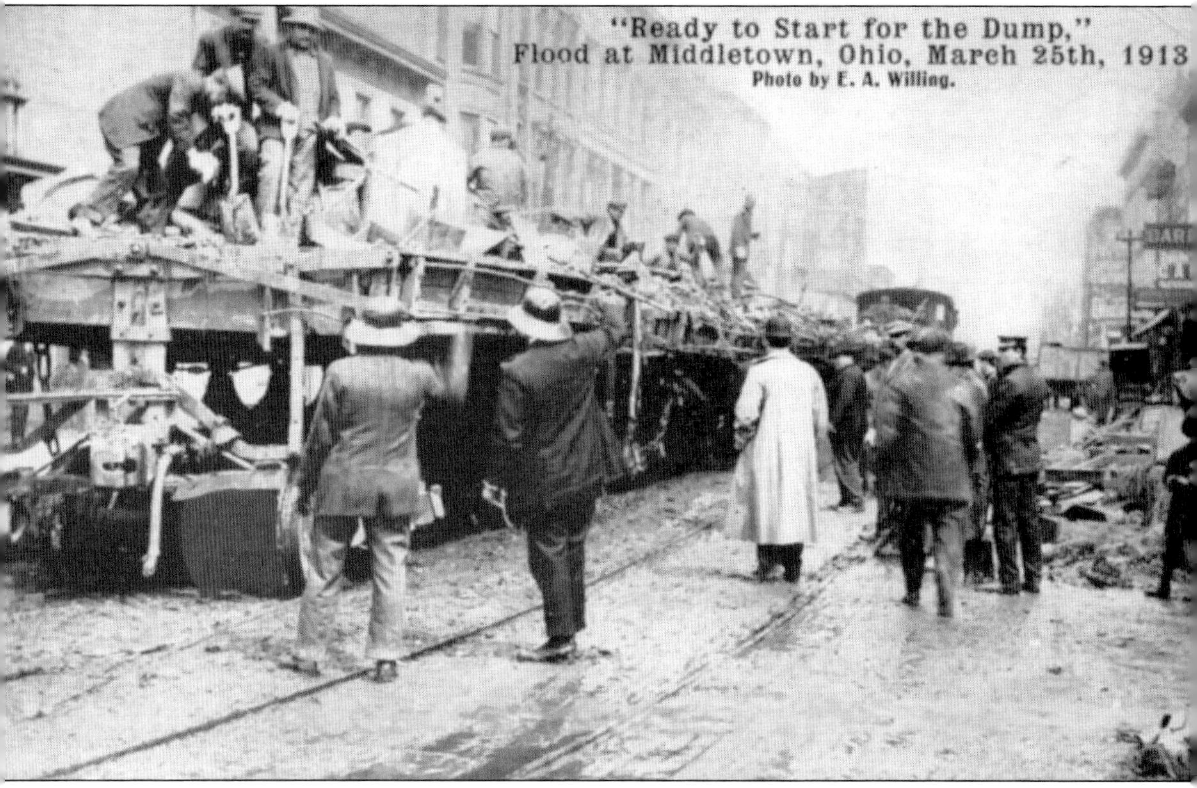

Broomise Lafayette figured out a way to put railroad equipment on the interurban line's track that went down Main Street. Trash did not need to be moved very far to be loaded onto railroad cars, making Middletown the first city in the Miami Valley to be cleaned up. Because of the Miami Conservancy District's flood control, there has never been a flood on the Great Miami River like that of 1913.

Four

Schools and Civic Interests

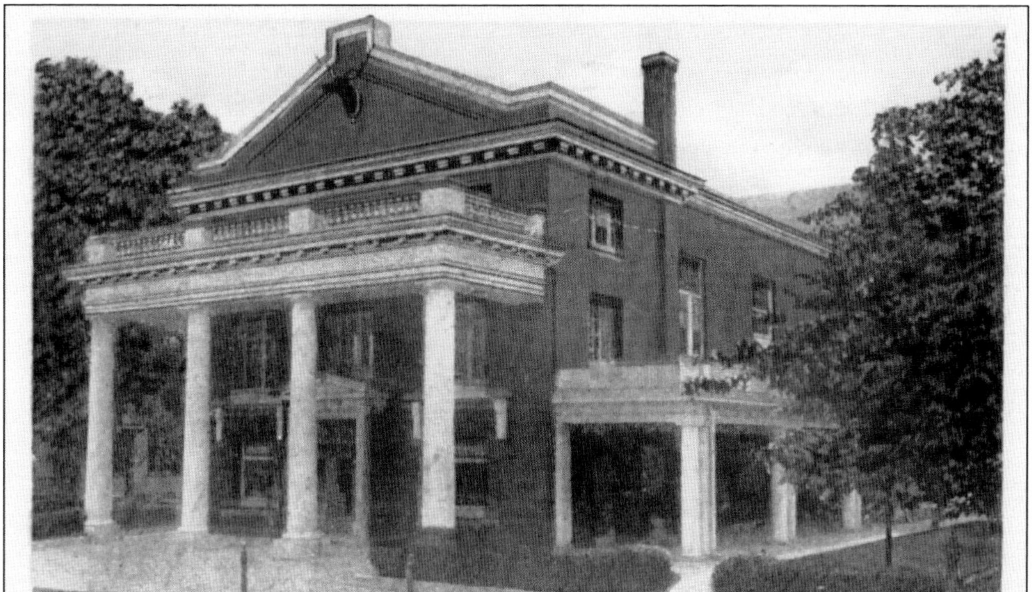

There have been several different postcards showing the Elks Temple, which has been torn down. The building was originally constructed as the Baptist church. Once the church relocated, the building was remodeled and enlarged for use by the Elks.

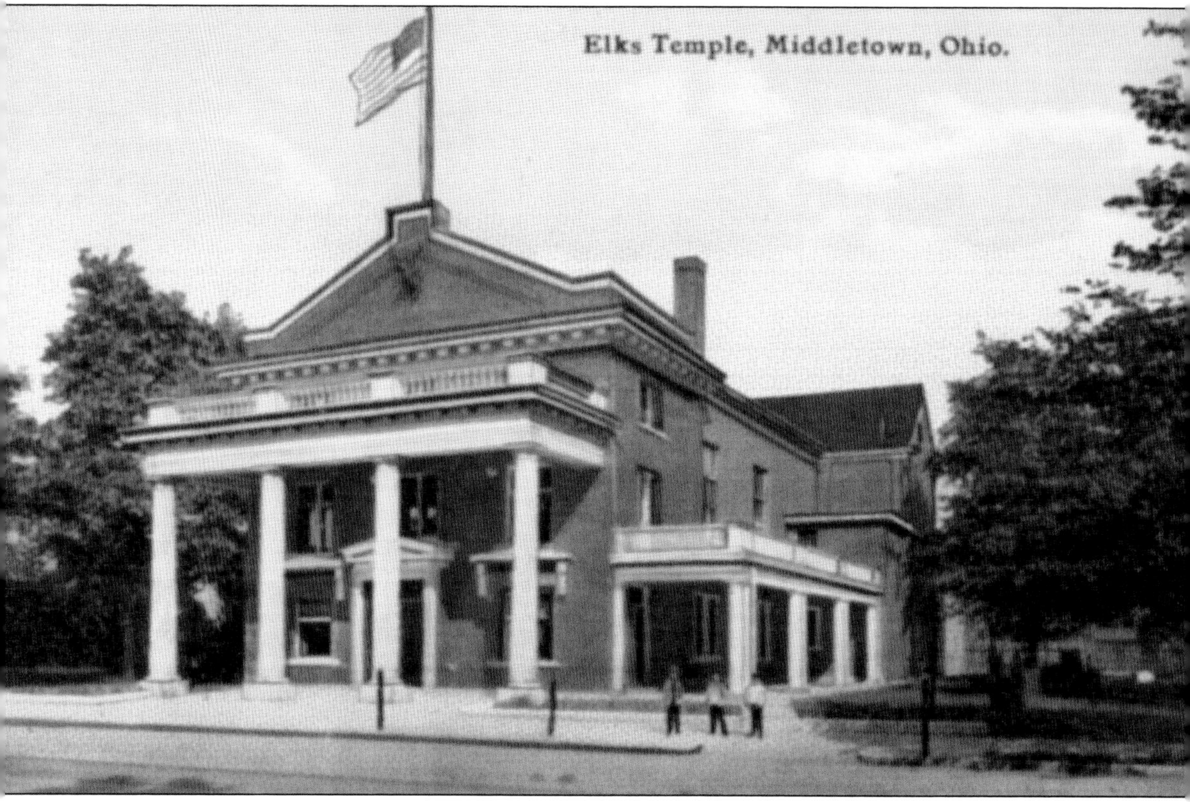

Although the local group of the Benevolent and Protective Order of the Elks (BPOE) was instituted in Middletown on March 22, 1893, the national organization traces its beginnings to 1867. This postcard was popular in the 1910s and 1920s.

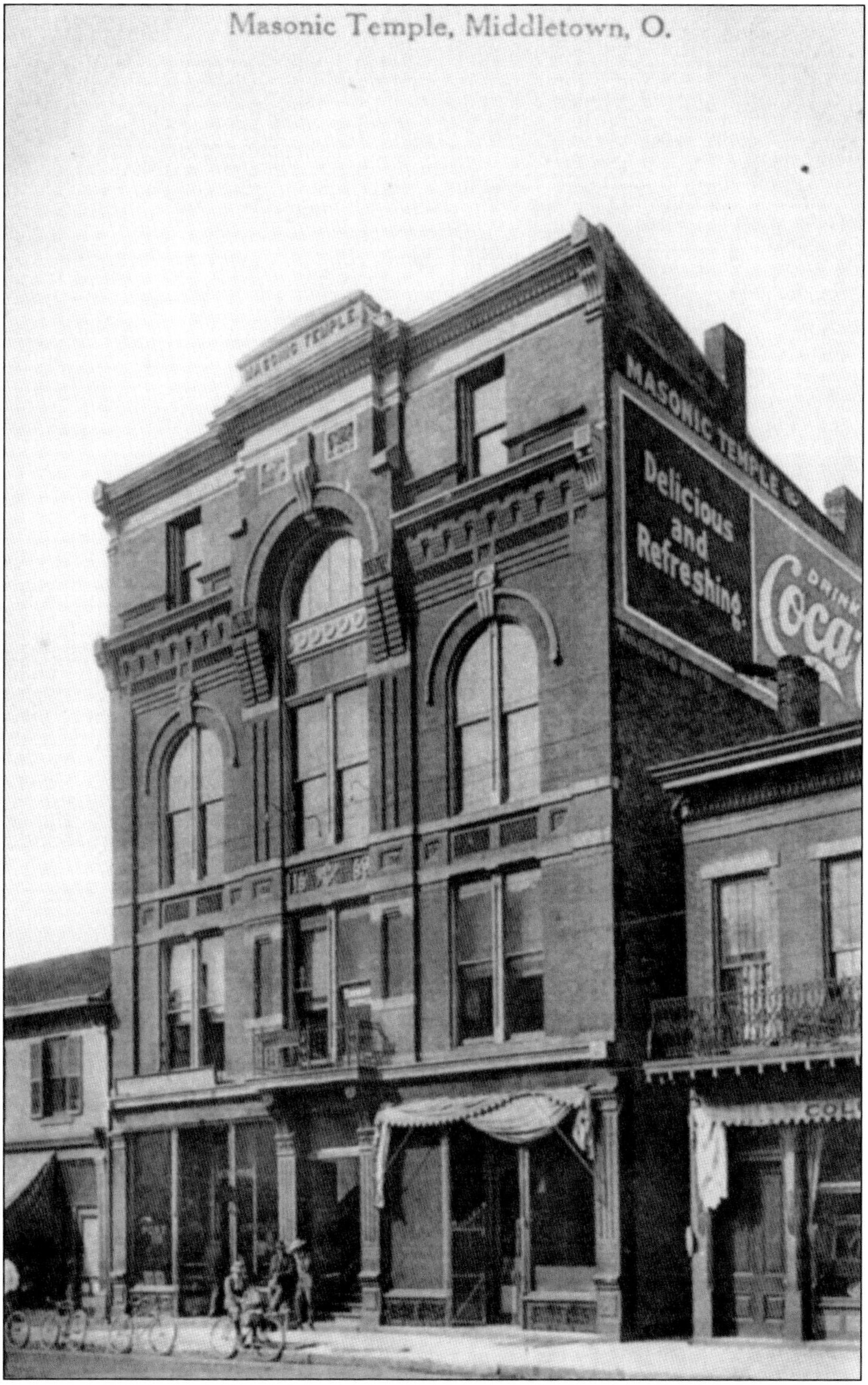

The Masonic Temple was erected by the Jefferson Royal Arch Masons in 1883. The signs on its side can still be seen on Main Street. In 1975, a new building on Marshall Road replaced this one. (Courtesy of Middletown Historical Collection, Middletown Public Library.)

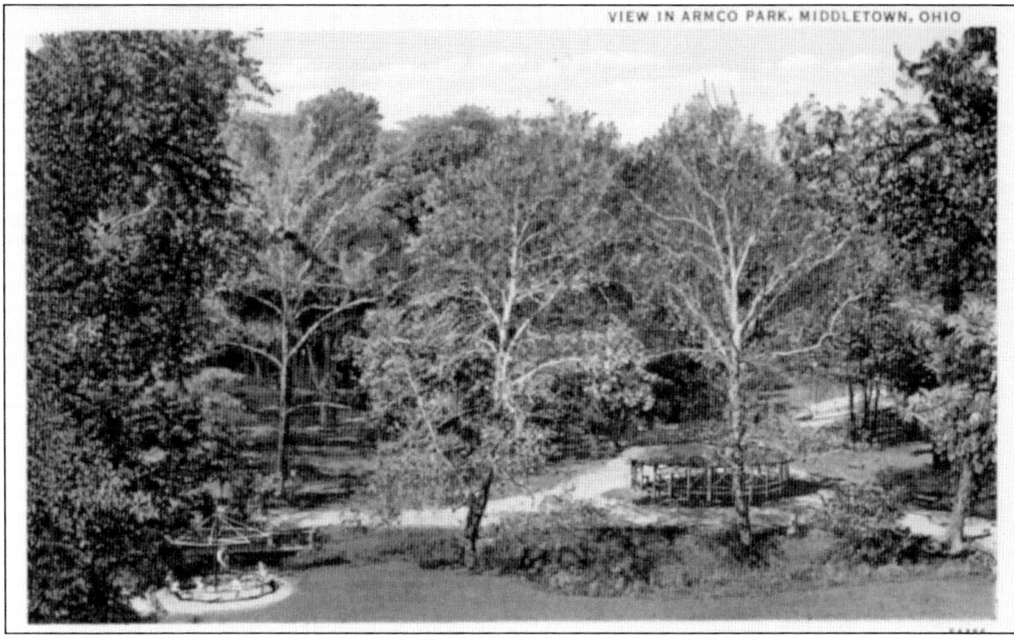

Armco purchased a large tract of land in the northeast part of town that the company developed into a park for all local citizens. One section, Bunny Hollow, was for very young park visitors.

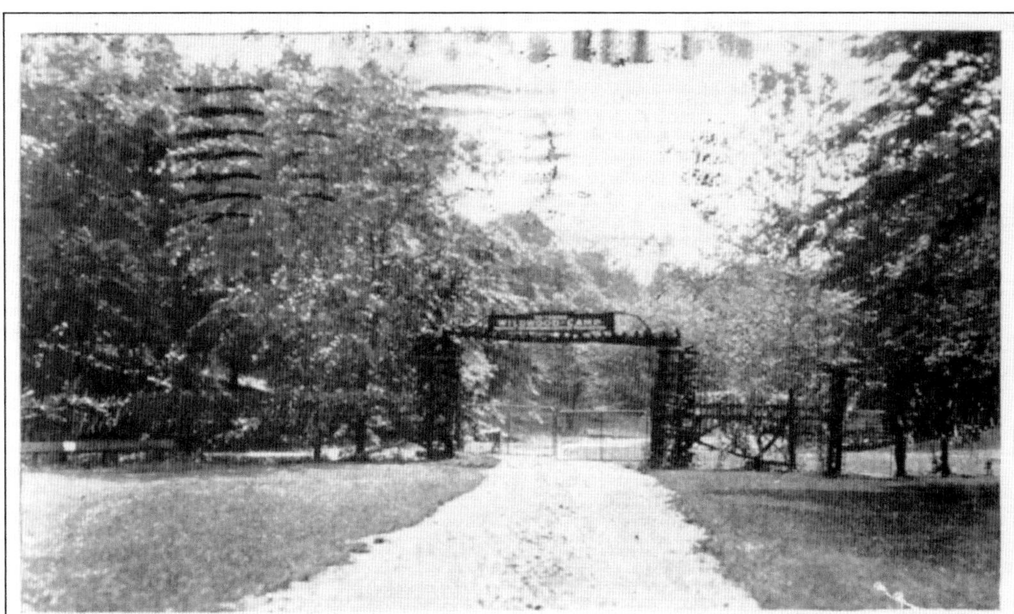

Postmarked August 18, 1927, this postcard shows a small area of what became Armco Park. At that time, this section was a camp area for young people, especially scouts.

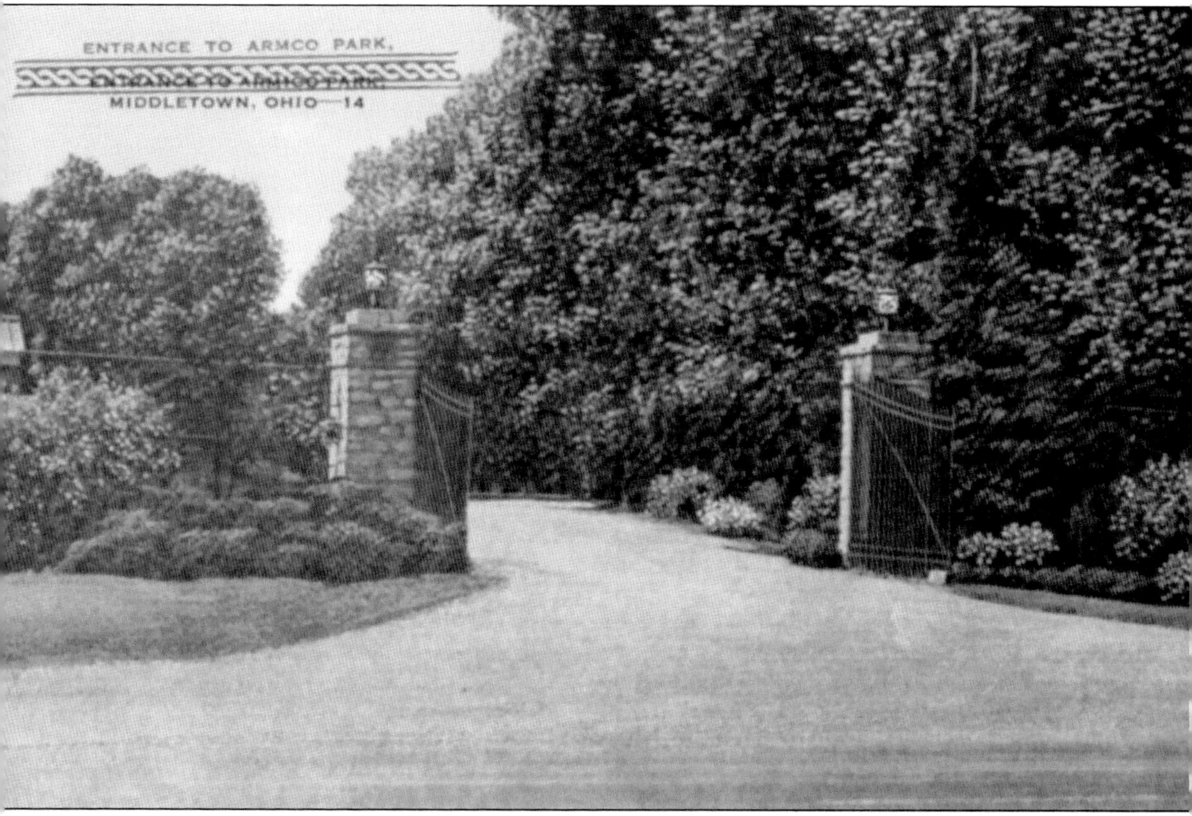

This card shows the entrance gates to Armco Park. Note that, because of a spelling error, the original caption was marked over, and a new one was printed on the card. Today, Armco Park is the home of Miami University Middletown (MUM) branch campus.

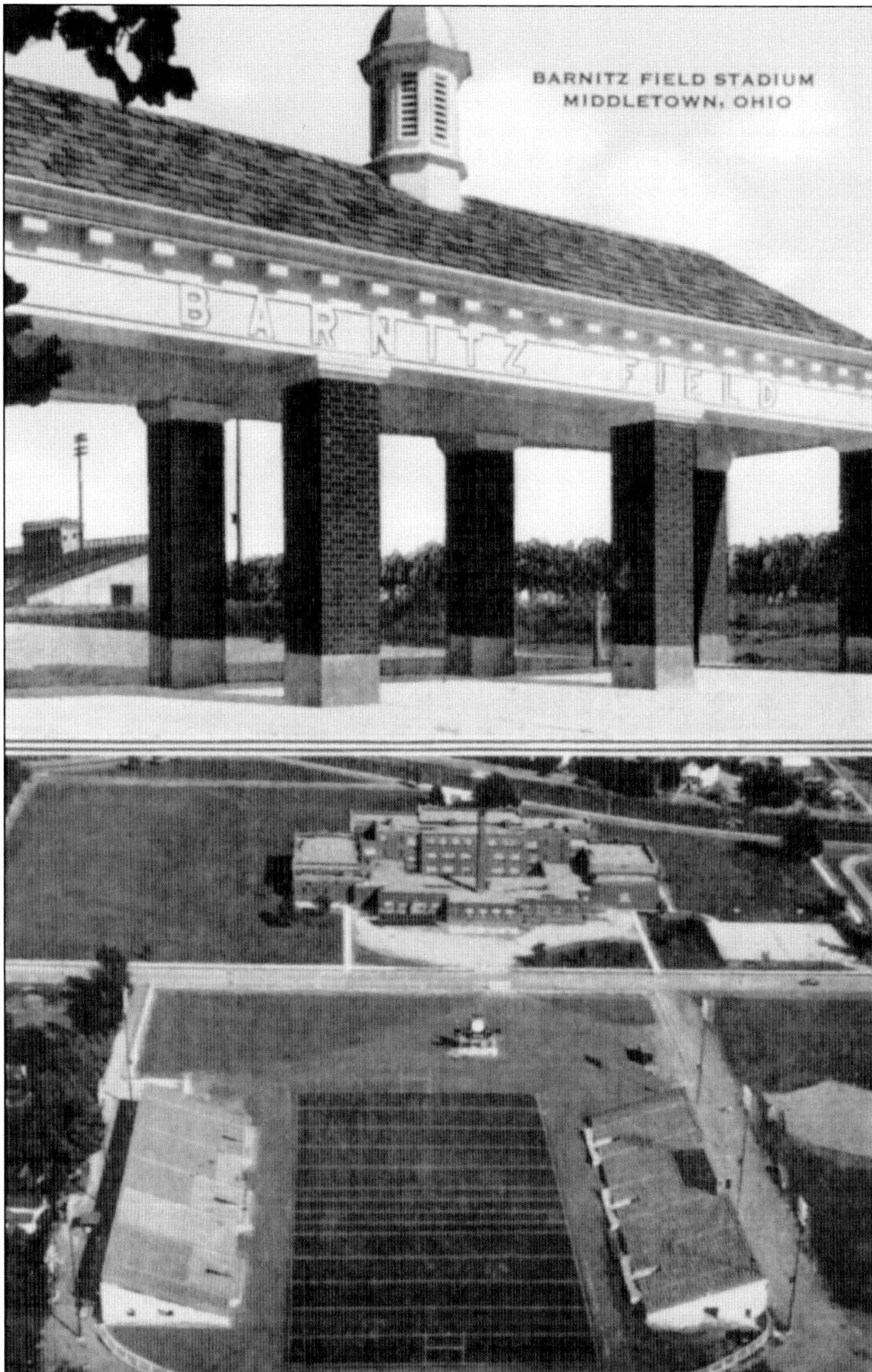

The Barnitz Field Stadium was constructed in 1950 for Middletown High School's football team. It seats 10,000 people. Other local schools, as well as civic groups, have made use of the stadium. The school in the background was McKinley Junior High School.

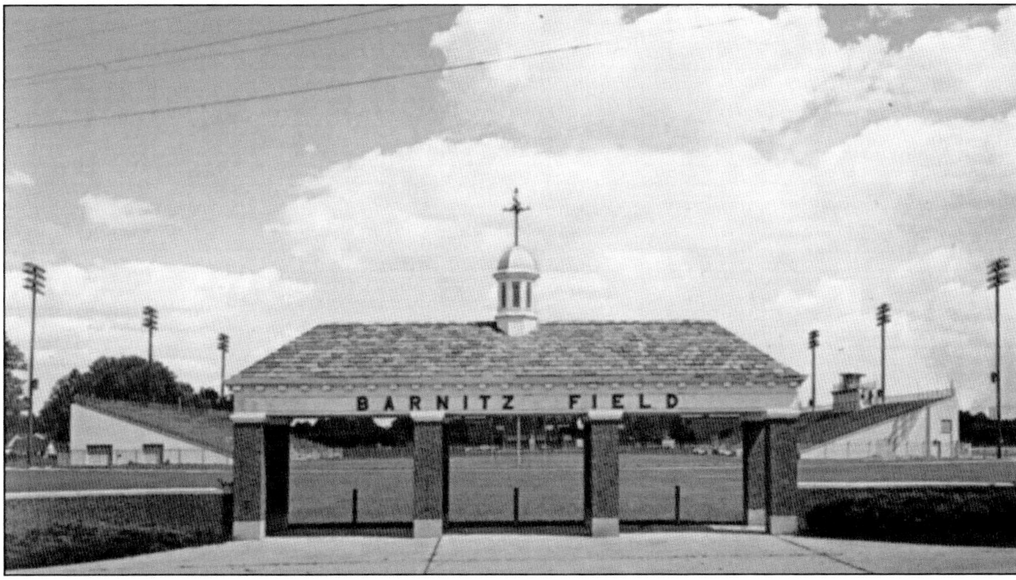

The land for Barnitz Field Stadium was owned by the well-known Barnitz family. The family had the entrance to the field built. It was later knocked down by a visiting team's truck.

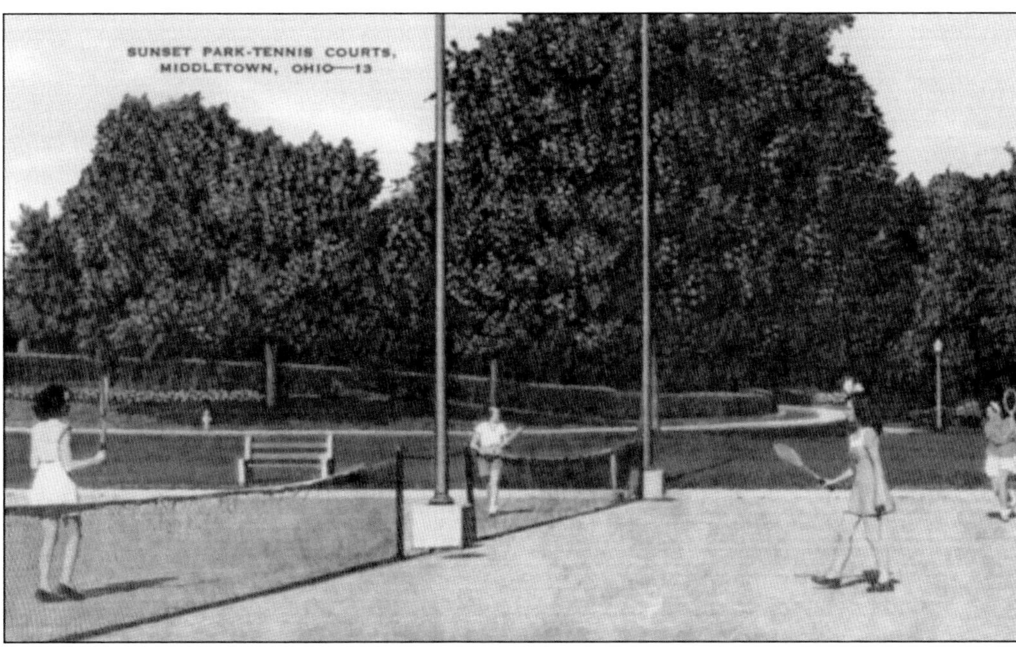

Middletown has many parks, one of which is Sunset Park, where these tennis courts are located. Another activity at the park was basketball, at which Middletown High School excelled during the 1950s. Many players learned and practiced here. The park also had a public swimming pool.

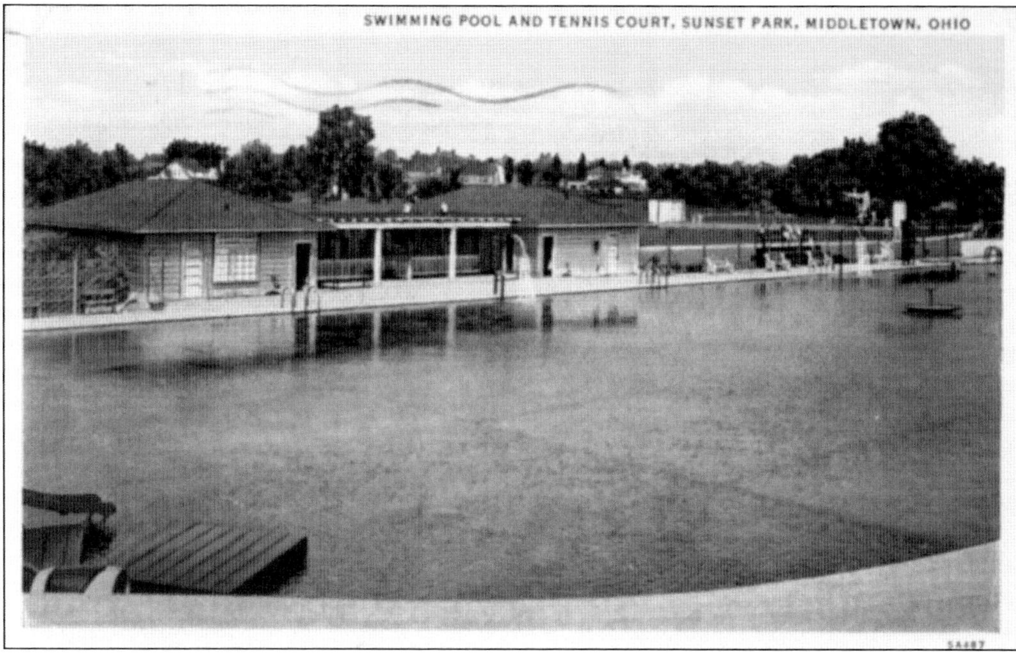

The first public swimming pool in the city was constructed in Sunset Park. It opened in 1928, replacing the swimming hole in Bull's Run Creek.

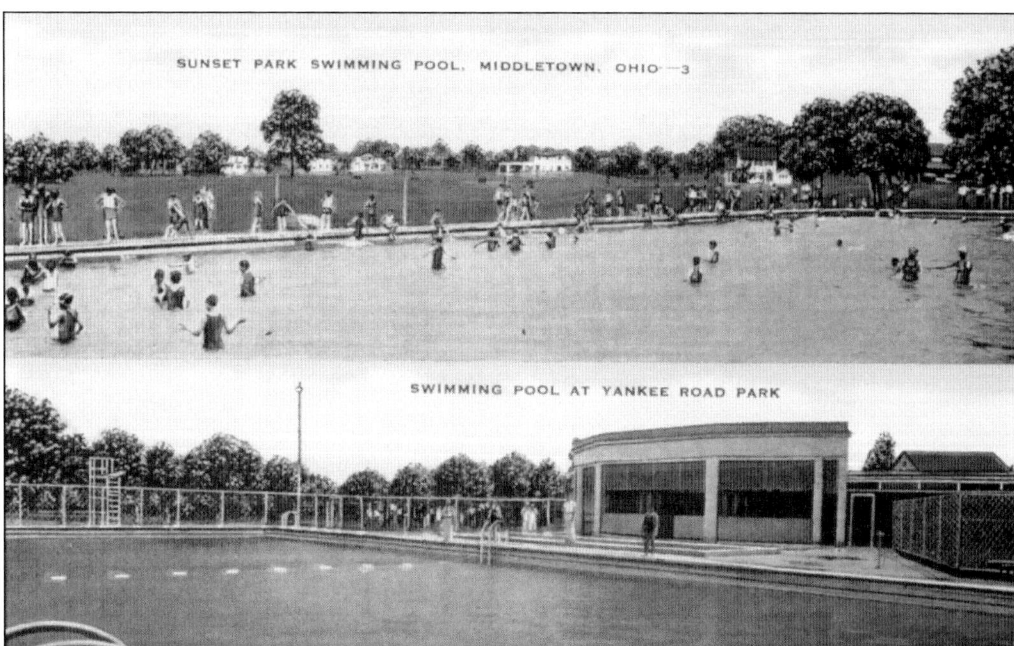

A second swimming pool was constructed in Yankee Road Park. This postcard shows both of the pools. Later, a third one was built in Douglas Park.

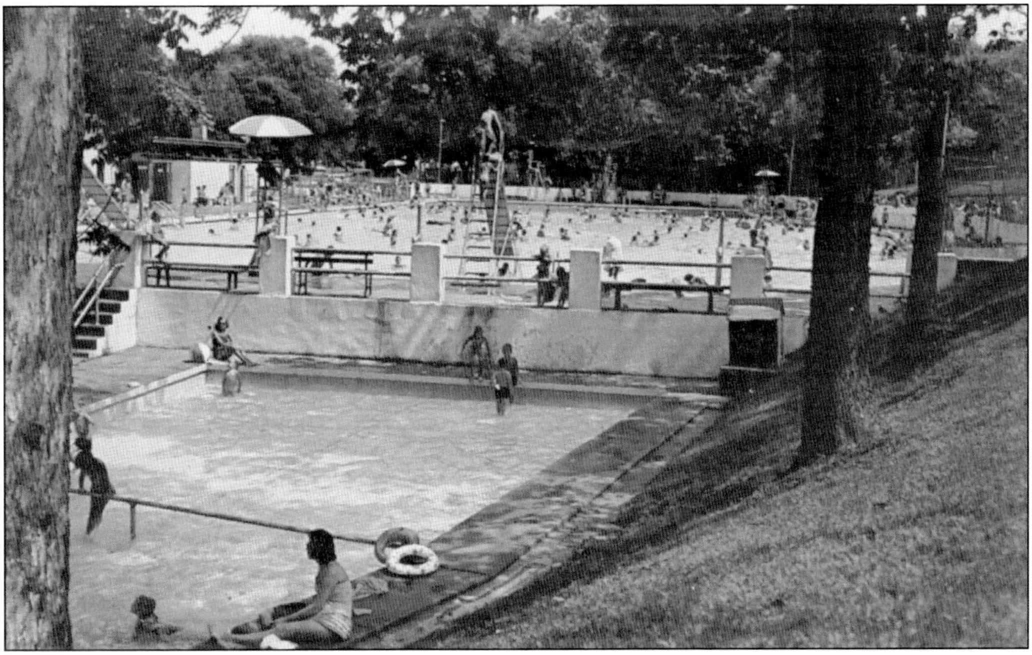

In 1979, the original Sunset Pool was replaced with a new one. It opened on Labor Day of that year and closed for the season the next day, however, it was ready for the next year.

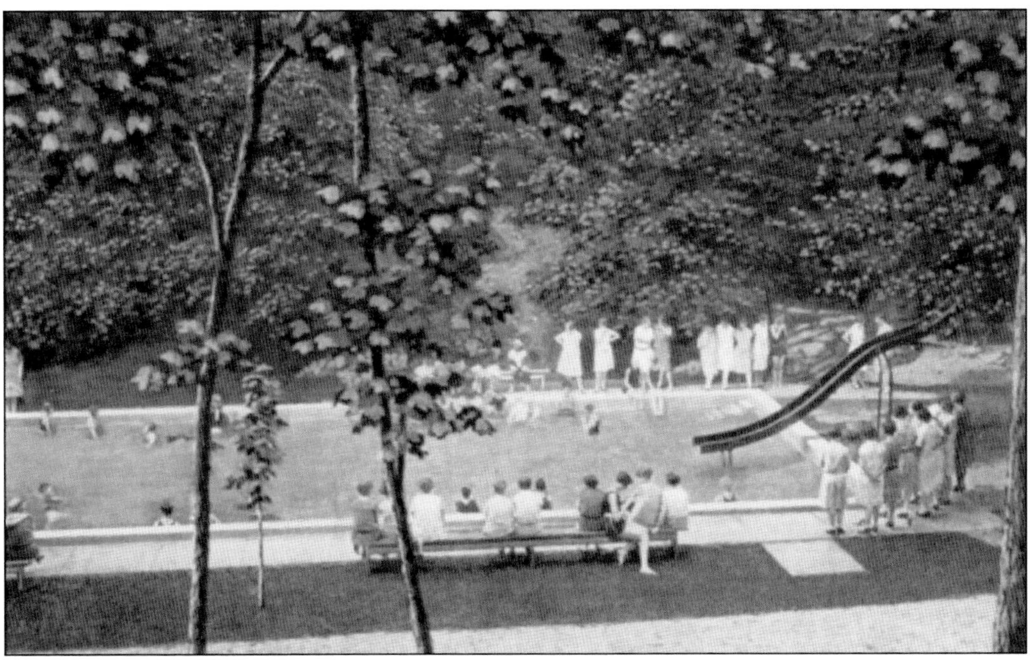

From the 1920s until the 1960s, the American Rolling Mill Company provided Armco Park for its employees and the citizens of the area. At one time, a section of the park was set aside for Forest Hills Country Club, where there was a private swimming pool.

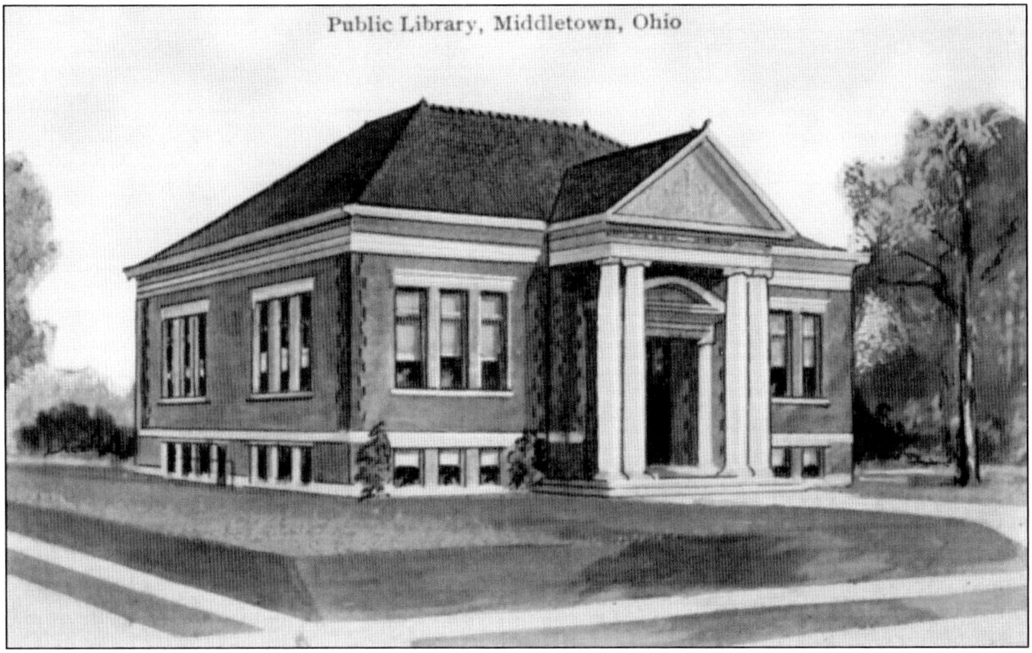

With a push from George M. Verity, founder of Armco, and the work of local attorney William H. Todhunter, the city finally got a library. Several ideas for a library showed up on postcards. This is one of the different ideas.

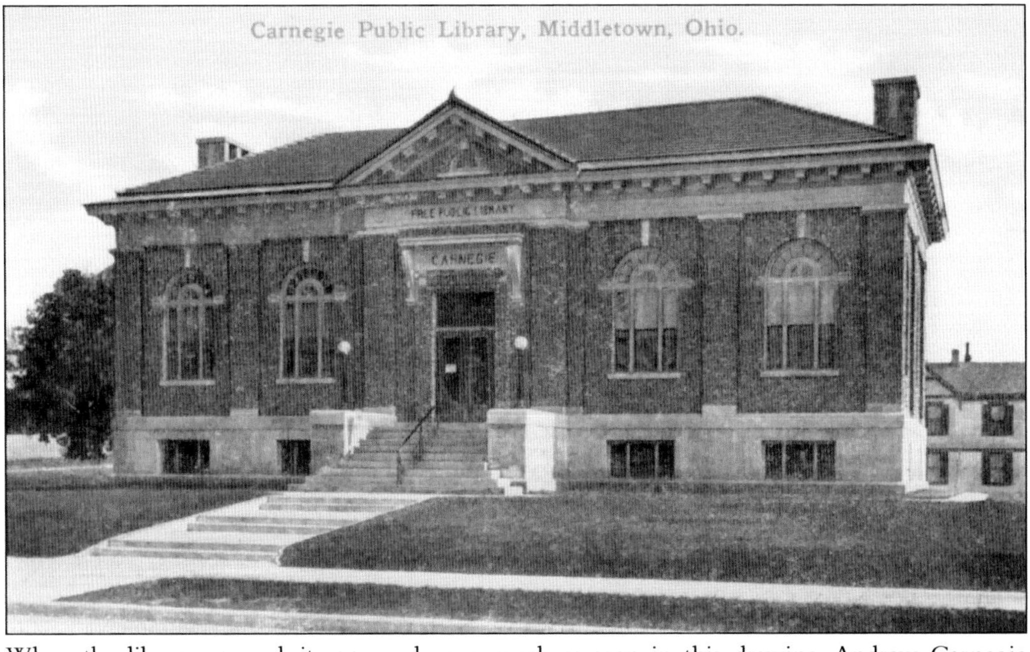

When the library opened, it appeared very much as seen in this drawing. Andrew Carnegie provided part of the funding. It opened January 2, 1913, and was enlarged several times.

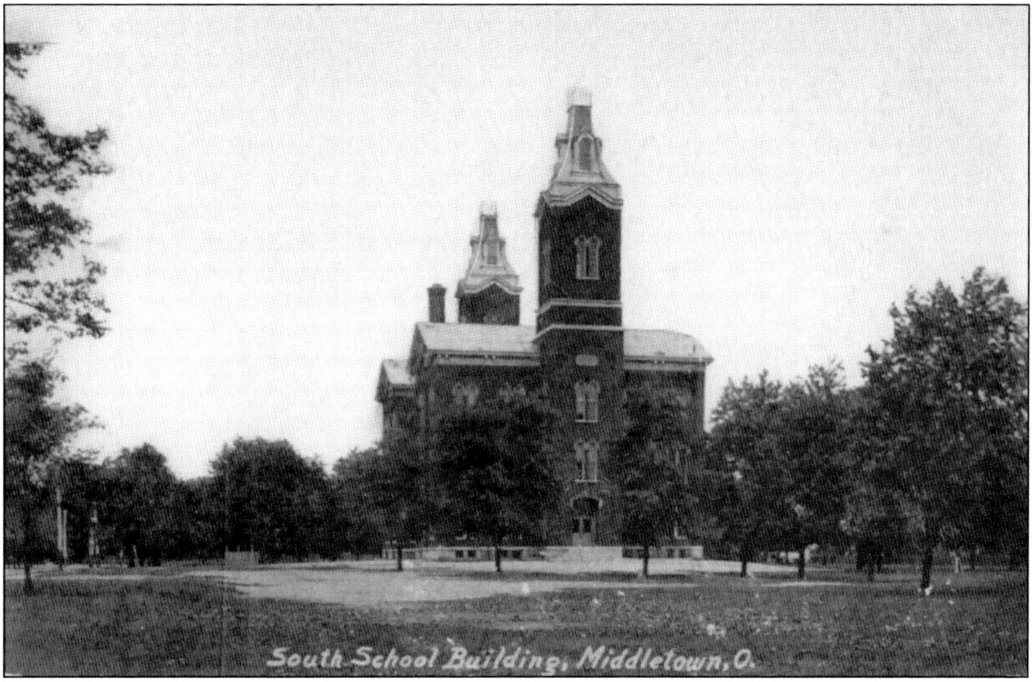

Best known as South School, this building opened in 1871 as Union School. Middletown's first true high school was on the third floor. It was in use as a public school until 1951 and was later used as the first home of Bishop Fenwick High School, a Catholic school.

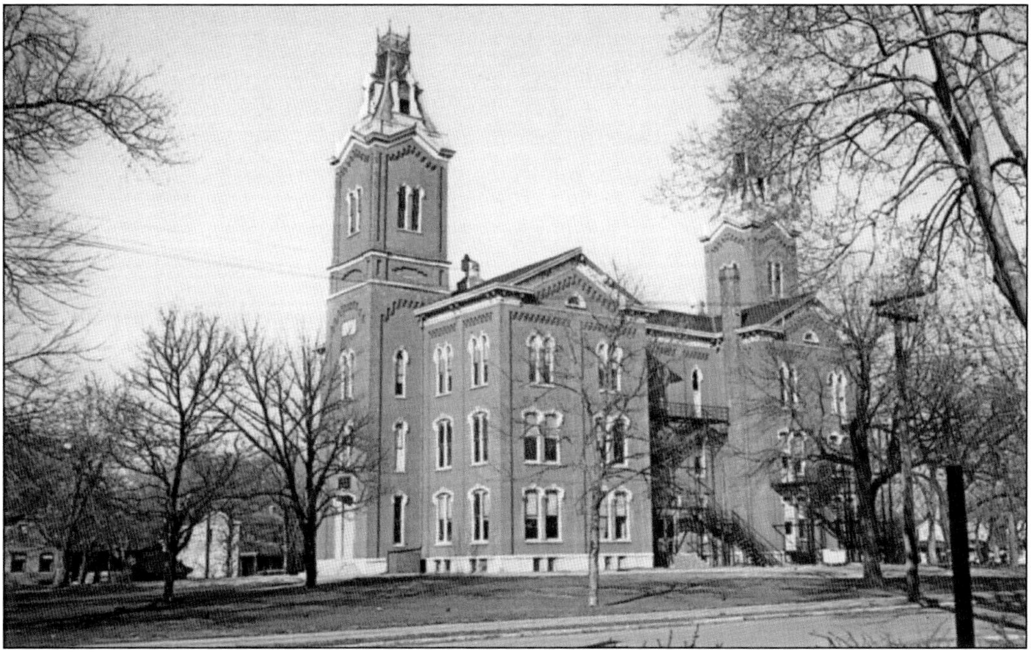

Several different postcards were made of old South School. Probably the last one was made by Middletown resident Glenn Perry. On April 23, 1965, the old building accidentally burned down.

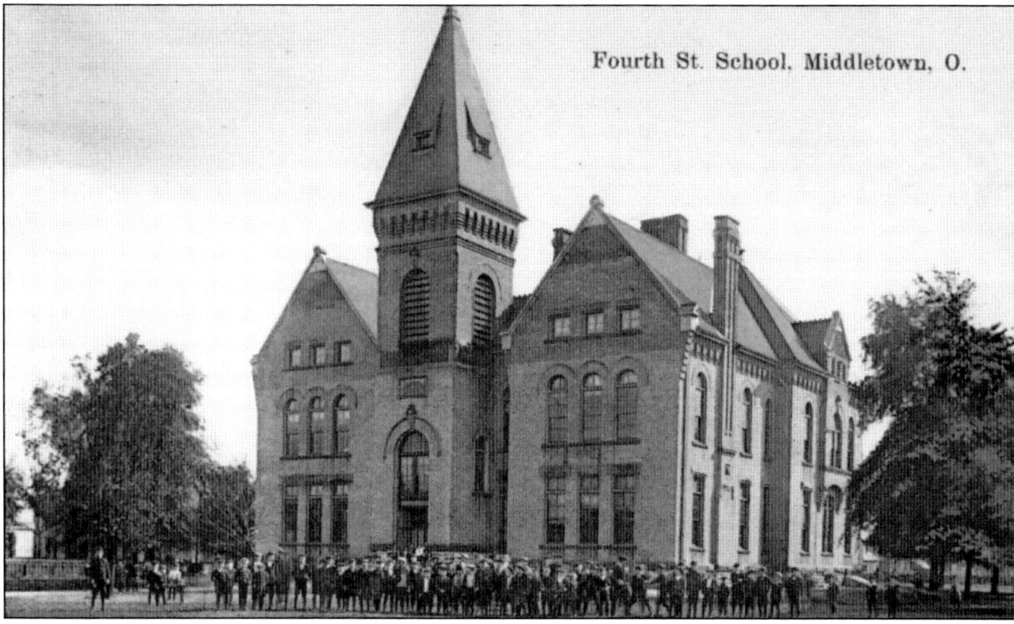

Originally known as Fourth Street School, Central School opened in 1885. Closed in 1958, it was replaced the next year with a new school on the same site and with the same name.

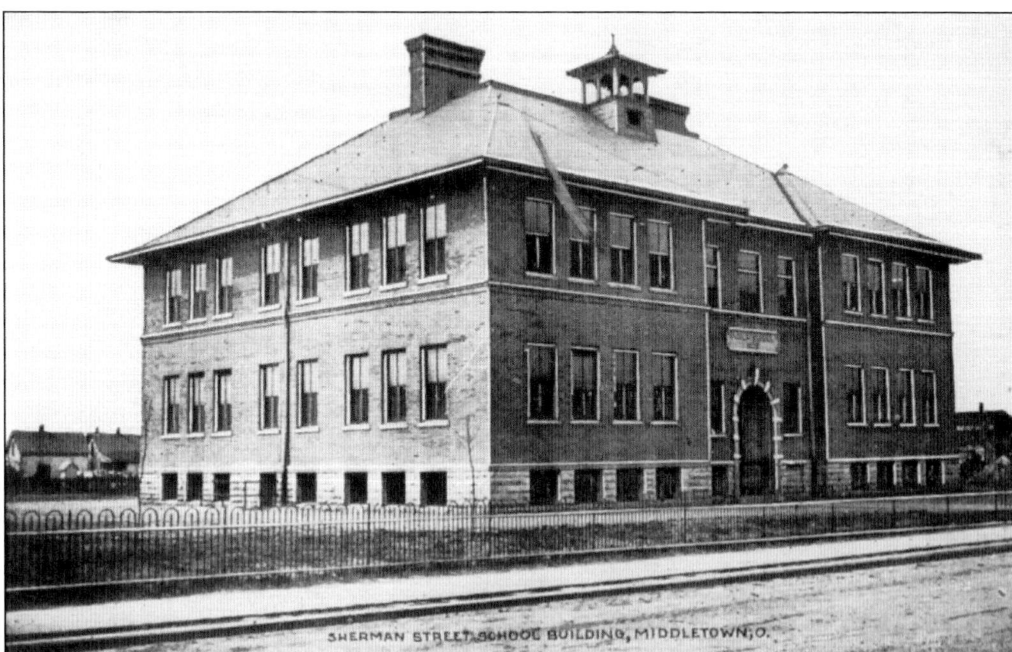

Opened in 1904, Sherman School was located on Sherman Street. In 1914, a second building was added to the east of the original structure. The buildings continued in use as an elementary school until 1981.

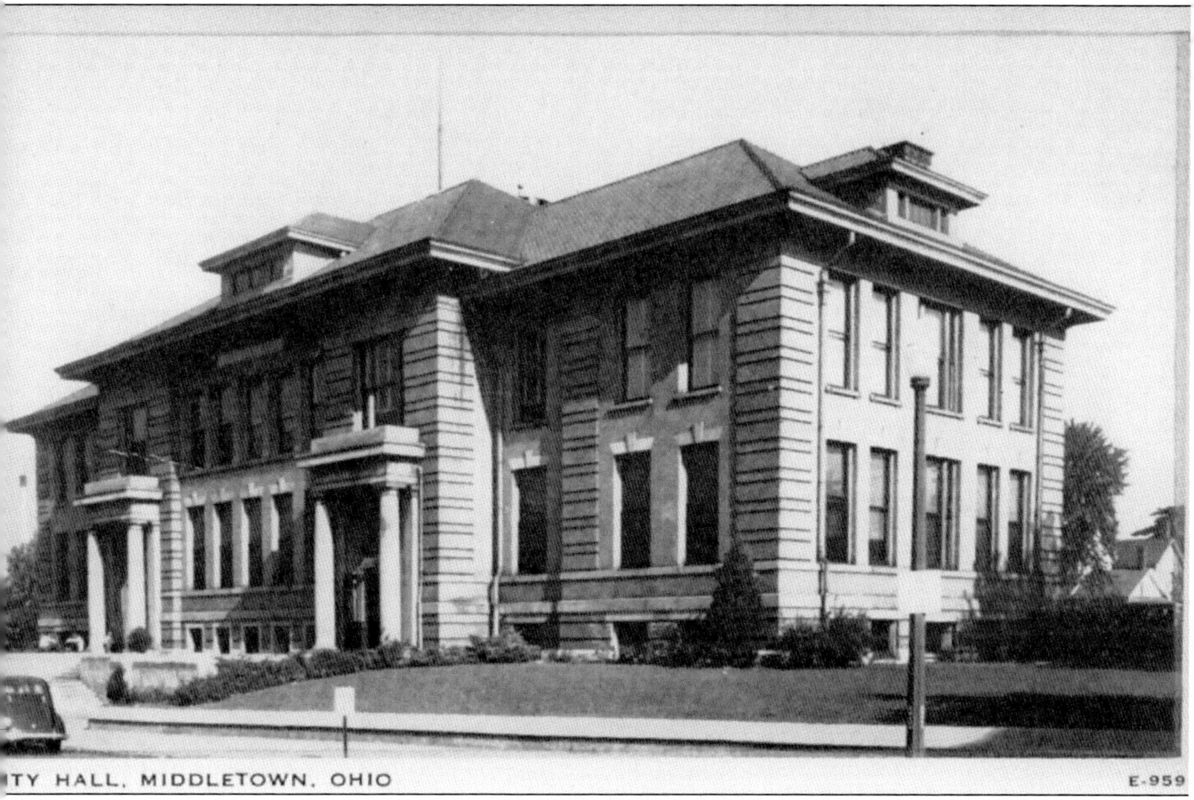

The first building erected as an exclusive high school opened in 1908 at the corner of Clark Street and Central Avenue. It was in use as a school building until 1931. After that, it was used as Middletown City Building until 1976.

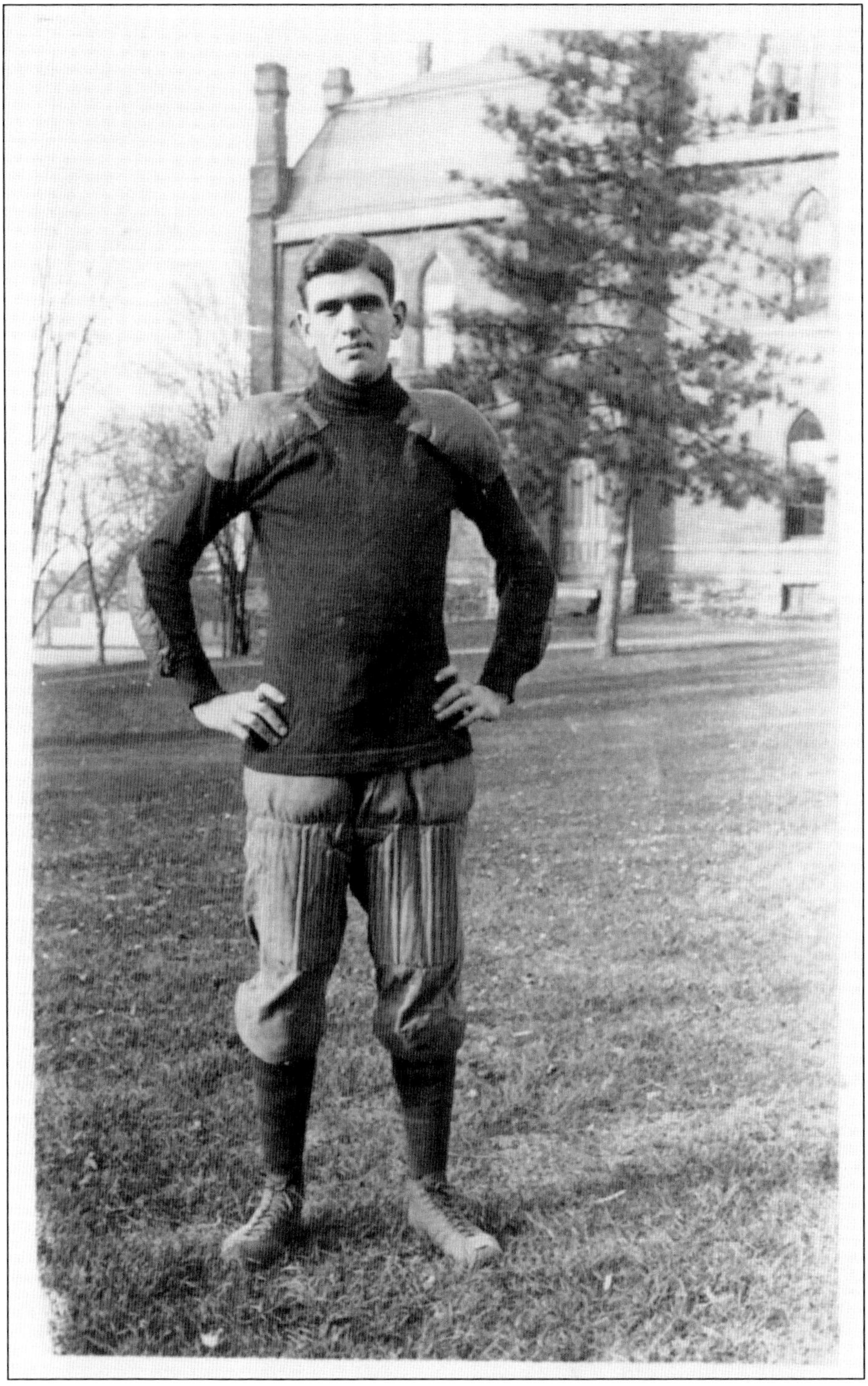

For 40 years, Elmo Lingrel served as a Middletown coach and athletic director. He began his career in 1923, with his football teams winning 149 games, losing 32, and tying 19. His 1934 team went undefeated in 10 games, while his 1936 team was undefeated, with some opposing teams unable to score against them. (Courtesy of Middletown Historical Collection, Middletown Public Library.)

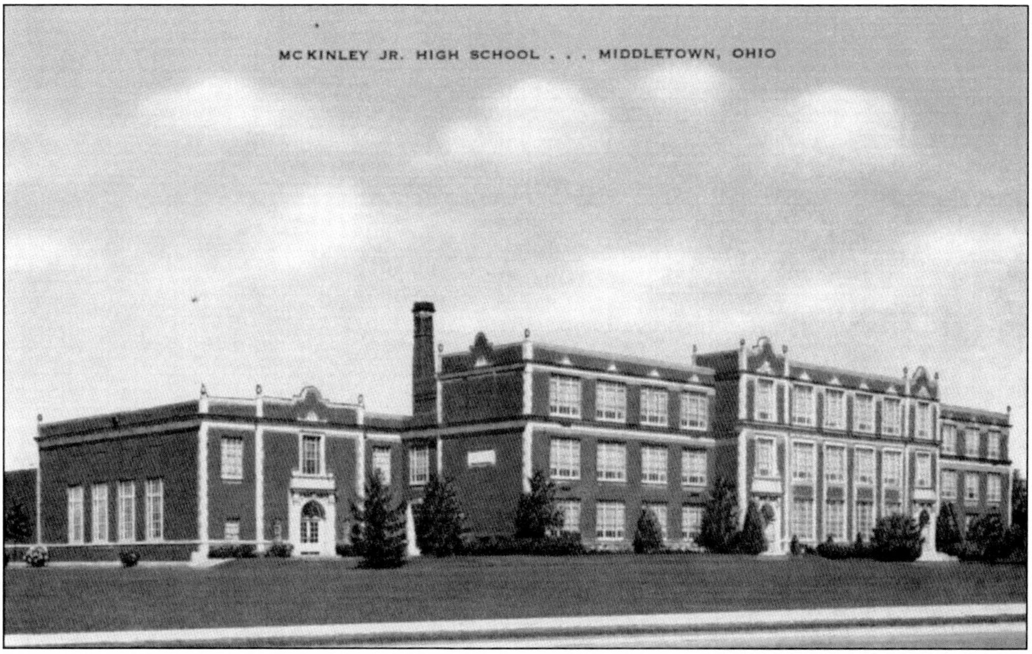

Two new junior high school buildings opened in 1930. They were named for former presidents Roosevelt and McKinley. McKinley was located on Verity Parkway in the south end of town. It has been torn down and replaced by Rosa Parks Elementary School.

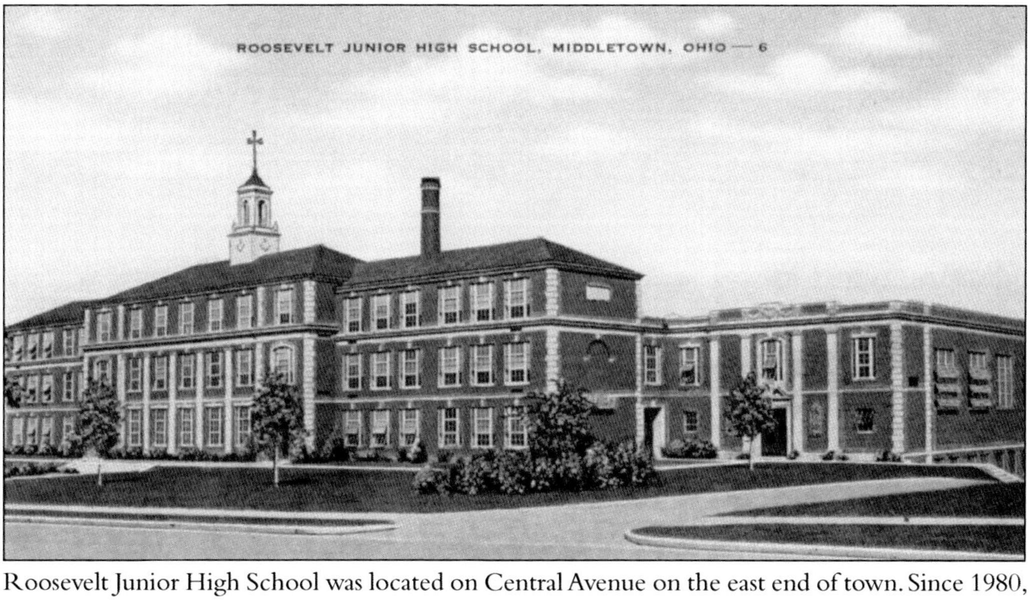

Roosevelt Junior High School was located on Central Avenue on the east end of town. Since 1980, it was used as an elementary school but has since been torn down. Two new buildings, Highview and Wildwood, have replaced it.

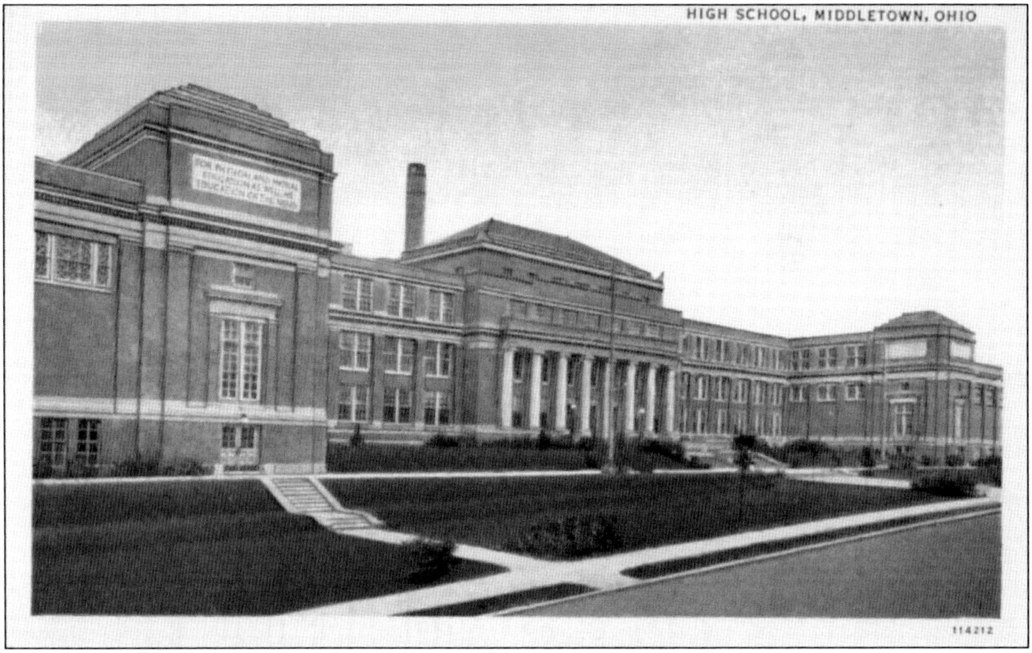

One of the finest and most expensive schools to open in Ohio was the new Middletown High School. It opened in the fall of 1923 and was the third building used as a high school. Today, it is Vail Middle School and is used for grades six through nine.

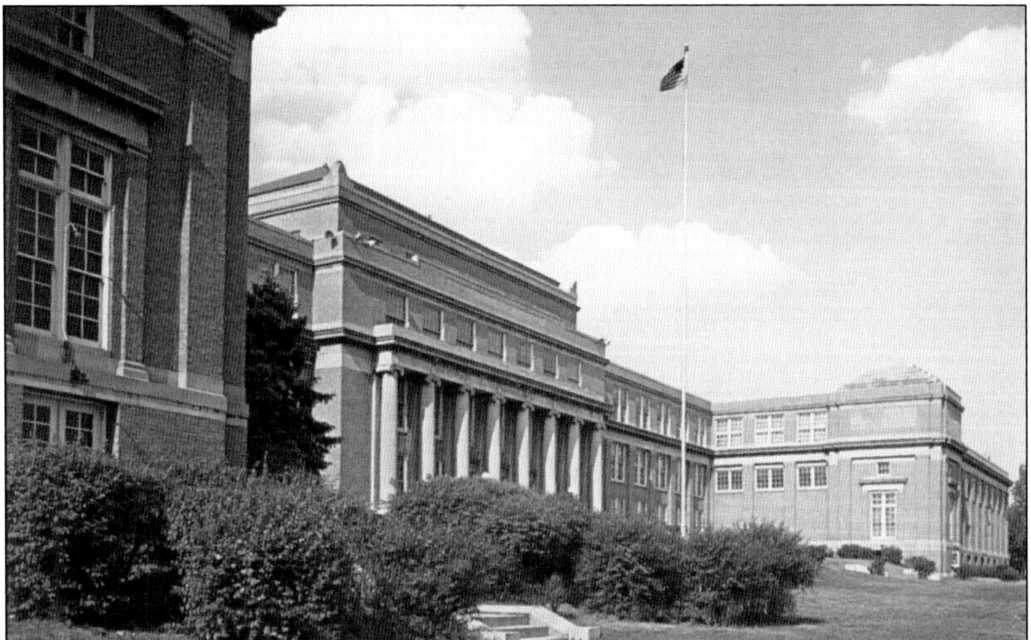

When the old Middletown High School was constructed, it was one the finest high schools in Ohio. It was made up of 55 classrooms, a lecture room with a projection booth, two huge study halls, a spacious and well-equipped science room, a greenhouse, and a gymnasium. R.W. Soloman was the school system's superintendent, and Wade E. Miller was the principal.

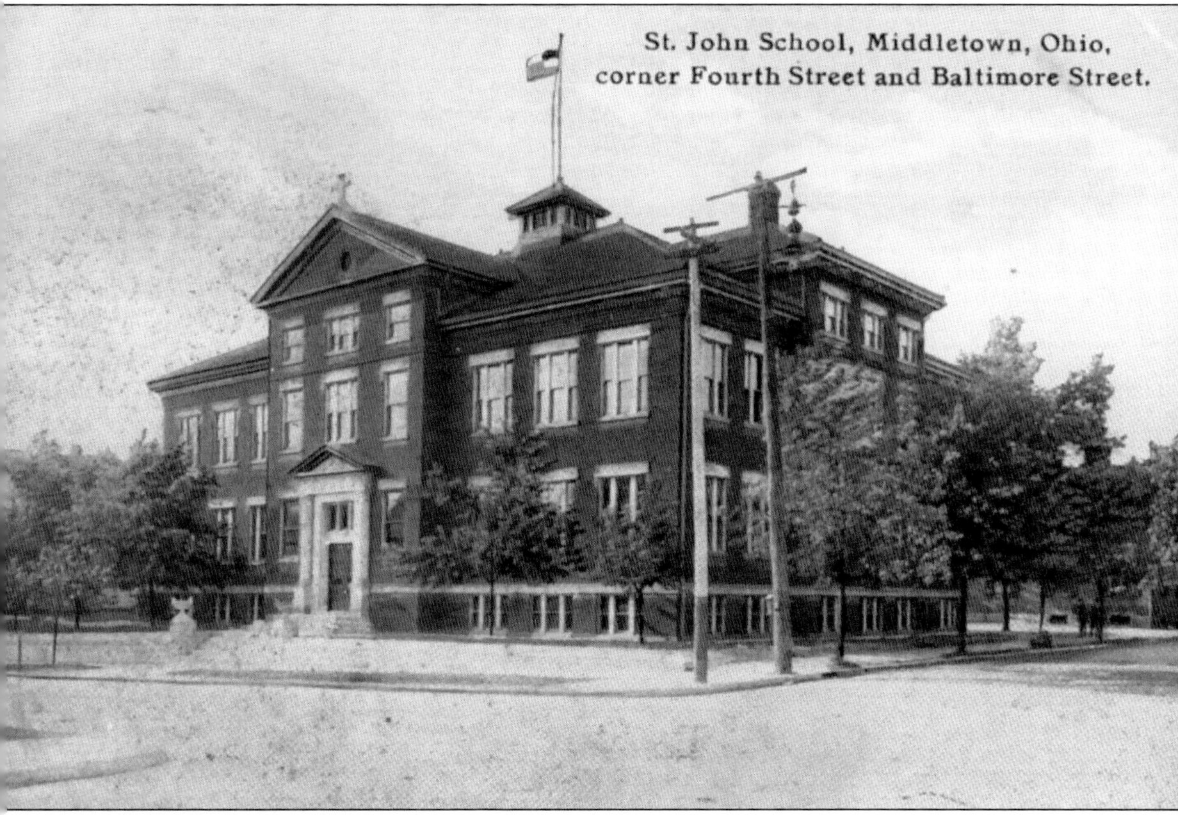

The Catholics have their own elementary and high schools. At one time, there were three Catholic elementary schools, one of them being St. John School. It was constructed in 1908 and closed in 1991.

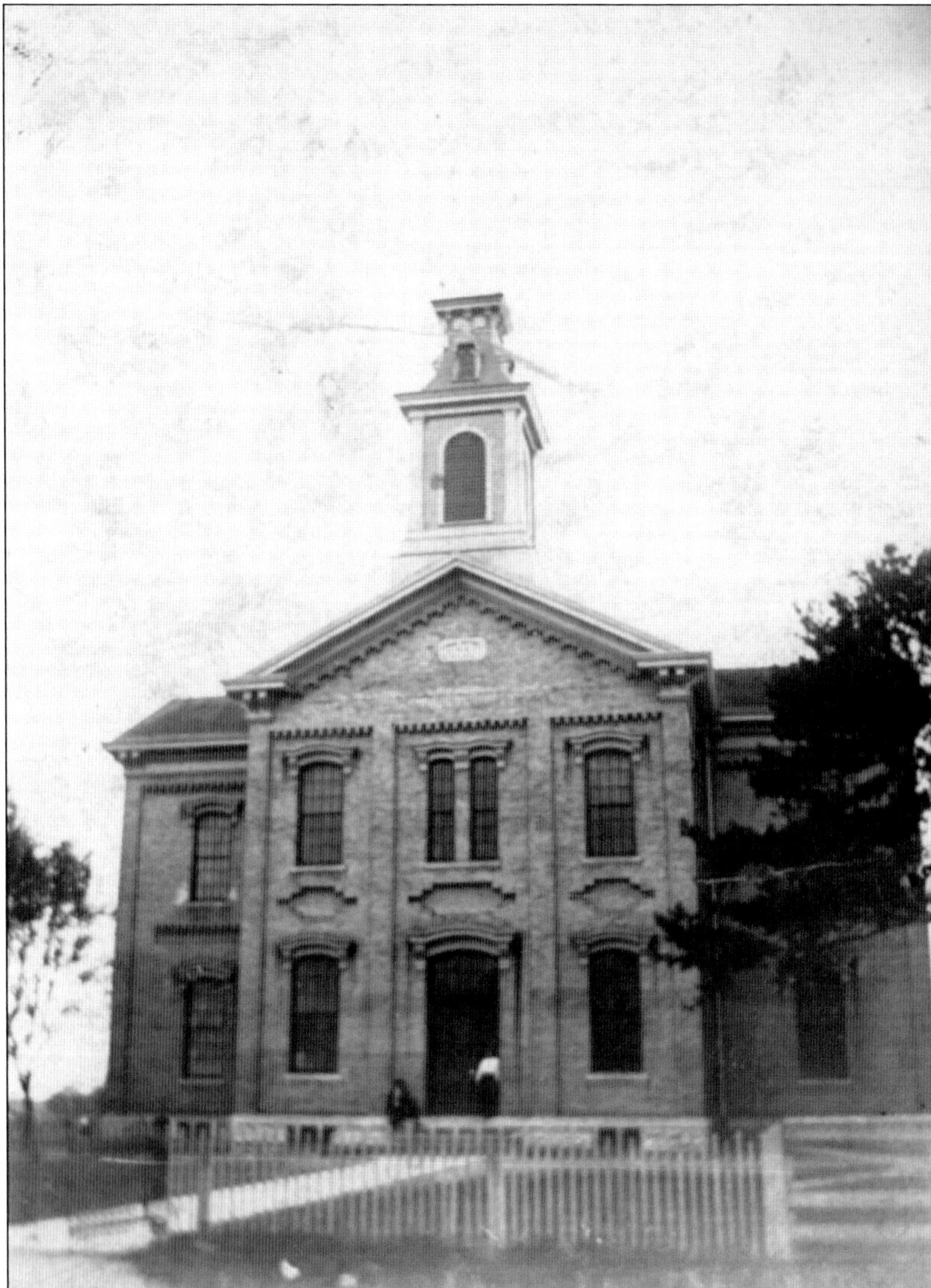

Amanda School was part of the Lemon Township School District. It was built in 1873 and housed elementary through high school. The building has been torn down, and the children of the area attend the nearby Amanda Elementary School that is part of the Middletown School System. (Courtesy of Roger L. Miller.)

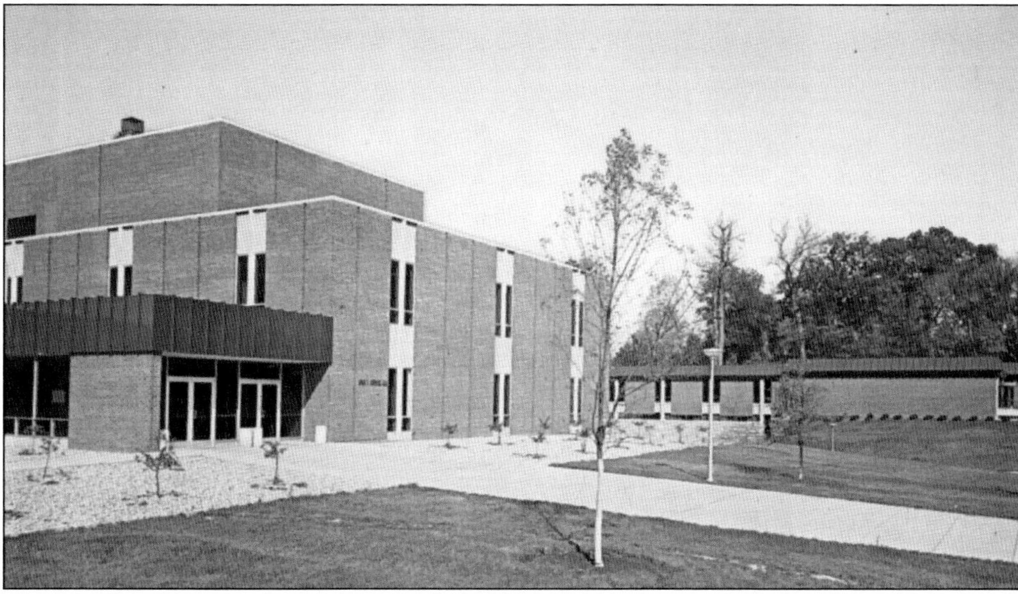

In 1966, the Middletown campus of Miami University of Ohio opened in the old Armco Park. It is best known as Miami University Middletown (MUM). Logan T. Johnston Hall was one of the first three buildings on the campus. The others were the Gardner-Harvey Library and the student center, which was the old Armco Girl's Holiday House but is now known as Verity Hall.

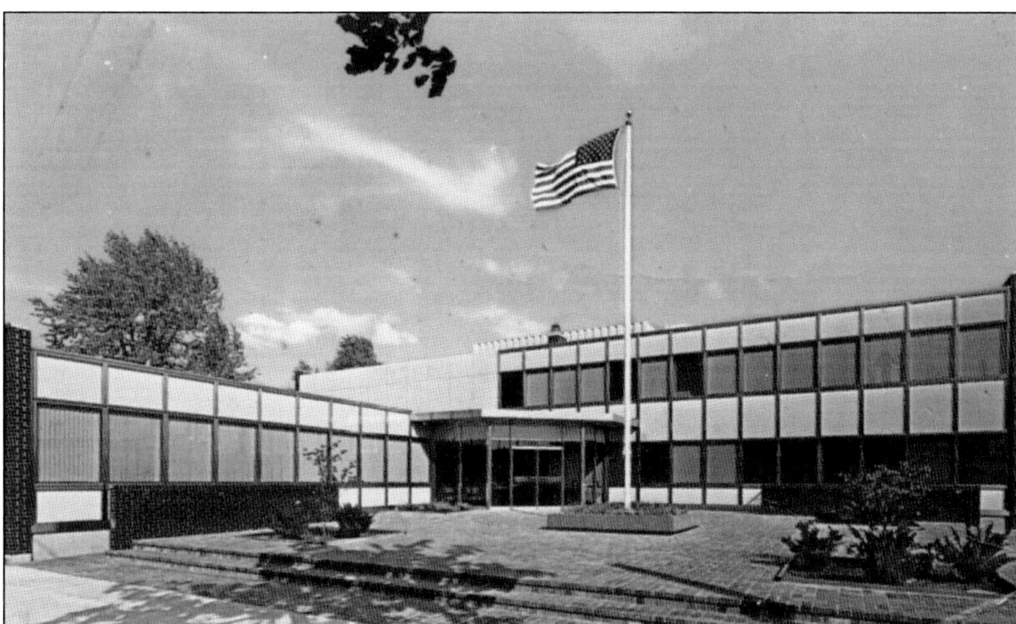

In 1923, the Middletown Civic Association, forerunner of today's Middletown branch of the United Way, was organized. This building was erected as a result of a campaign held in 1957. It opened in May 1964, became the Middletown Area United Way in 1974, and later merged with the Cincinnati United Way. Although it recently moved from this building, the organization continues to support many local health, welfare, and recreational agencies.

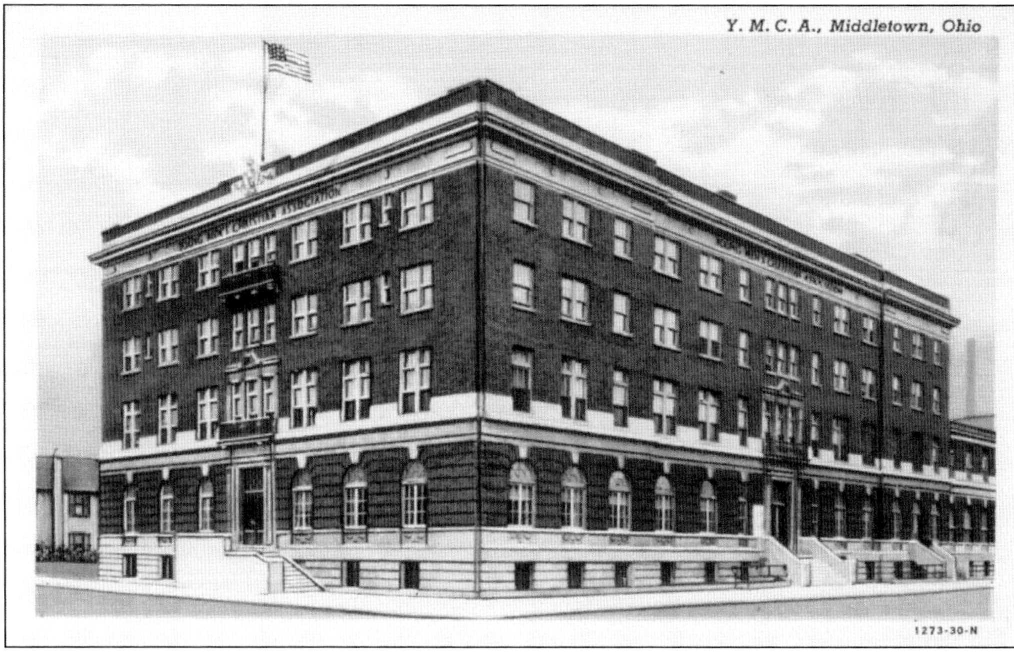

On March 21, 1867, Middletown's first YMCA was organized. It was not successful, but the third reorganization of the group was successful, and this building opened on the corner of Broad Street and Manchester Avenue on October 15, 1923. An addition was completed in 1985. What is seen here was torn down, but the newer section is still in use. A new branch has opened at the Atrium Medical Center.

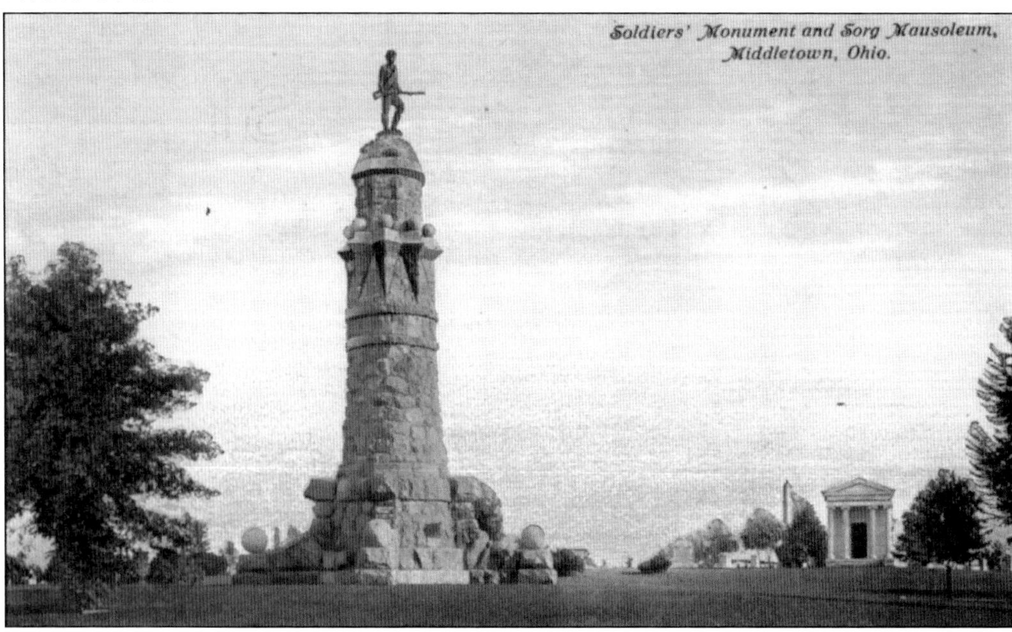

Middletown's leading industrialist, Paul J. Sorg, challenged the citizens to construct a monument in honor of the soldiers and sailors who fought in the Civil War and the Spanish-American War. Constructed in Woodside Cemetery and Arboretum, it was dedicated on December 24, 1902. Sorg, who died before the monument was completed, is interred in a nearby mausoleum.

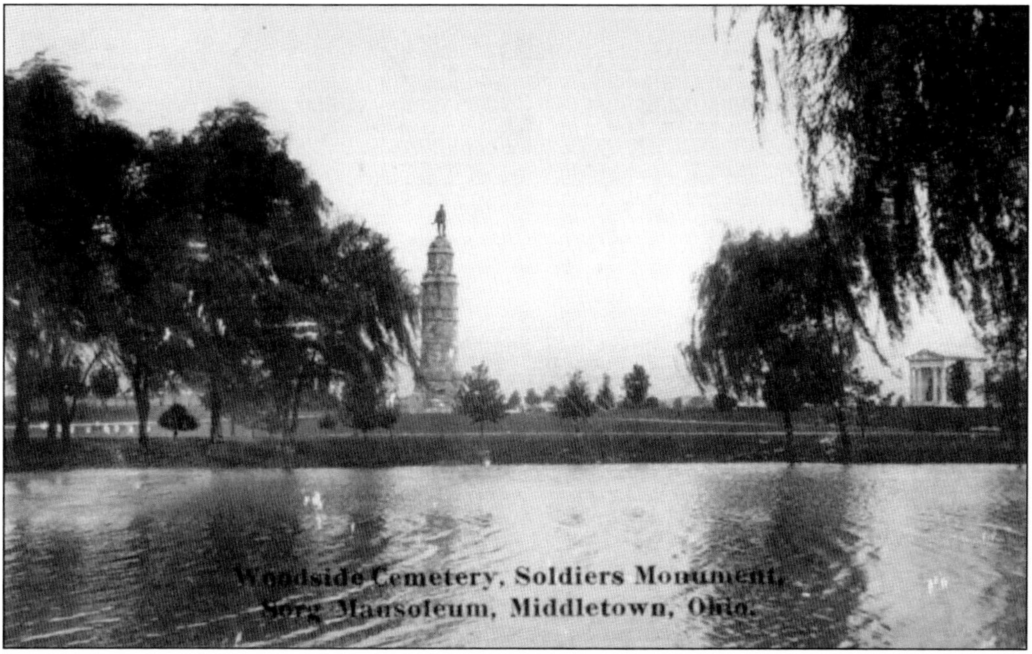

Woodside Cemetery and Arboretum is a beautiful cemetery. The first burial here took place on December 31, 1891. At one time, there were several ponds in the cemetery.

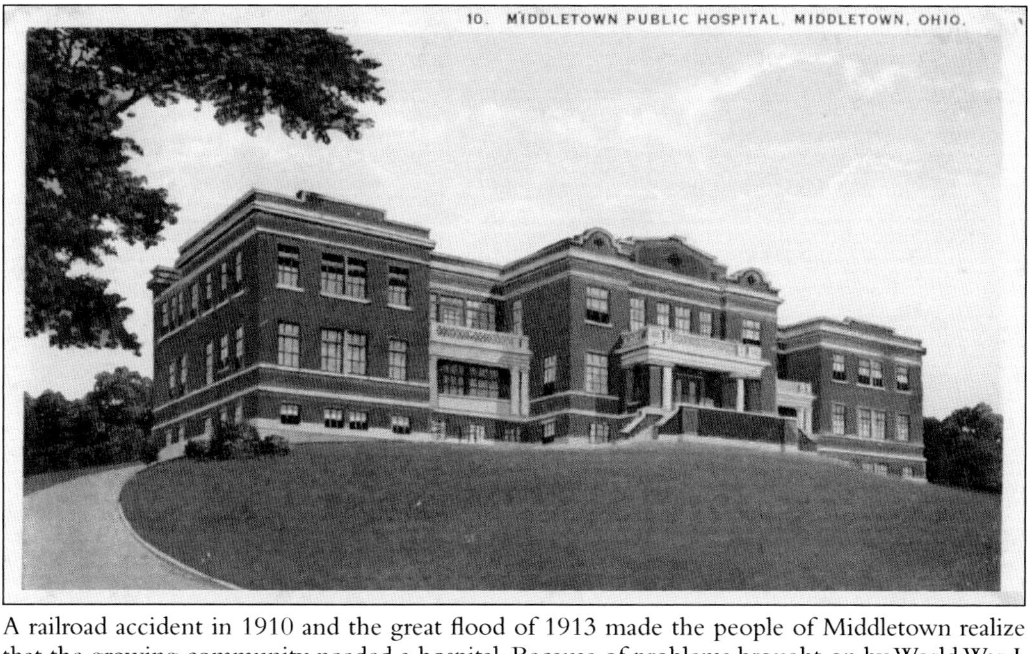

A railroad accident in 1910 and the great flood of 1913 made the people of Middletown realize that the growing community needed a hospital. Because of problems brought on by World War I, the hospital did not open until 1917.

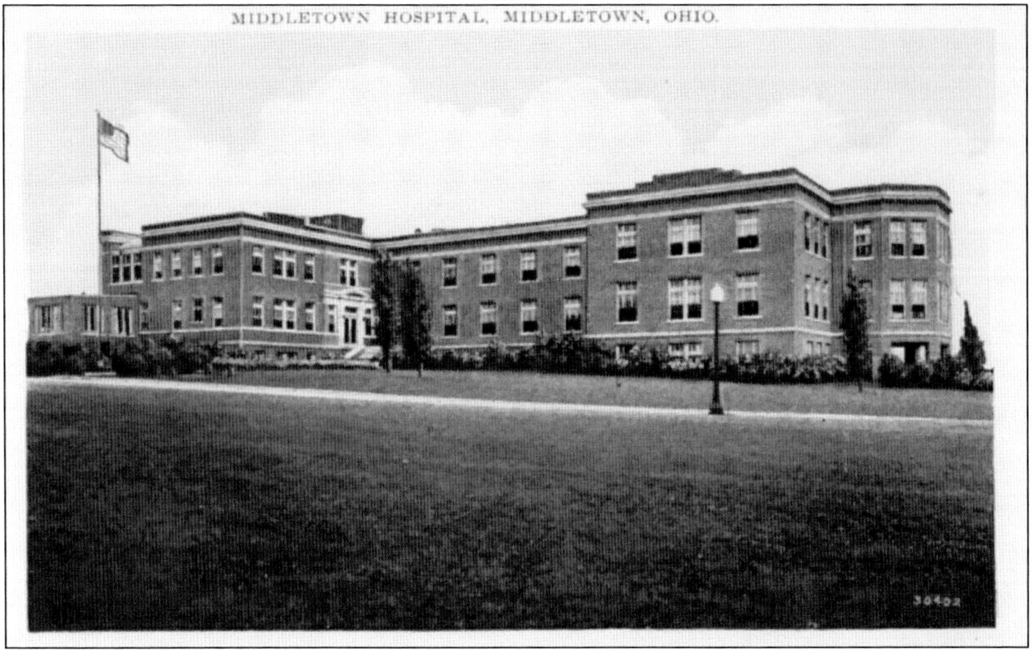

Over the years, several additions were made to the hospital. In December 2007, a new hospital opened on the east side of the city. The old hospital was torn down to make room for housing.

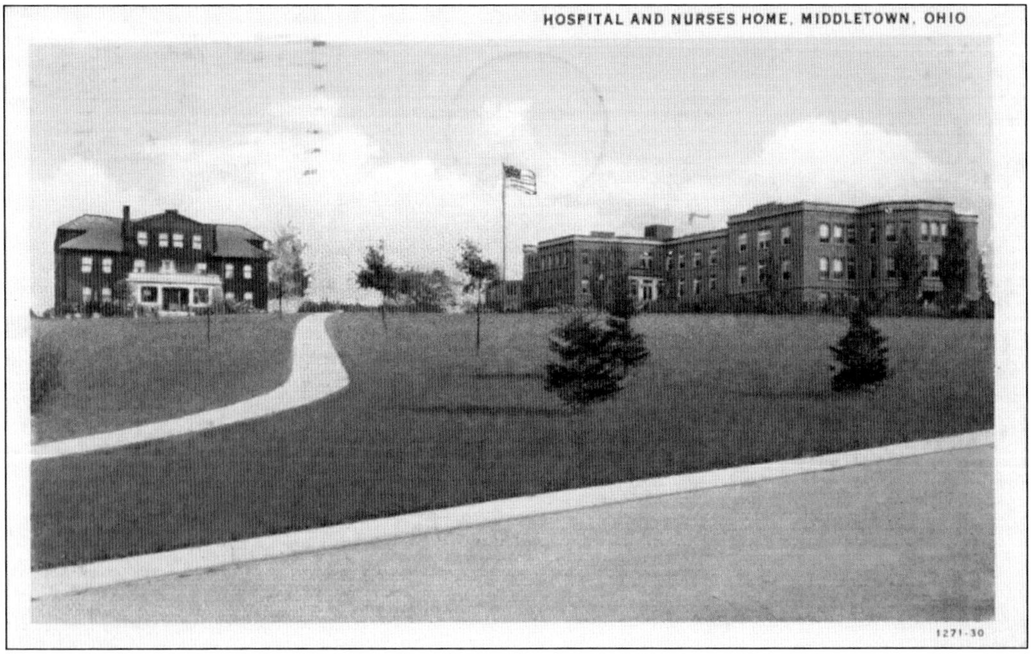

The Middletown Hospital had an excellent nursing school. The nurses' home was erected in 1918, and the School of Nursing was started in 1924, with the first class graduating in 1927. The last graduation took place in 1972.

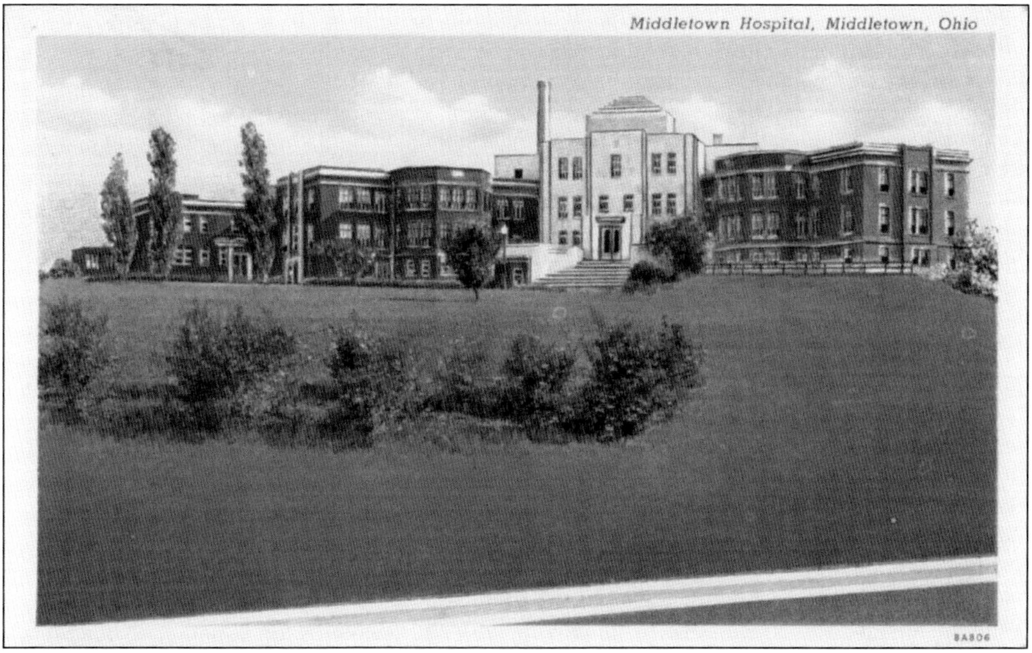

When the hospital was constructed, many people thought it was too far from the center of town; they soon found the city growing past it. The hospital sat upon a hill overlooking the city. In 1938, a large addition was made to the hospital.

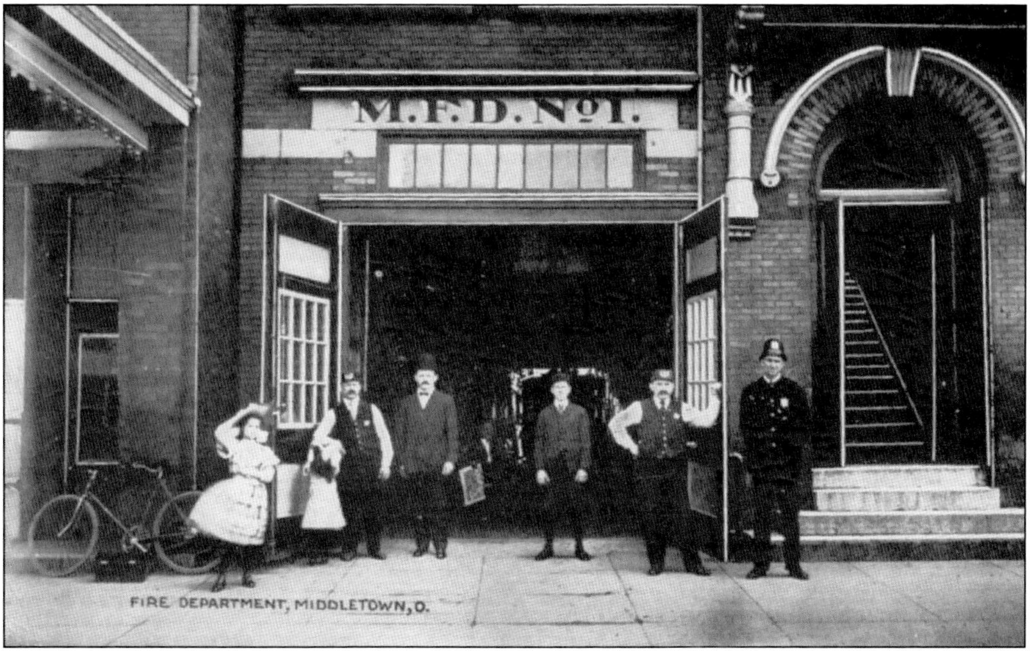

The Middletown Fire Department was organized in 1882. This building not only served as Middletown's first city building but it included the fire department, police station, and mayor's office. In 1897, a second fire station opened east of the railroad, thus, making this Middletown Fire Department No. 1 Fire Station.

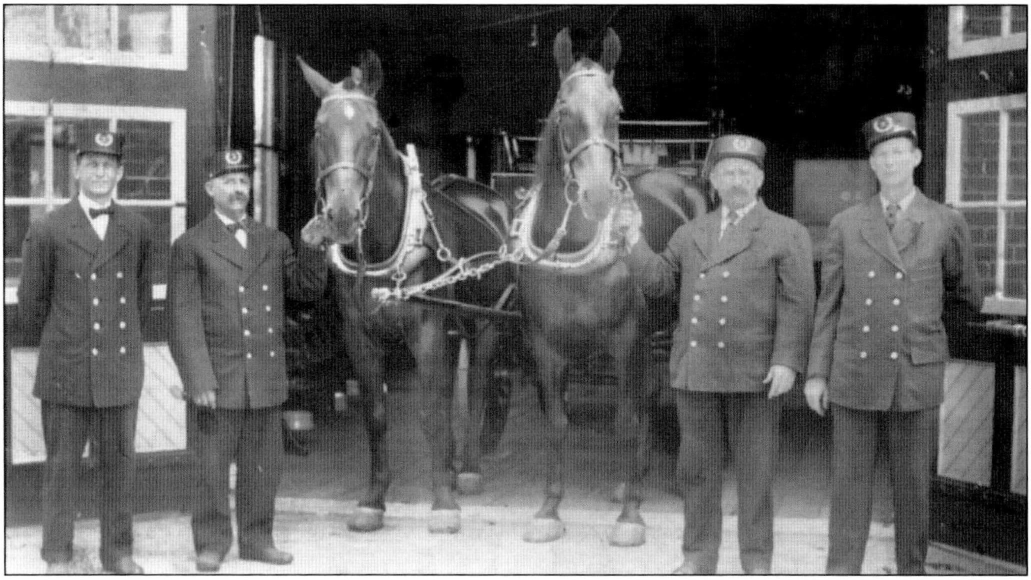

Fire horses Joe and Prince and, from left to right, firemen Orville Buckingham, Louis Keiser, John Ross, and Tom McCue stand in the doorway to No. 2 Fire Station. Horse-drawn fire equipment was first used in 1886 and continued in use until 1914. (Courtesy of George C. Crout Collection, Middletown Public Library.)

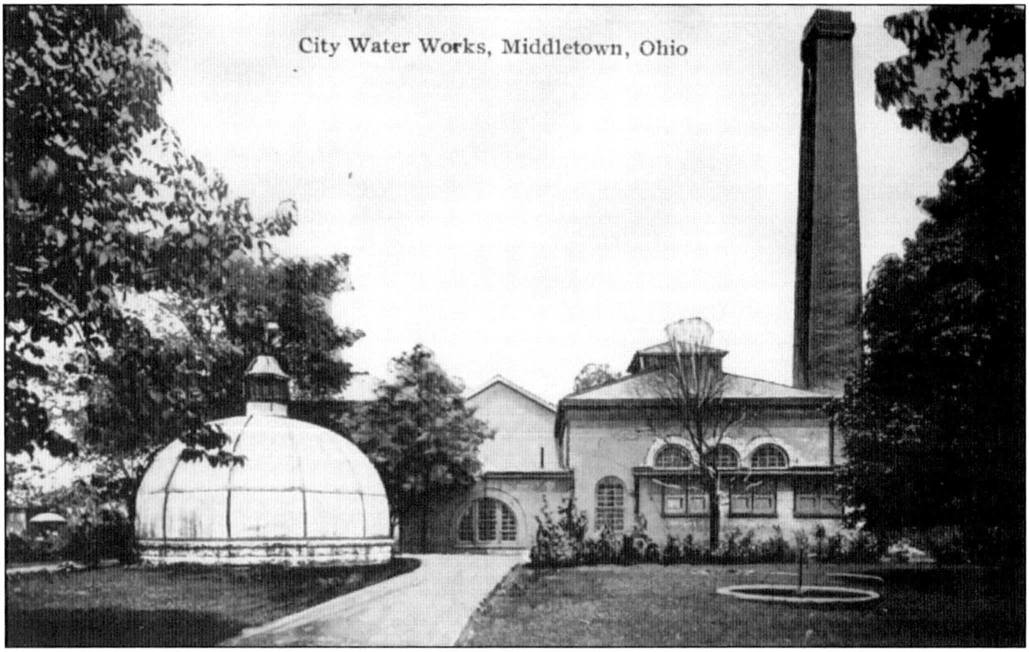

In 1874, at a cost of $72,000, the town put in the Holley Water Works. It provided an inexhaustible supply of good, cool, clear, and pure water with pressure sufficient to throw water 100 feet high.

Five

Religion Plays Its Part

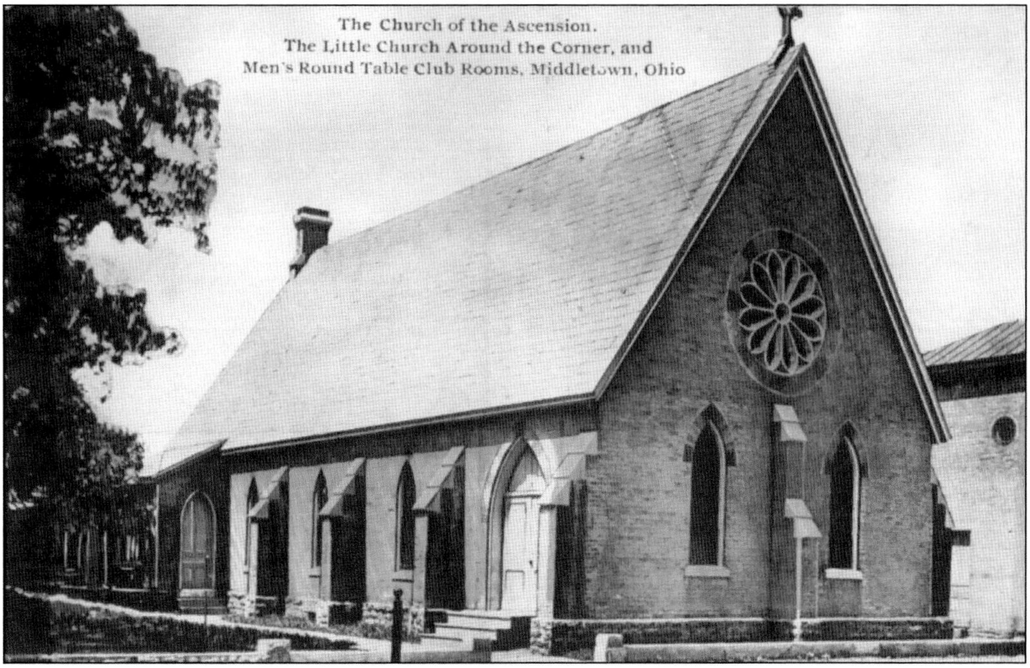

Located between Main and Broad Streets on First Street, "The Little Church Around the Corner" (as noted on the face of the postcard) was the first home of today's Episcopal Church of Ascension. Later, this building was the home of another church that became Zion Lutheran Church.

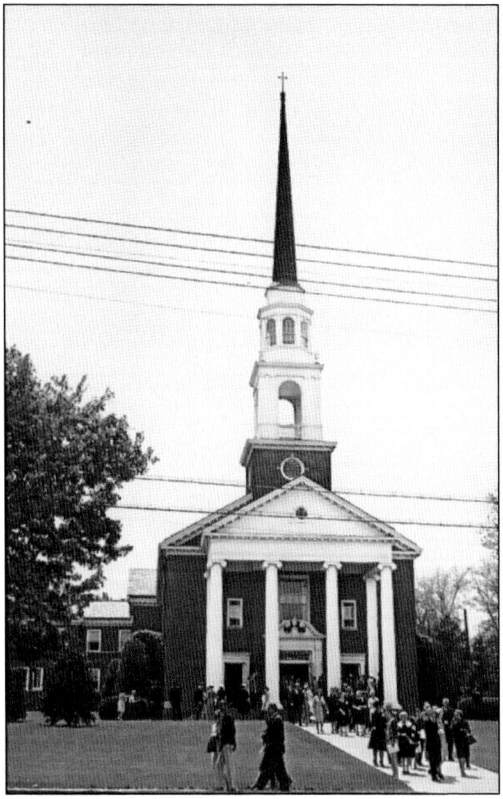

Middletown has many beautiful churches, including this one, the First Presbyterian. The Presbyterians, Baptists, and Methodists were the earliest religious organizations in the community. In 1952, the Presbyterians moved from South Main Street to this building on Central Avenue.

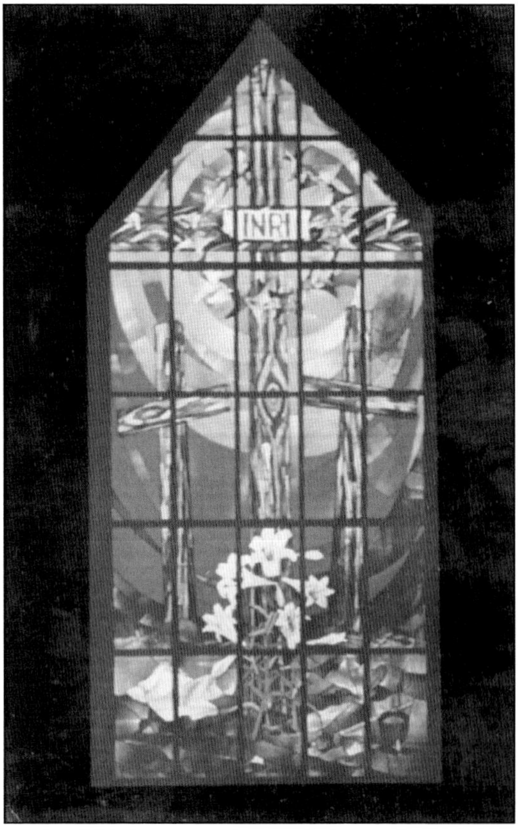

The Resurrection Window at the Zion Lutheran Church is a beautiful stained-glass window. It was designed and constructed by two members of the congregation, Arlene C. Klafter and Wylie G. Senften. The new church was dedicated February 12, 1961. (Courtesy of Roger L. Miller.)

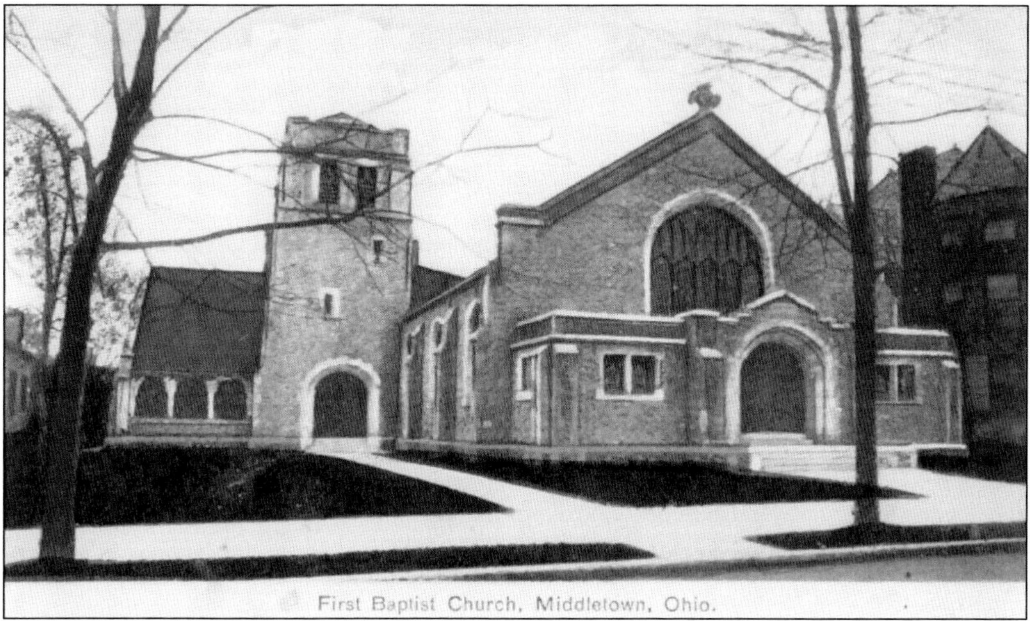

The Sorg family had a large influence in the construction of the First Baptist Church. In 1906, the congregation moved from North Main Street into this building on South Main Street. Added onto several times, this beautiful building is not being used at present, and the back of it has received fire damage.

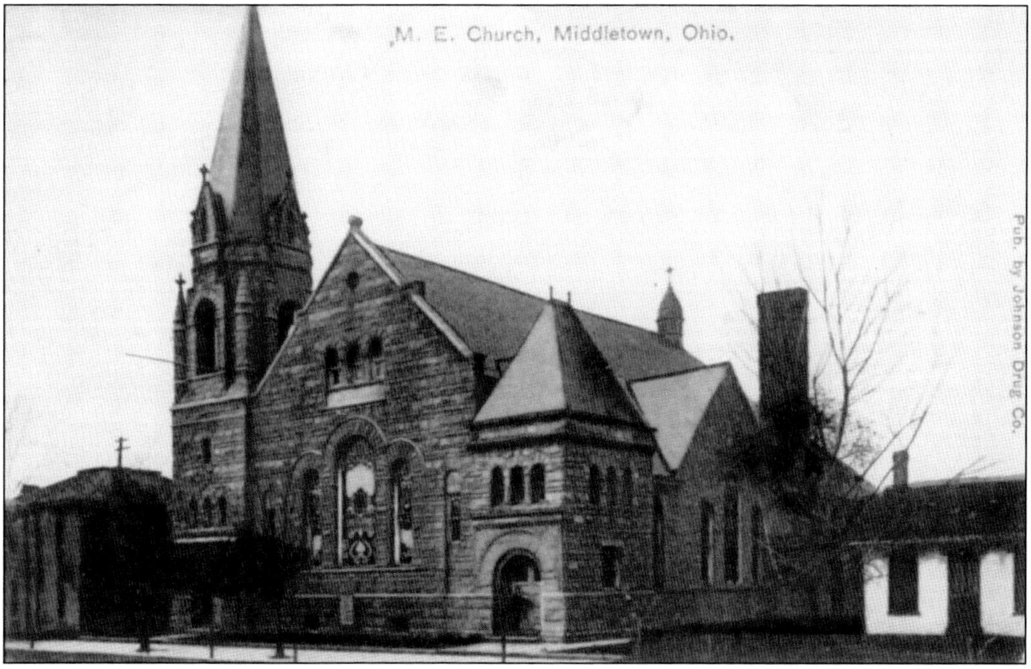

The local Methodists trace their history to 1805. In 1891, the Methodist Episcopal Church constructed Middletown's first stone church. Today, it is the home of First United Methodist Church. (Courtesy of Roger L. Miller.)

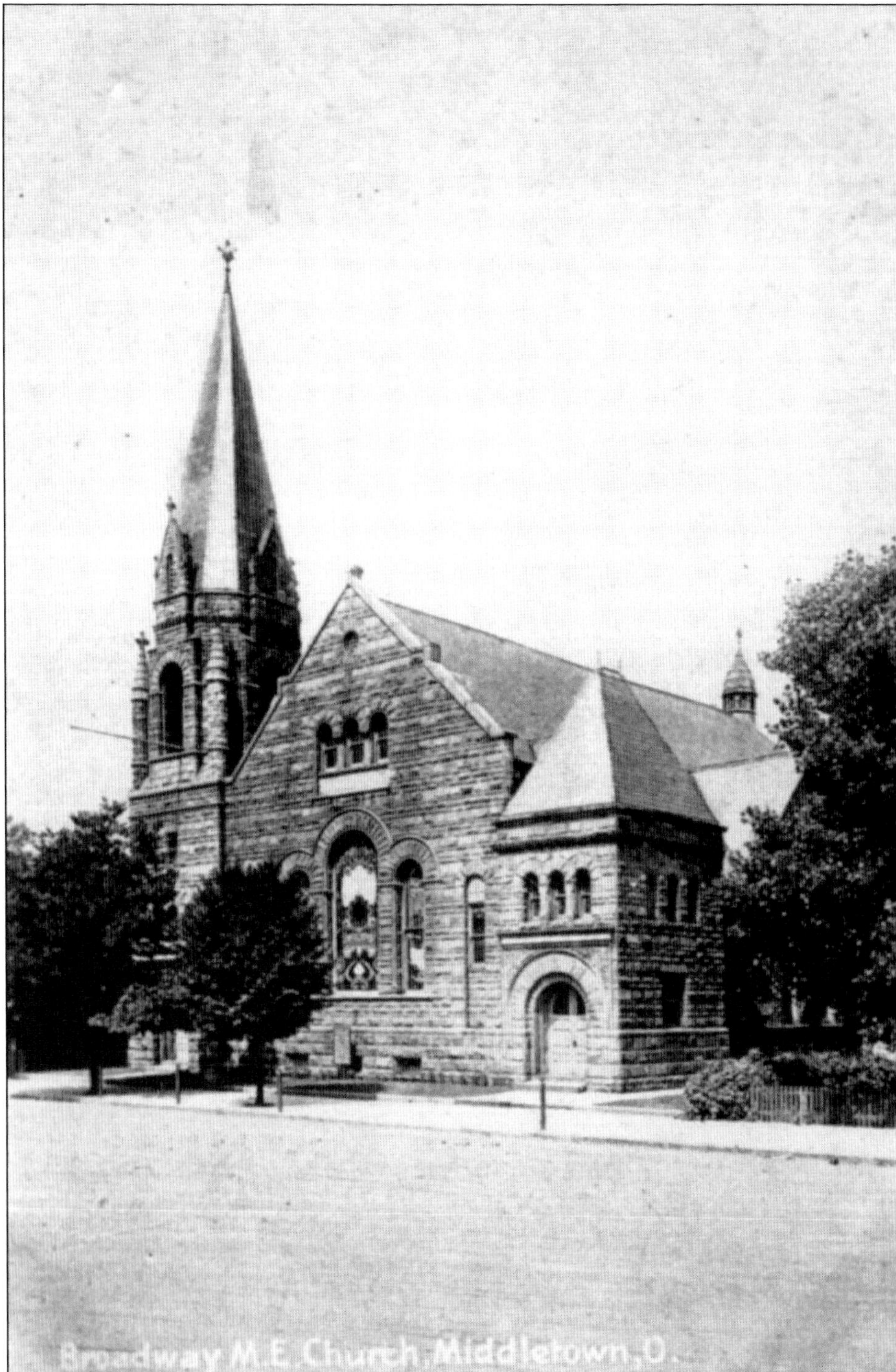

Located on the northwest corner of Broad Street and Second Avenue, the Methodist Episcopal Church once used Broadway as part of its name. Located about two blocks north was the Methodist Protestant church, which was also known as Calvary Methodist Church.

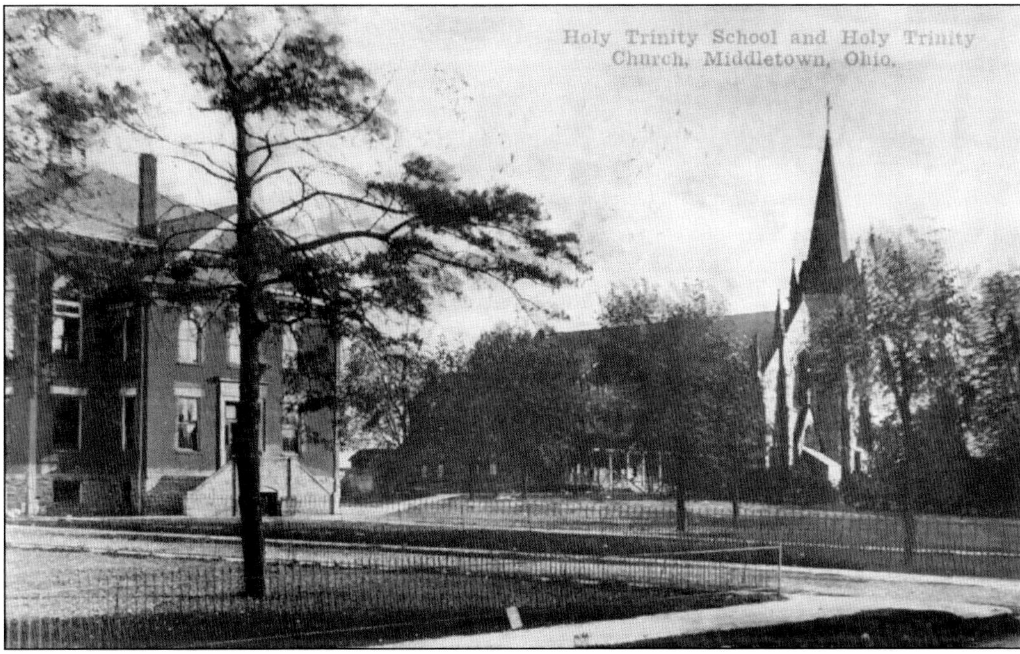

The early Catholics in Middletown were Irish. They built their church and school in a section of Middletown that was settled by the Irish; the area was known as "Dublin." Their history in the area can be traced back to April 1852, and their first church was built on this site in 1869.

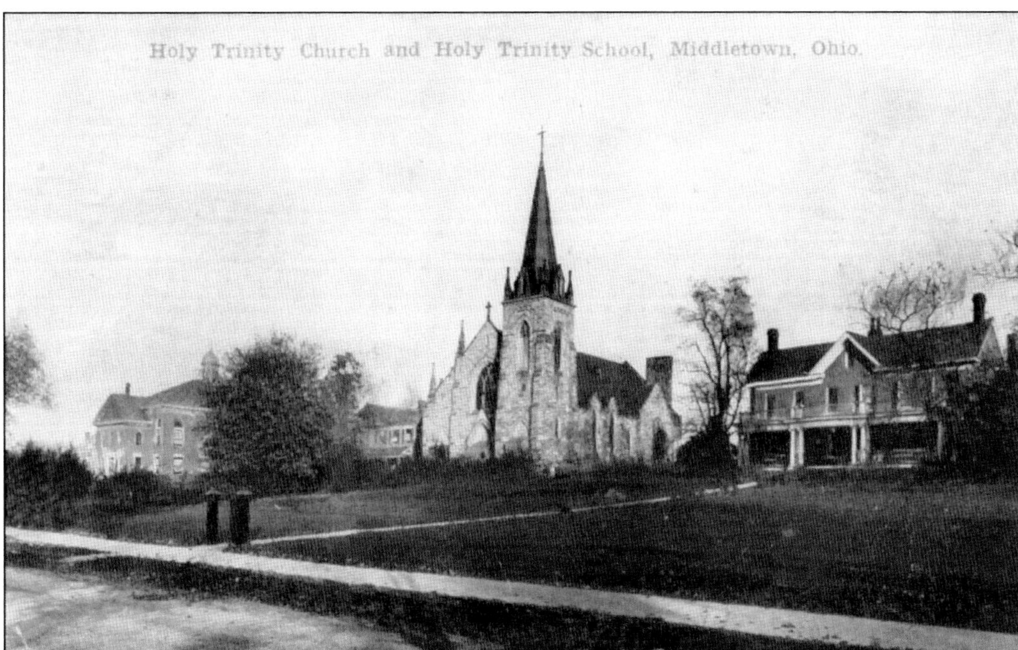

The Irish named their church Holy Trinity. It sits high on Clark Street hill, which was at the edge of the 1913 flood. The church seen on this card was constructed in 1899 and is still in use.

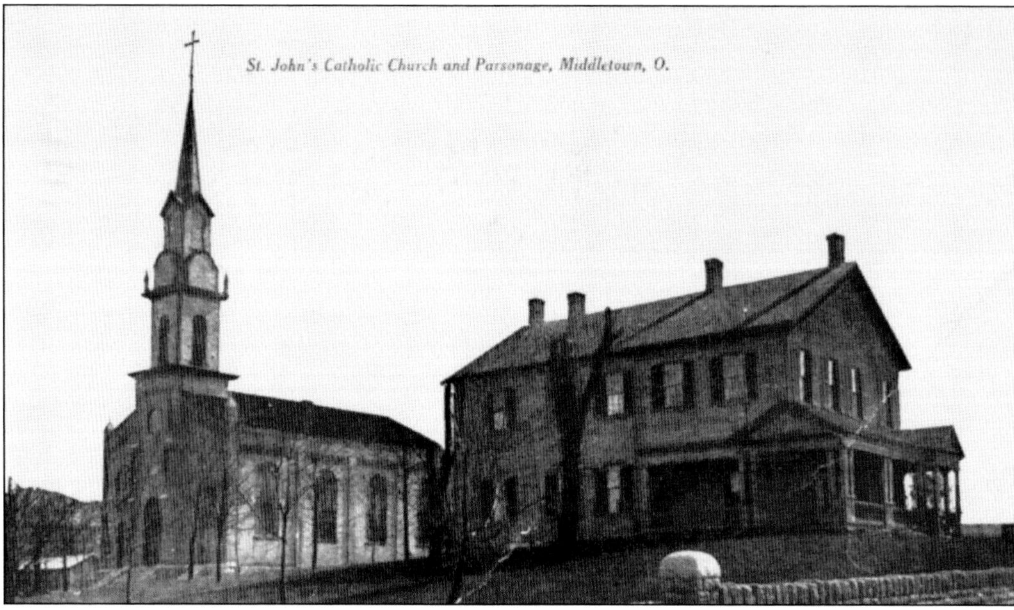

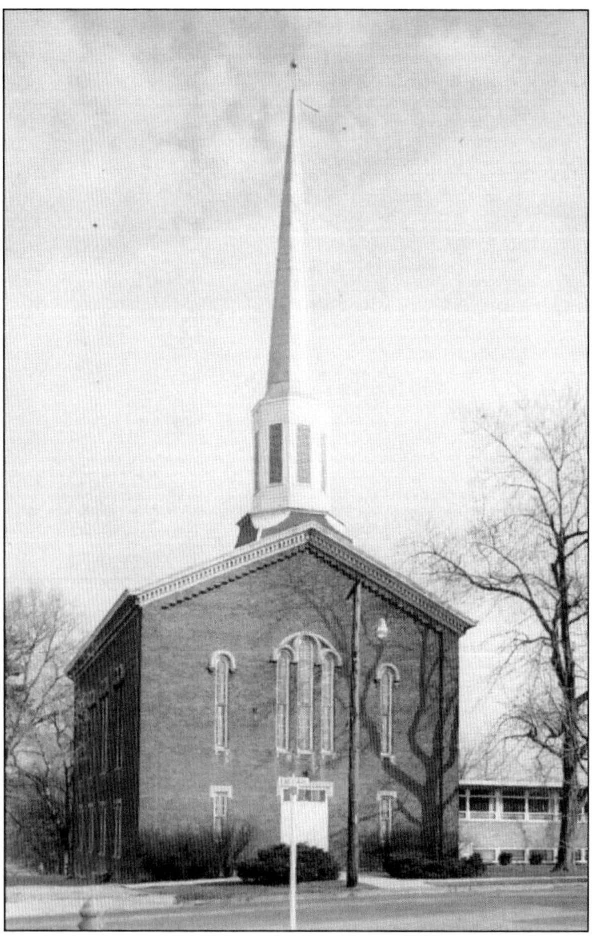

Located on Curtis Street, St. John the Baptist Catholic Church was constructed by the German Catholics. For a time, the Edward Jones home was used as the church's parsonage. In 1927, a beautiful new building was dedicated on this site. Both Holy Trinity and St. John buildings are being used, but the congregations have merged, becoming Holy Family Catholic Parish.

At the nearby community of Monroe is the Monroe United Methodist Church. With its 86-foot steeple, this building was completed in February 1860 and stood until destroyed by a tornado in 1969. A new building was constructed on the same site. (Courtesy of Roger L. Miller.)

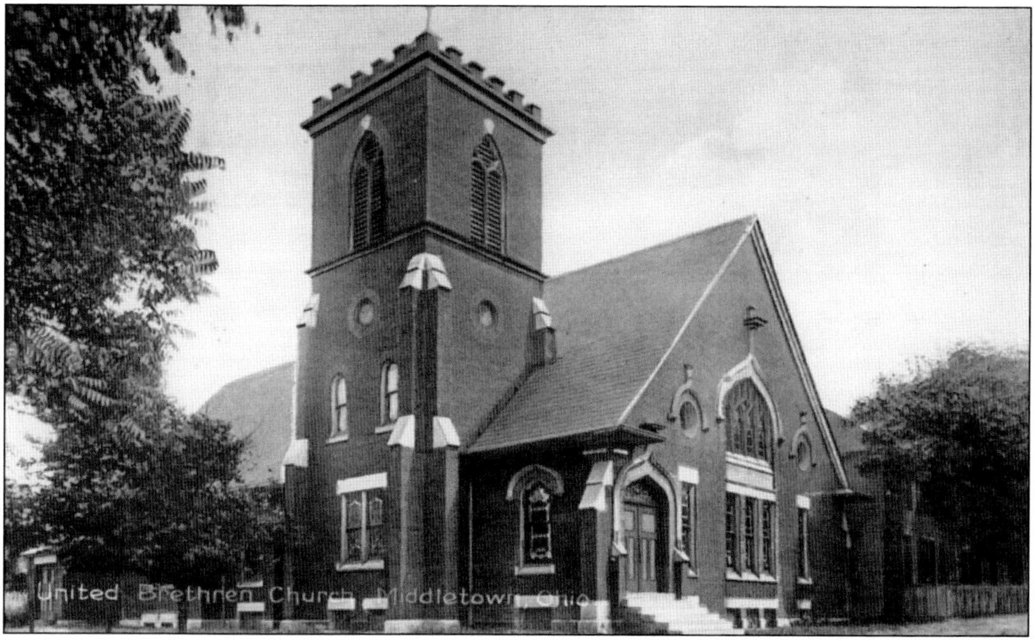

Until 1889, United Brethren in Christ Church members had to worship at the Pleasant Ridge United Brethren Church located on top of West Middletown hill. In 1900, this building replaced the United Brethren's first church building, the "Little Tin Church."

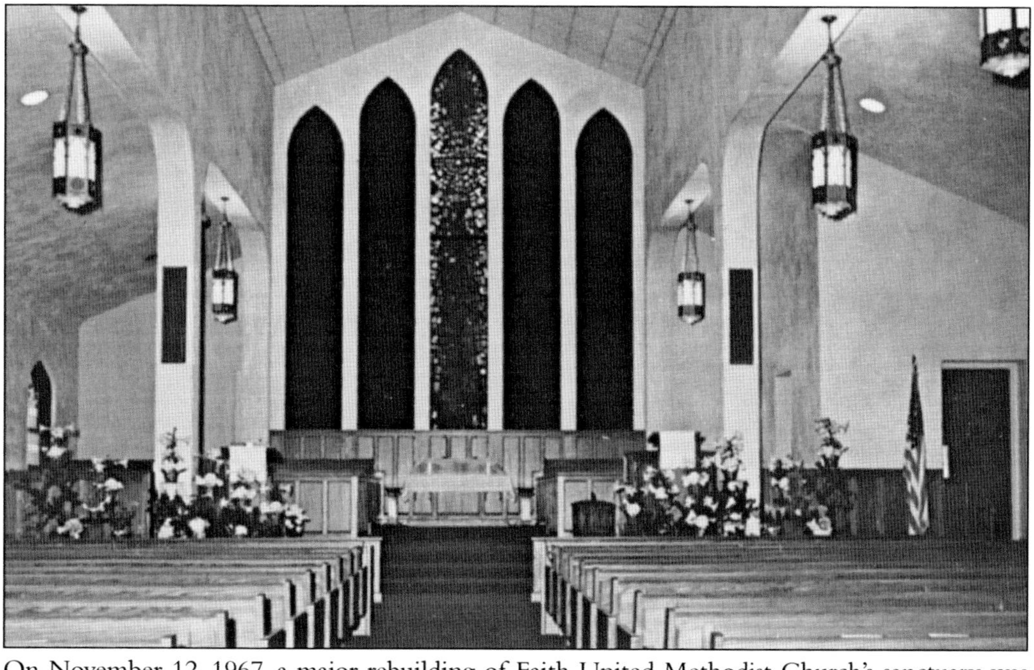

On November 12, 1967, a major rebuilding of Faith United Methodist Church's sanctuary was dedicated. They have merged with Hunter Community United Methodist Church to form Hope United Methodist Church, and the old church building is now used by Faith United Church. (Courtesy of Roger L. Miller.)

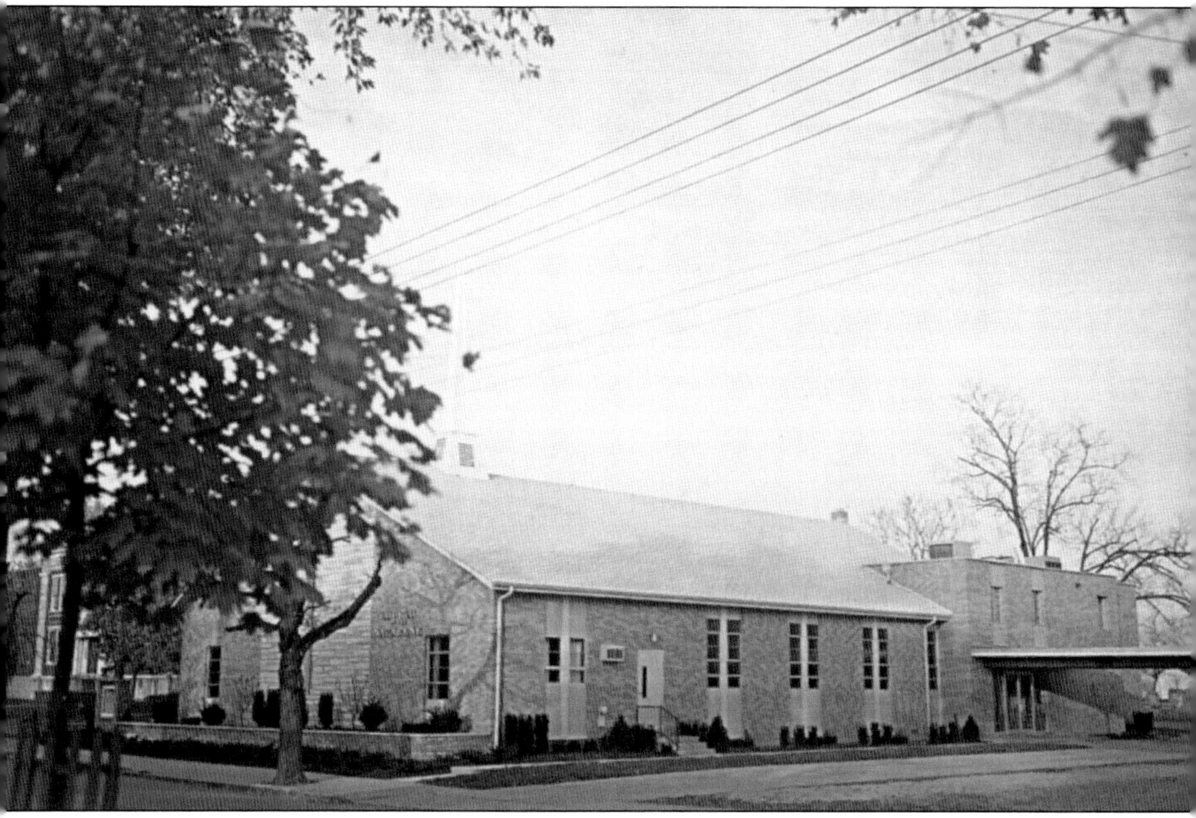

This is the Trenton Church of the Nazarene. The church was organized January 18, 1942, and constructed this building in 1965. Trenton is another community that is near Middletown. (Courtesy of Roger L. Miller.)

Six

Homes Are Important

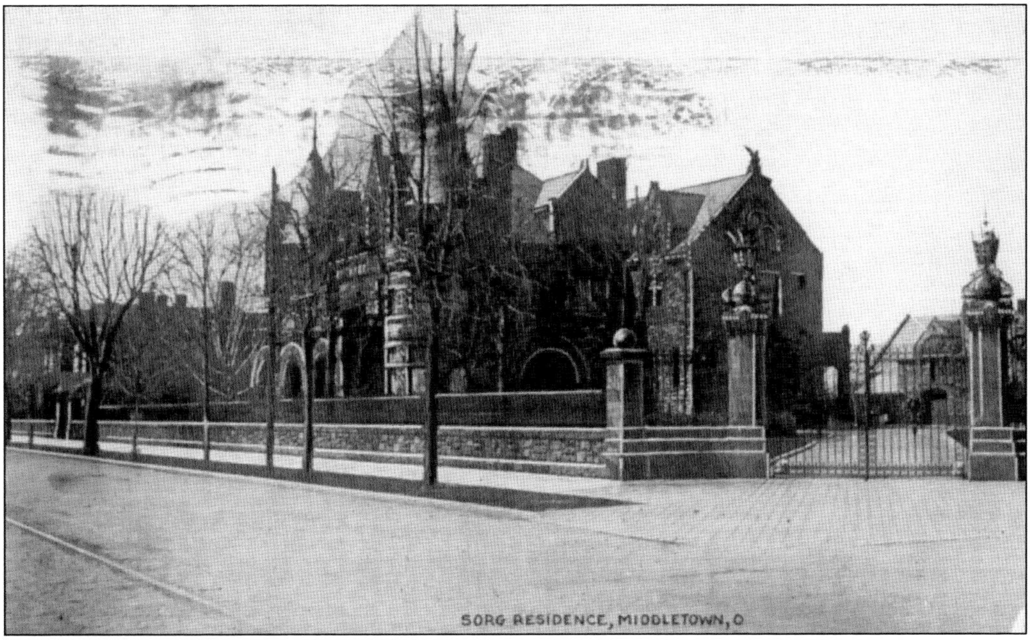

The Sorg mansion was the home of industrialist Paul J. Sorg and his wife, Jenny. In 1888, the Sorgs moved into the original section of the house, which was constructed of red sandstone. In 1902, an addition made the house into that seen on this postcard.

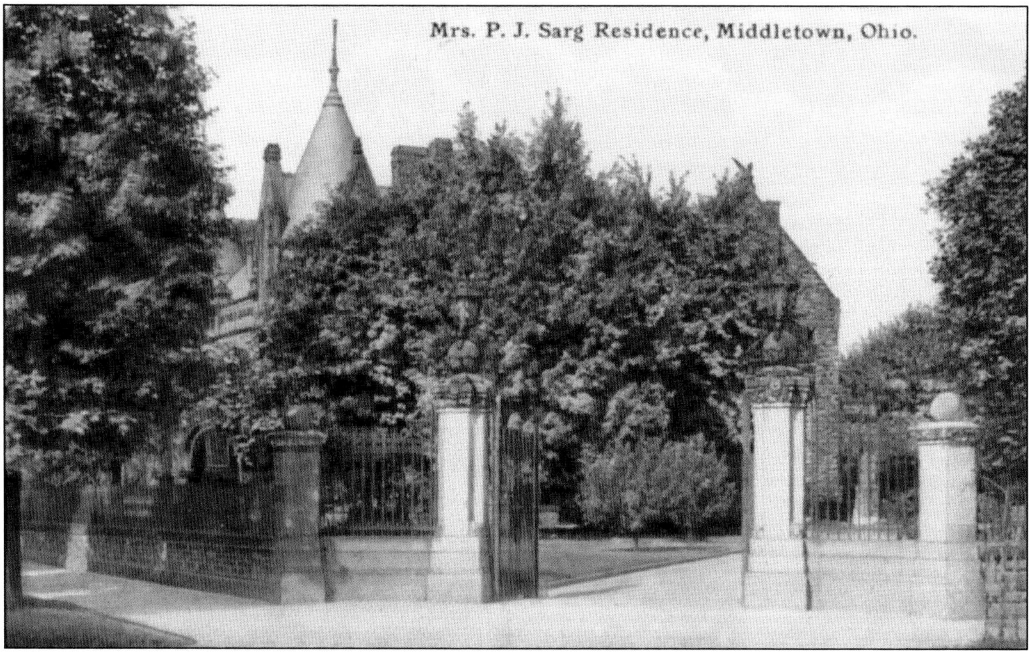

In the early 1900s, the Sorgs and their South Main Street neighbors set the social scene for the community. Today, this area is known as the South Main Street Historic District.

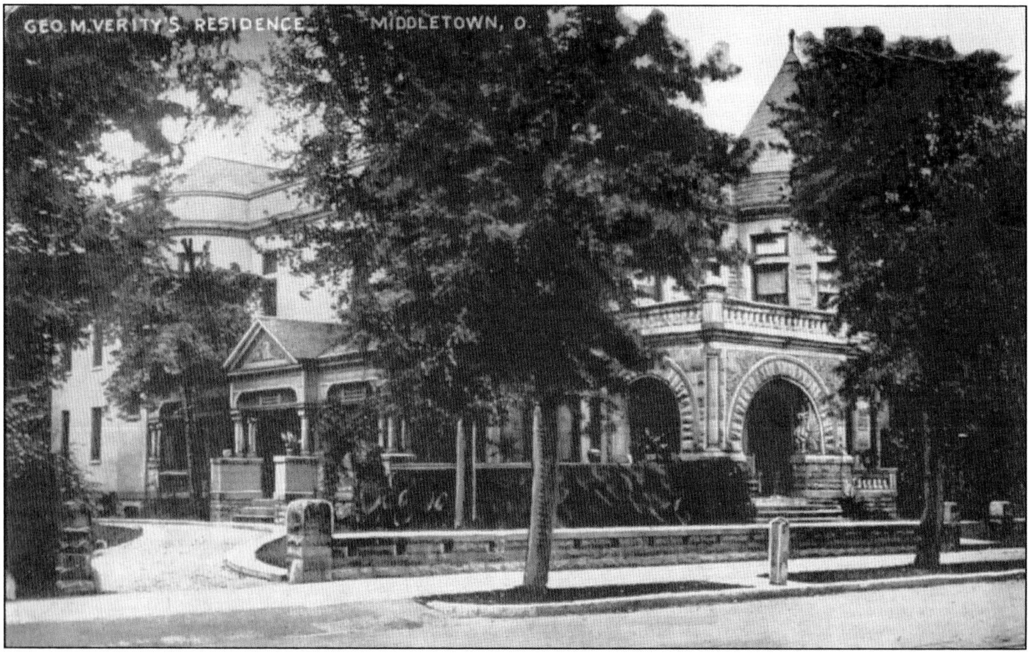

George M. Verity came to Middletown and formed the American Rolling Mill Company. He purchased this South Main Street home and raised his family here.

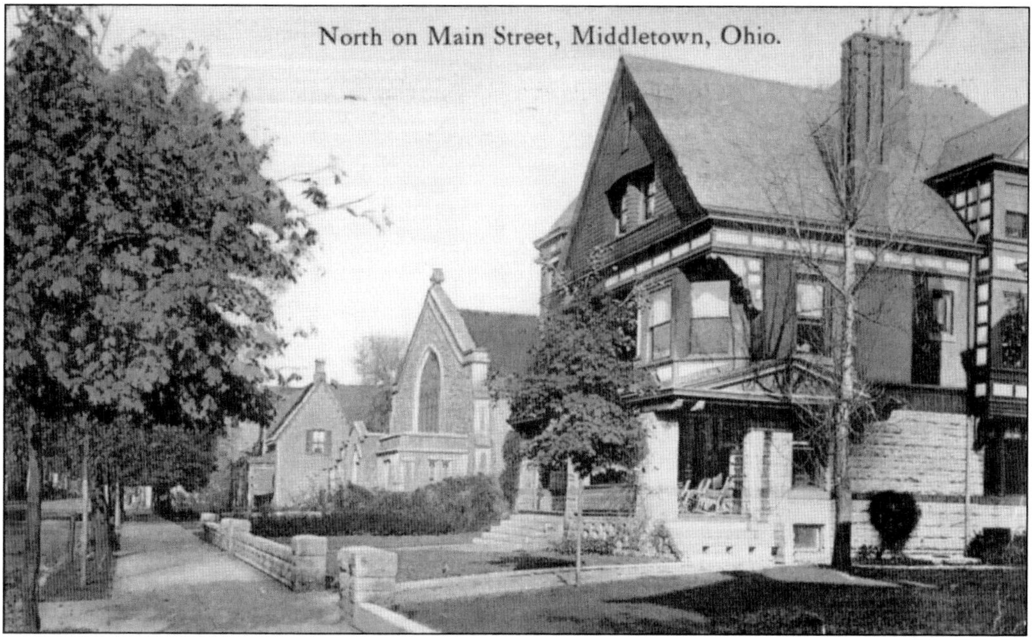

The east side of Main Street north of Second Avenue looks much as it did when this postcard was mailed in 1916. The large house was originally Simon Goldman's, while the church was First Baptist Church, dedicated in 1906.

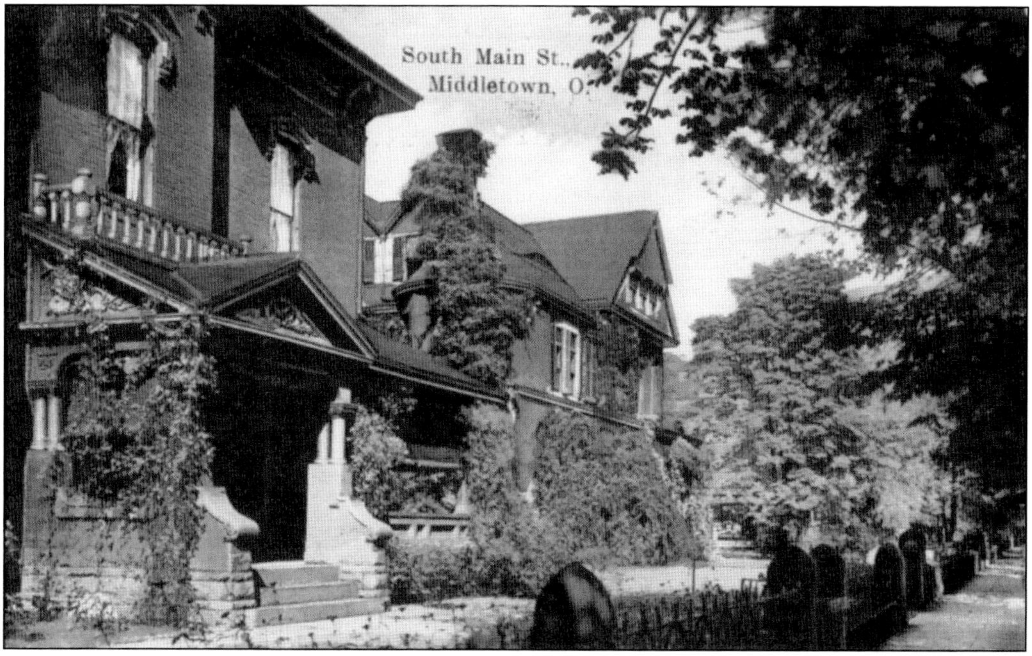

This scene is the west side of Main Street looking north. The building on the left is the home of druggist C.B. Johnson, while the home of John Butler Tytus, inventor of the continuous rolling mill, is the far one. In between, at 306 South Main Street, is the Isaac Wolverton home.

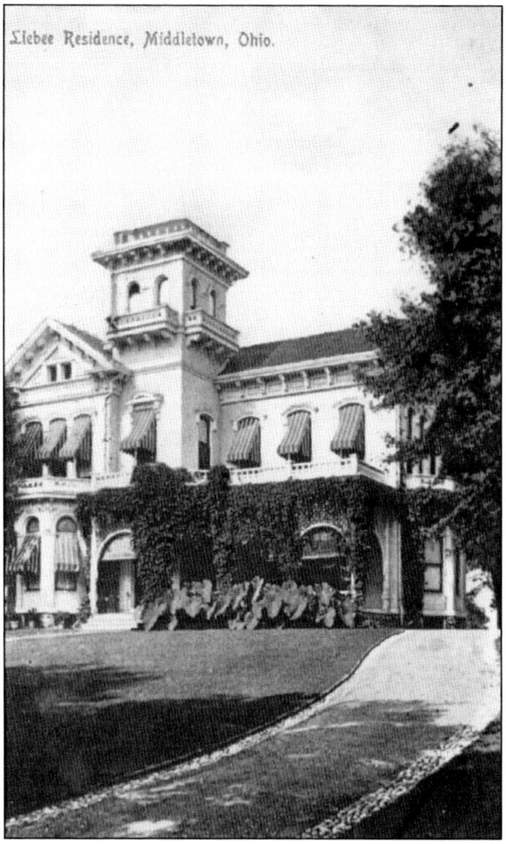

One of the fine homes on Main Street was that of H.P. Leibee (note the spelling error on the postcard). He was a very successful businessman. The Leibee family members were merchants and also involved in construction. This home has been restored and is located in the South Main Street Historic District.

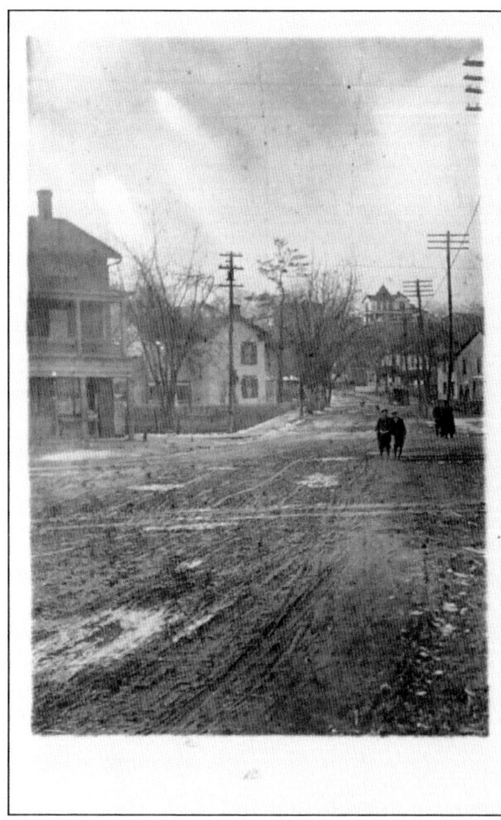

Across the river, the road to Winchester (Gratis) went through West Middletown, which was earlier known as Heno or Madison City. The arrival of the first railroad in the area made it important. The Madison Inn can be seen on the left, while several homes are visible in the distance. (Courtesy of Middletown Historical Collection, Middletown Public Library.)

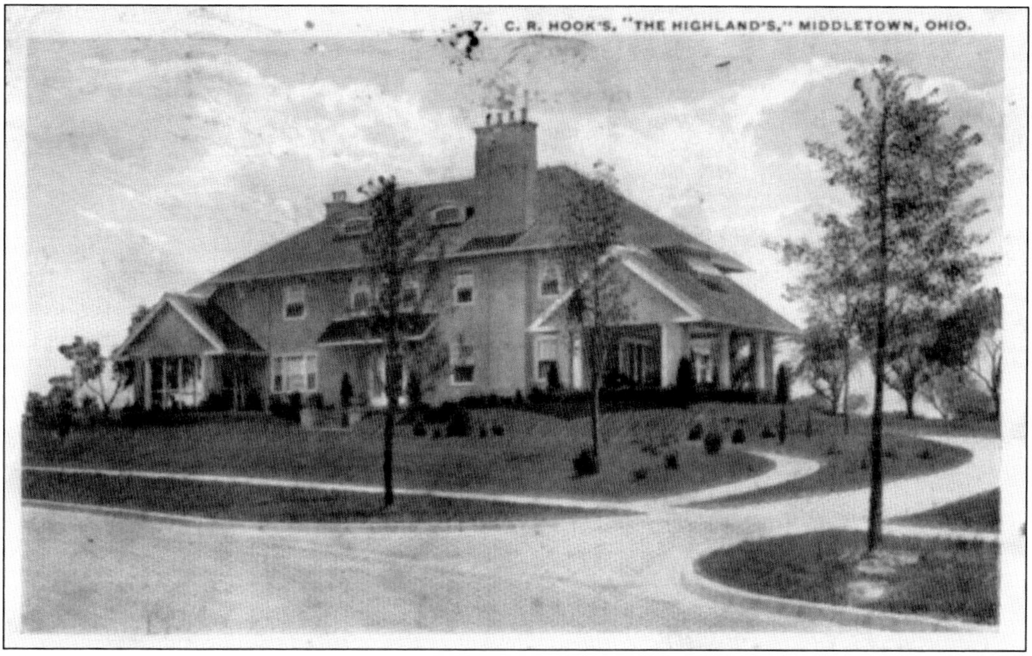

The Highlands subdivision developed around the Middletown Hospital, which was located on a hill well east of downtown. Civic and industrial leader Charles R. Hook built this very nice home in the area.

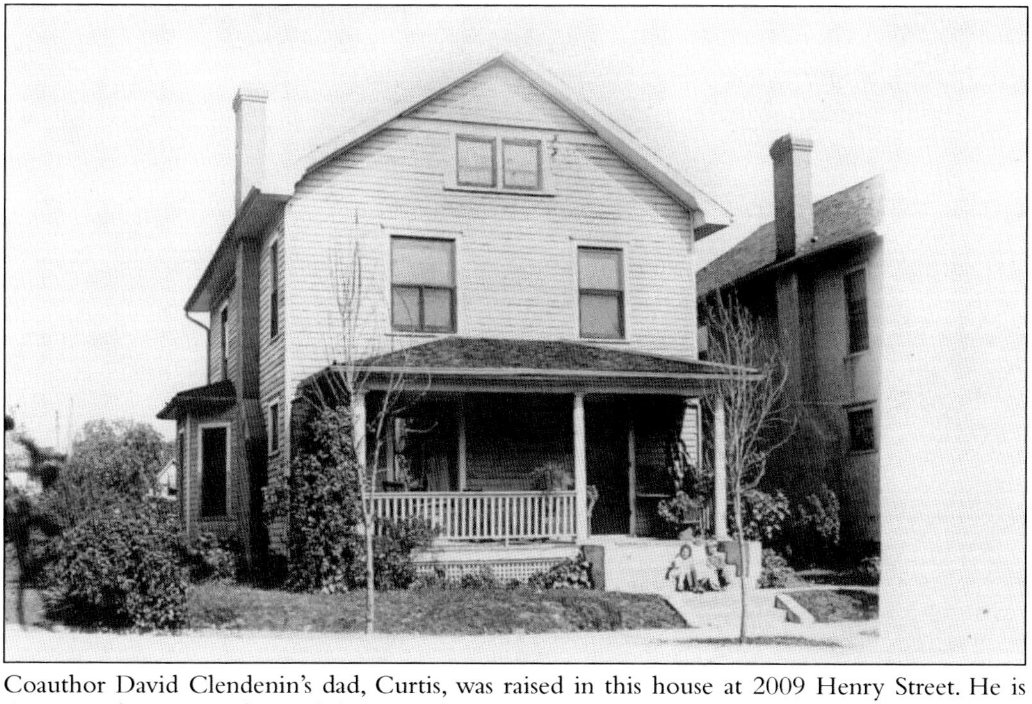

Coauthor David Clendenin's dad, Curtis, was raised in this house at 2009 Henry Street. He is sitting on the steps (right) with his twin sister, Charlotte, and older sister Wilda (center).

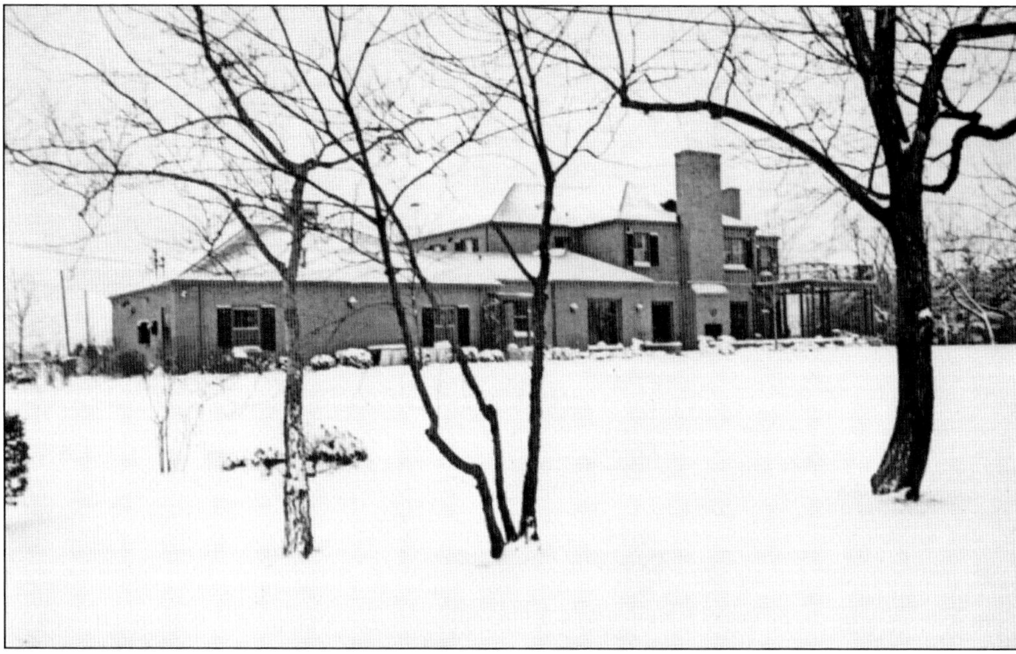

Located at 4309 Rosedale Road, Loynita was the home of Anita and Loyal Juengling. It is also located in a very nice area of the city. (Courtesy of Roger L. Miller.)

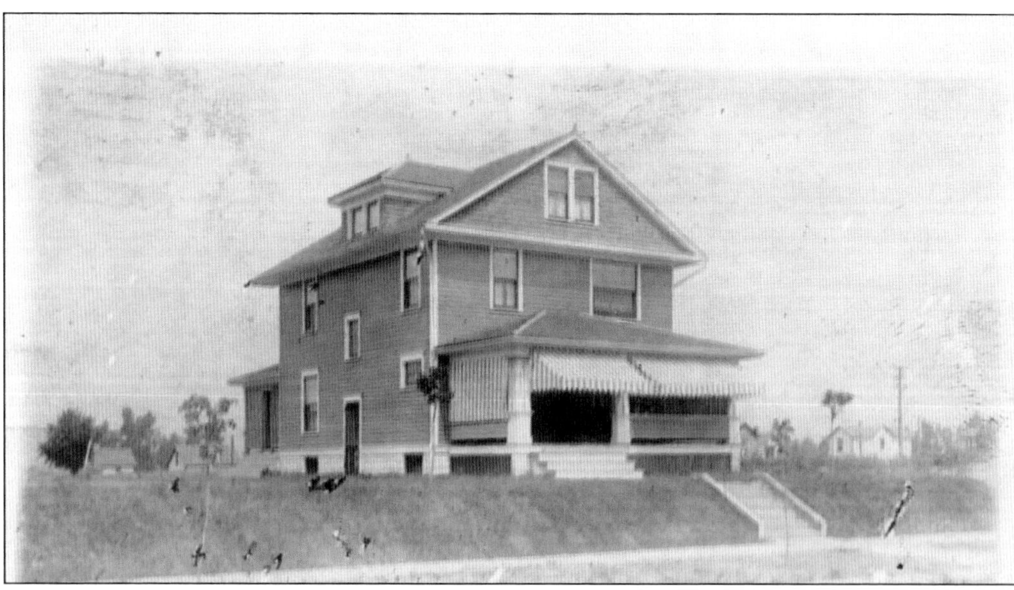

During July 1912, a series of 10 postcards advertising the Highlands as a good place to live was mailed to John C. Phillips. At the time, he lived on Sutphin Street, but the 1914 city directory shows him living on Alameda Avenue, one of the streets in the Highlands.

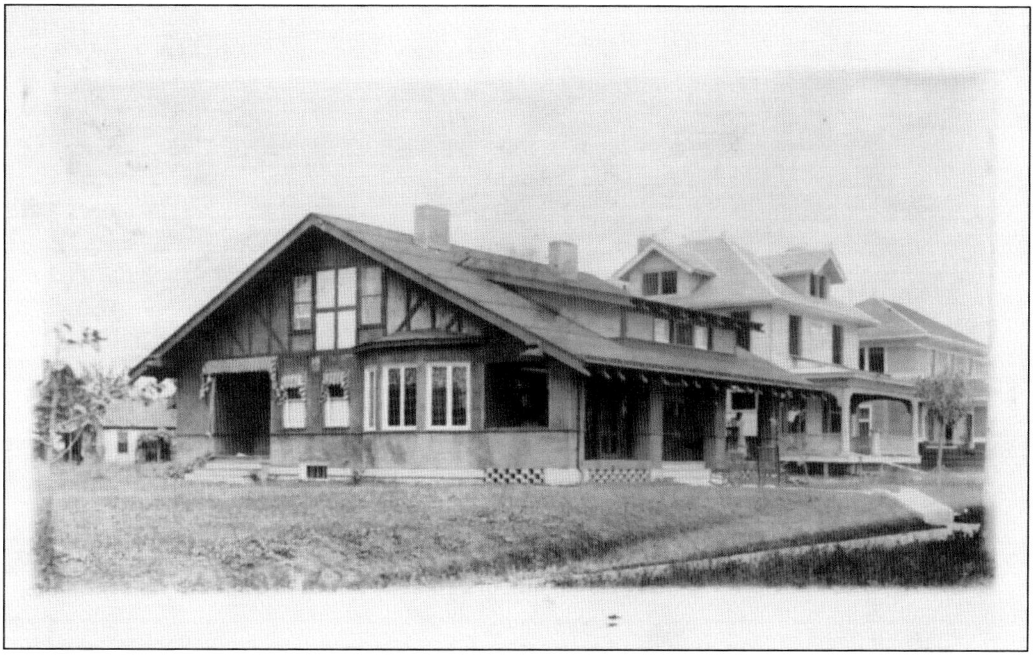

This is one of the postcards advertising the Highlands that was mailed to Phillips. These houses would have been owned by middle-income residents. Those on the north end of the subdivision were much larger.

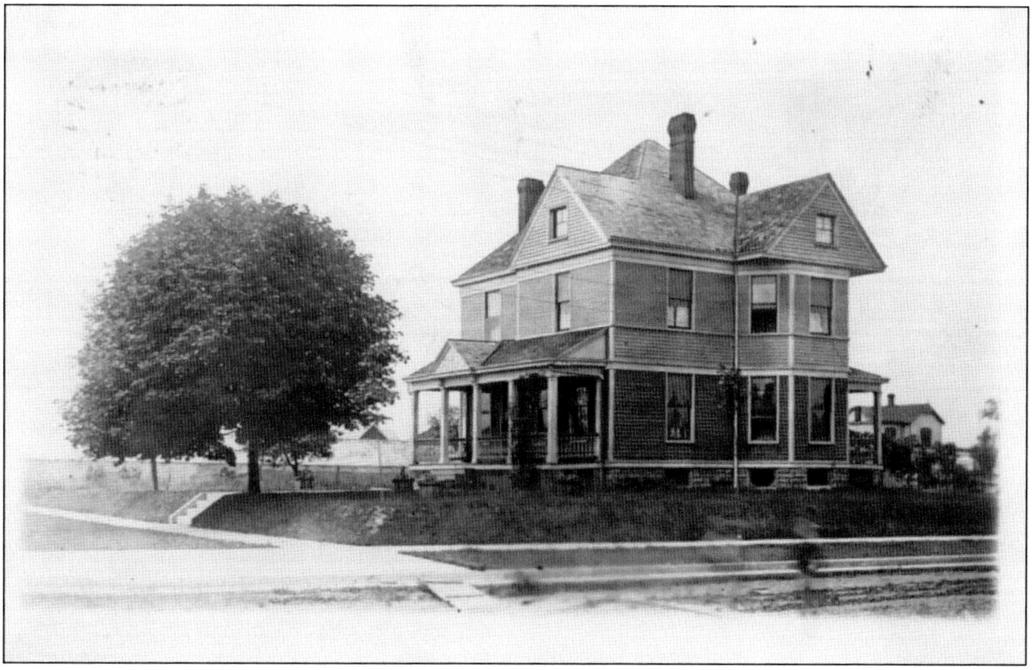

This is another one of the houses built in the Highlands. One of the city's prominent merchants, Simon Goldman, owned the land that was developed into the Highlands. His son Charles platted and sold the lots. They also gave the city land for a park.

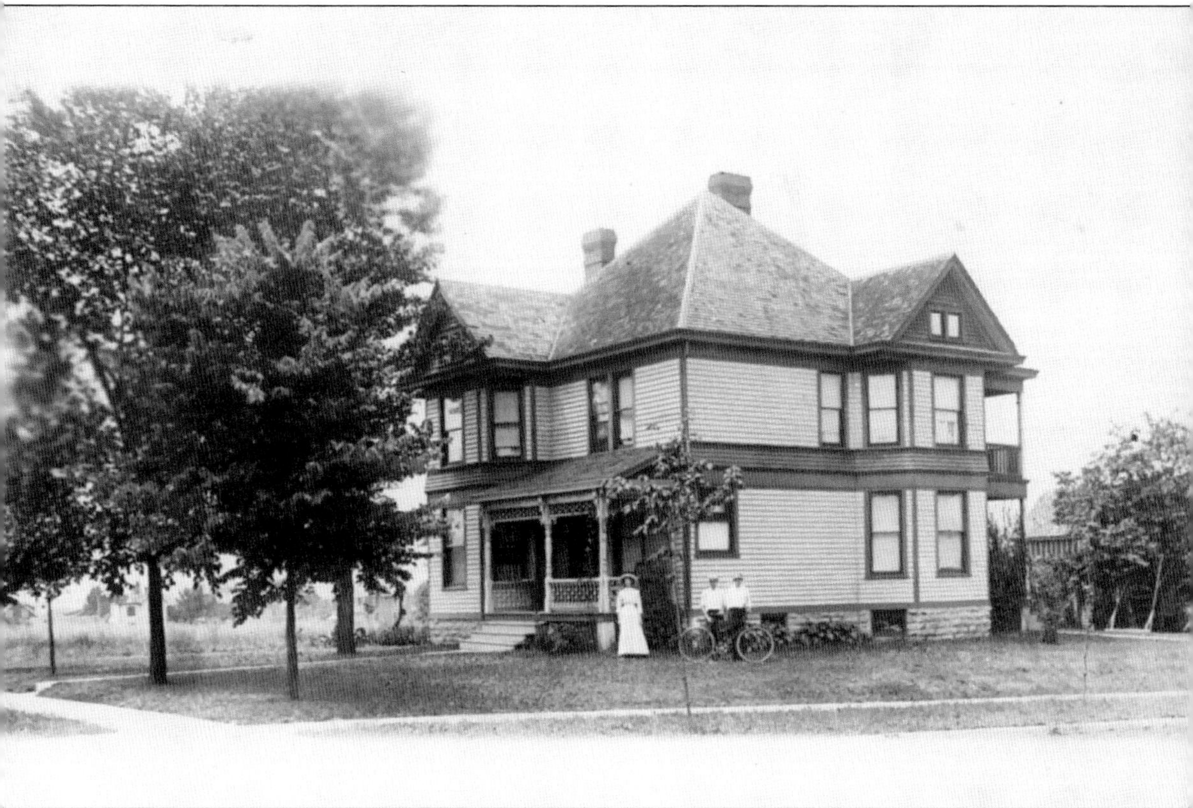

Like this one, many of the lots in the Highlands were very large. Additional houses have been constructed on several of them. Some of the present owners of these houses are interested in having the area declared a historic district.

Seven

Nearby Amusement Parks

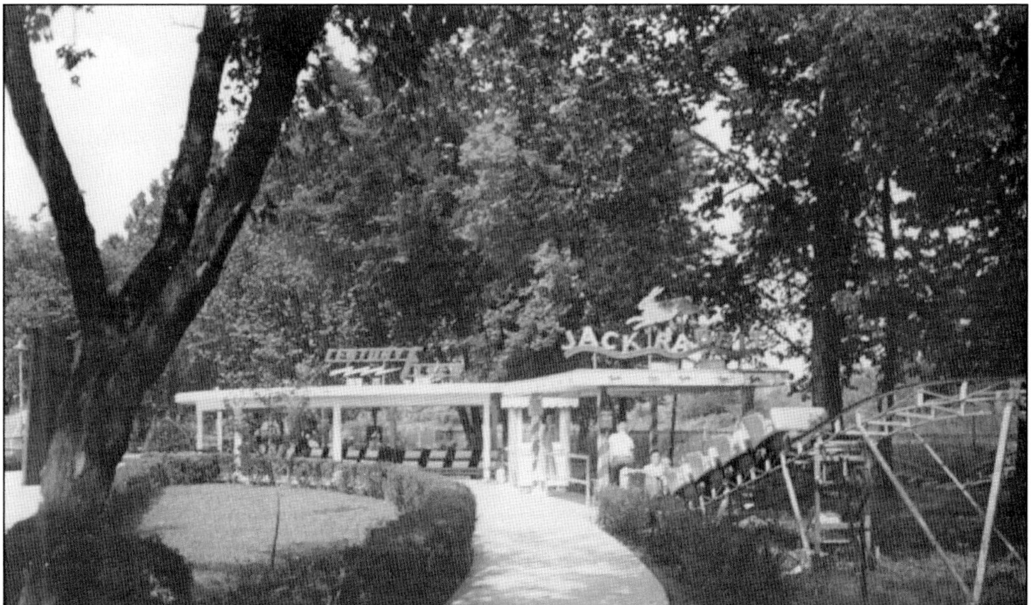

Located south of Middletown, LeSourdsville Lake Amusement Park first opened in 1922 as a picnic area before developing into a full-fledged amusement park. This c. 1950 postcard shows the children's area.

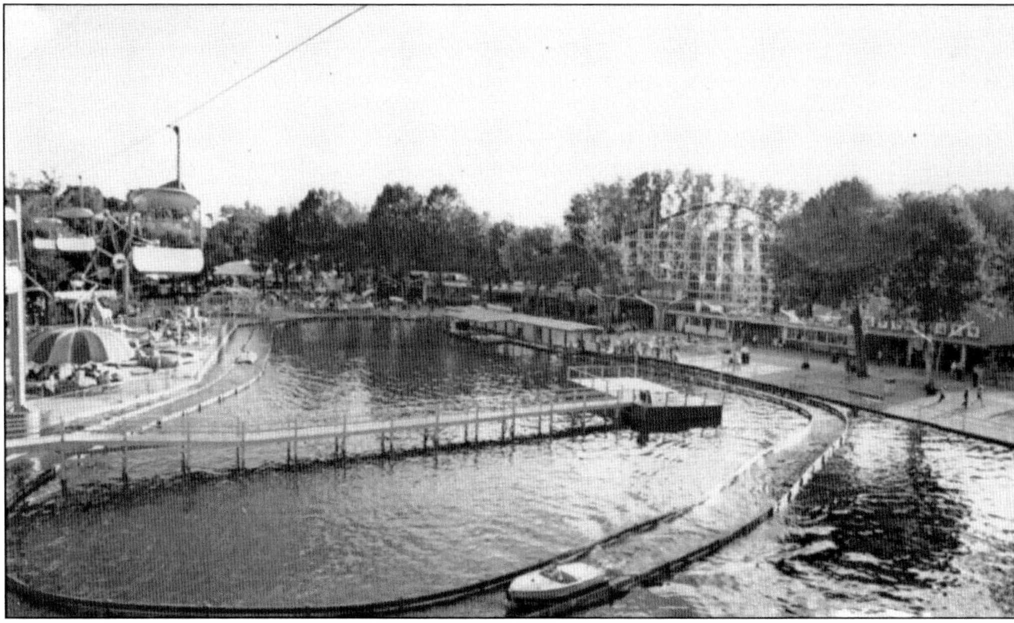

LeSourdsville Lake was much more than a park for children; this c. 1968 scene depicts the 19-acre freshwater swimming lake and some of the park's 27 rides.

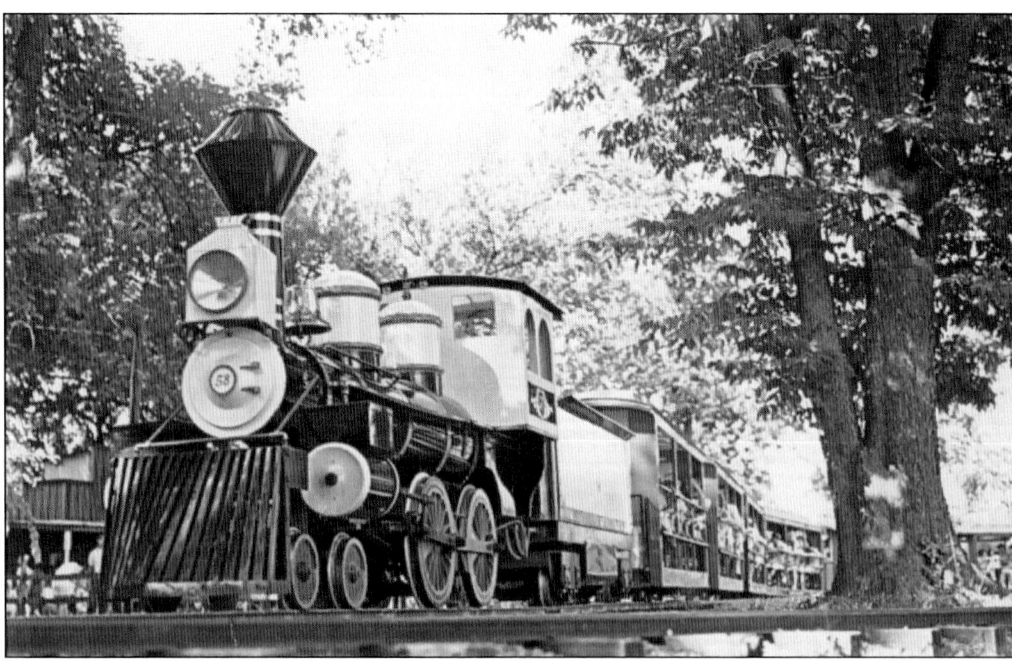

One of the rides was the Iron Horse. It made a tour of much of the park, which was developed by Edgar Streifthau.

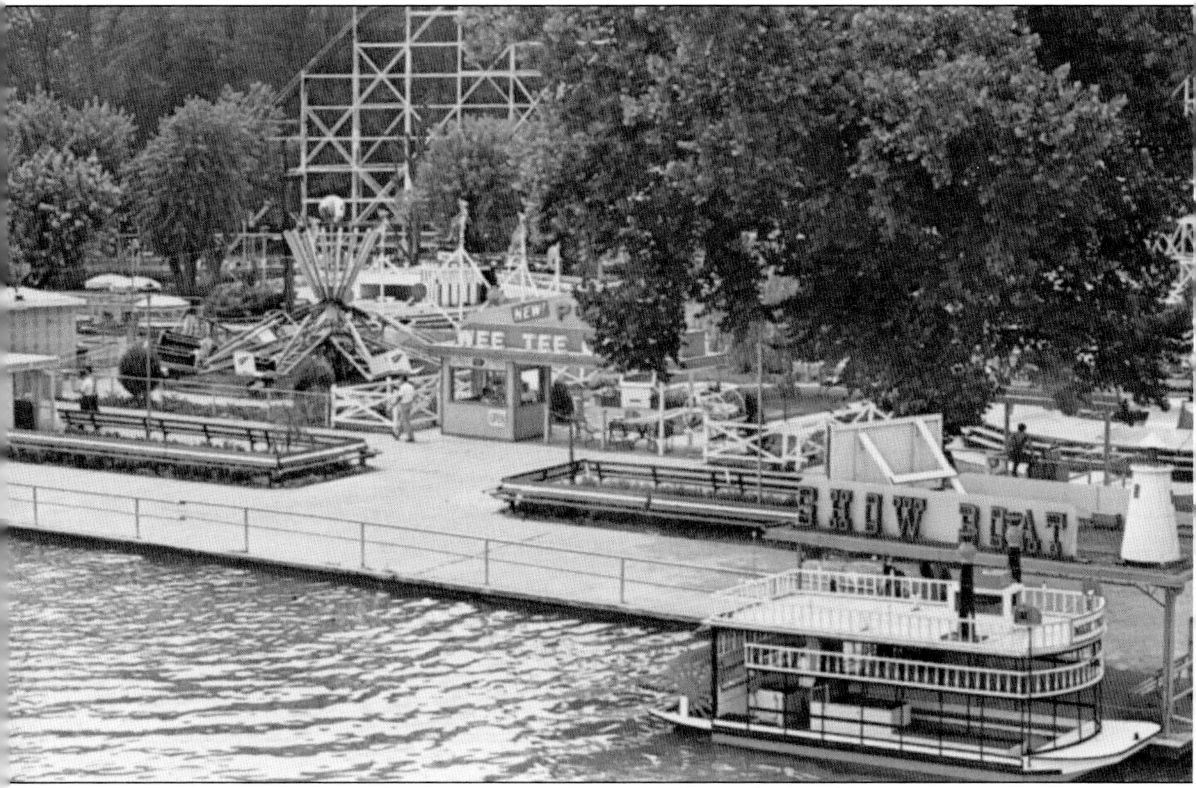

Some of the rides and the "mall" are seen here. The *Show Boat* toured a large section of the lake. Industrial and business concerns often used the park for their annual picnics and outings.

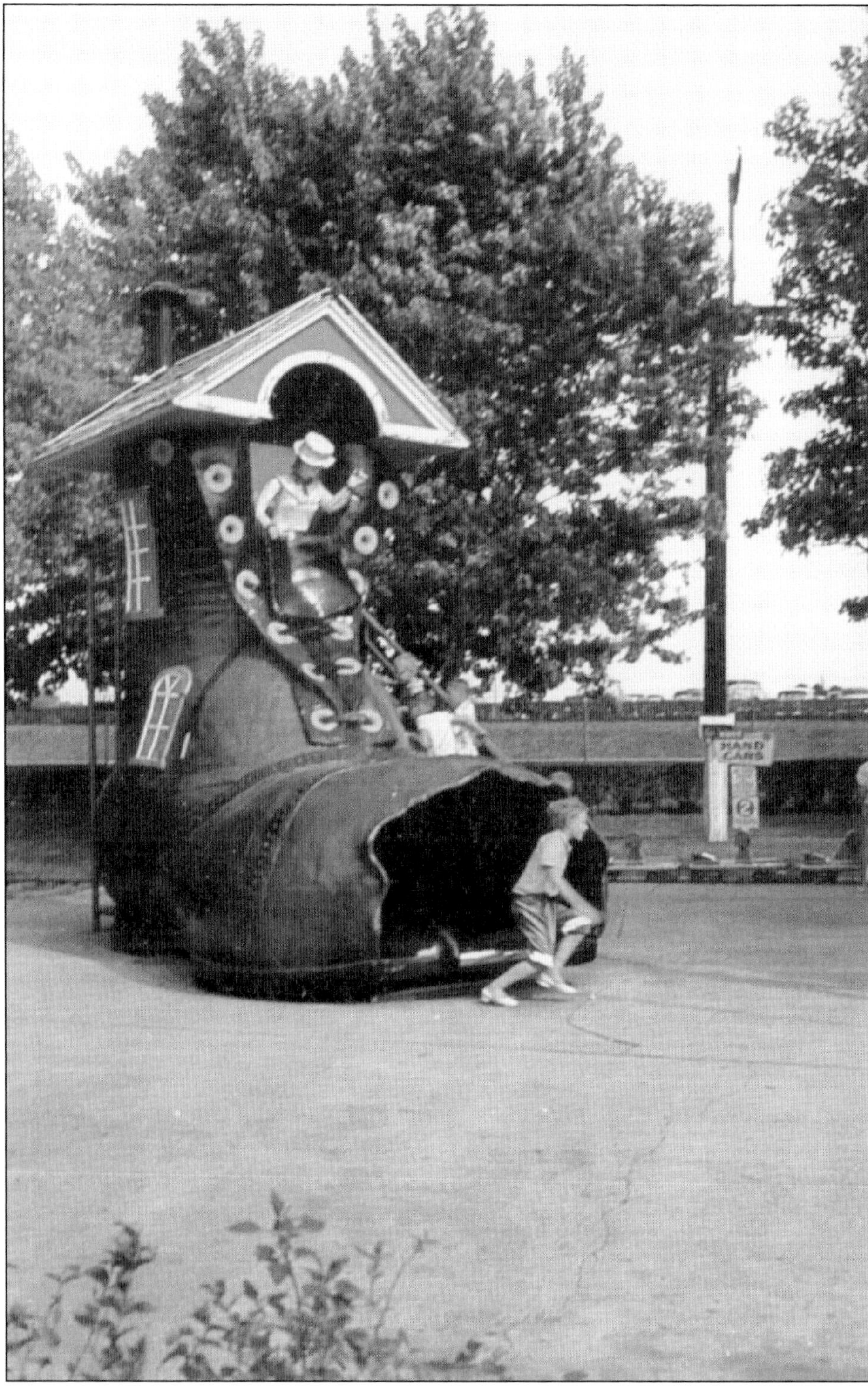

The "Old Lady in the Shoe" was one of the feature rides of the children's area of LeSourdsville Lake. After Streifthau sold the park, it became Americana Amusement Park.

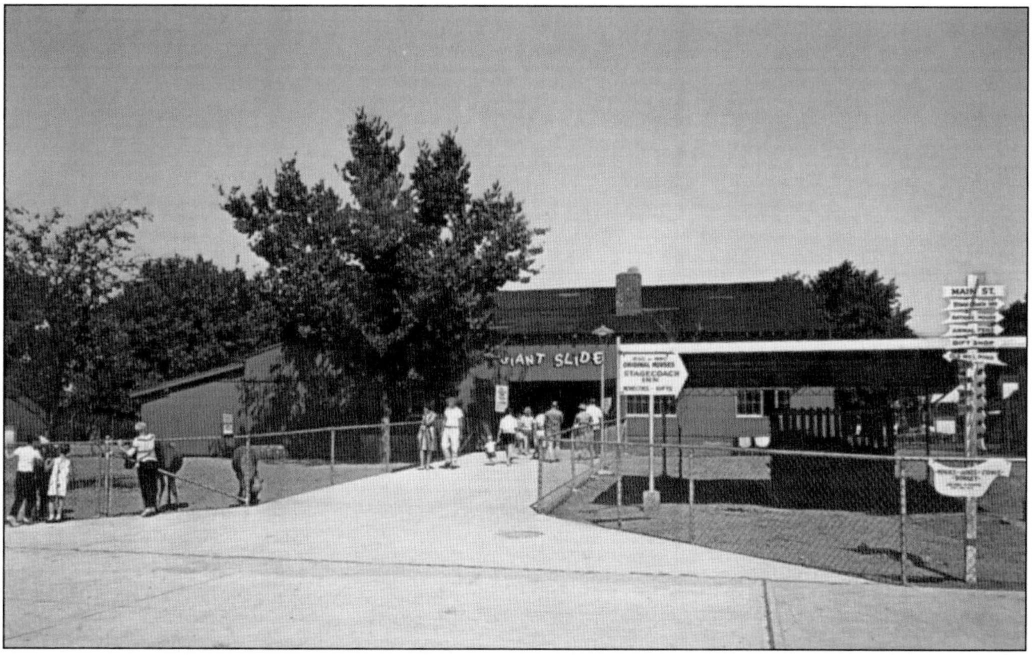

After the sale of LeSourdsville Lake, Edgar Streifthau built another park, Fantasy Farm. With smaller rides and many animals, the new attraction was designed as a children's park. The Big Red Barn featured antique farm machinery, a blacksmith forge, a cow-milking stall, and a giant slide for thrills.

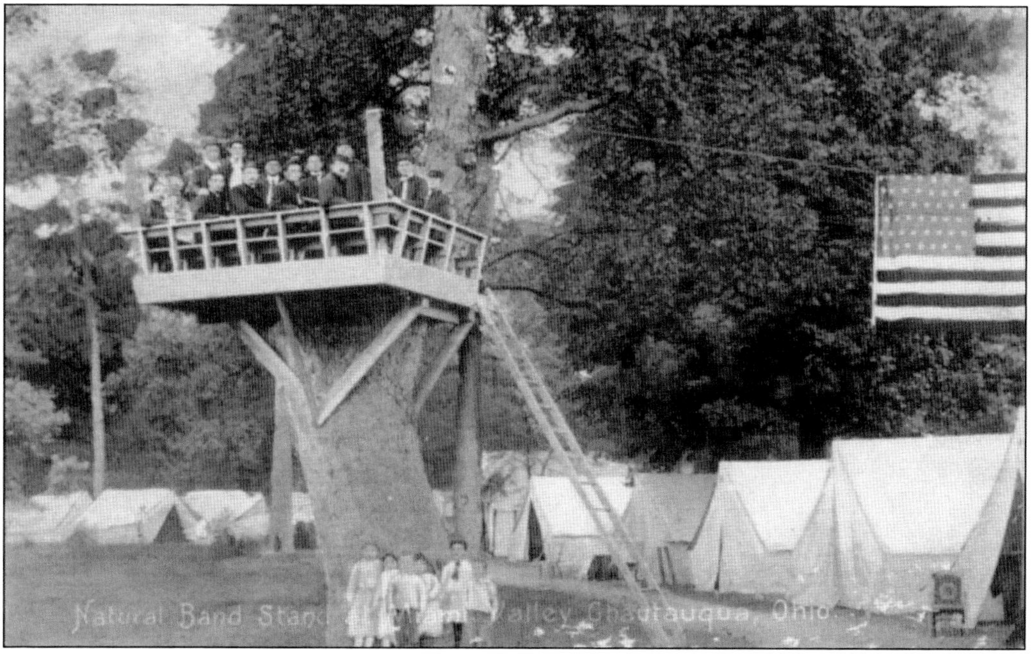

The Miami Valley Chautauqua was another area where people went to relax. It was located on the west side of the river, just north of Franklin. Many people took the traction car and then walked across a bridge to the park. (Courtesy of Middletown Historical Collection, Middletown Public Library.)

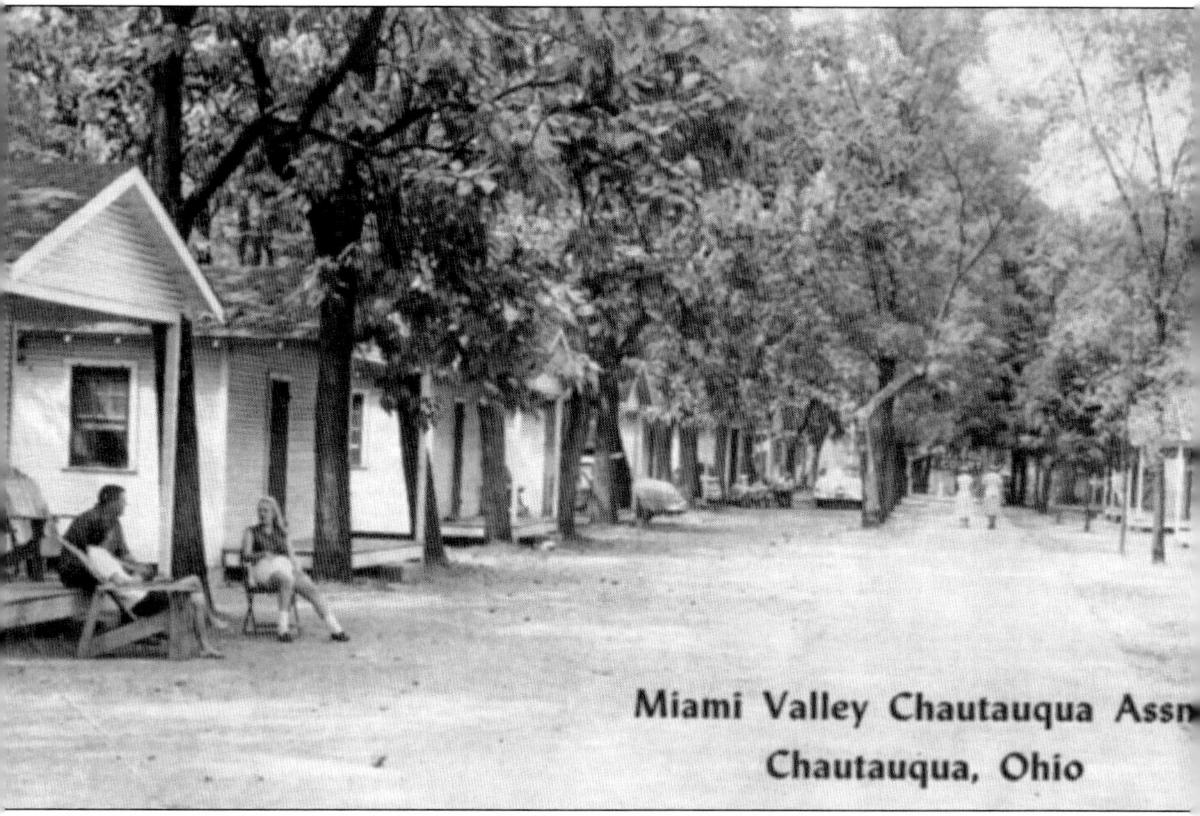

When this postcard was issued, the Miami Valley Chautauqua Association had cottages, a dining room, a swimming pool, and "kiddy land" in addition to other attractions, and patrons could boat, skate, or bowl, which were suitable activities for the whole family. One of its mottos was: "A Place To Spend Your Vacation."

Eight

The Business Community

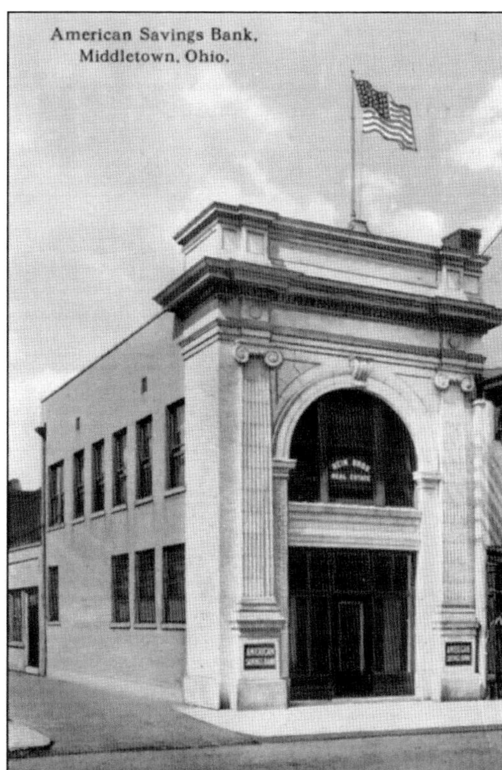

The American Savings Bank was located at 120 East Third Street (1020 Central Avenue). Eventually, it became part of the First National Bank.

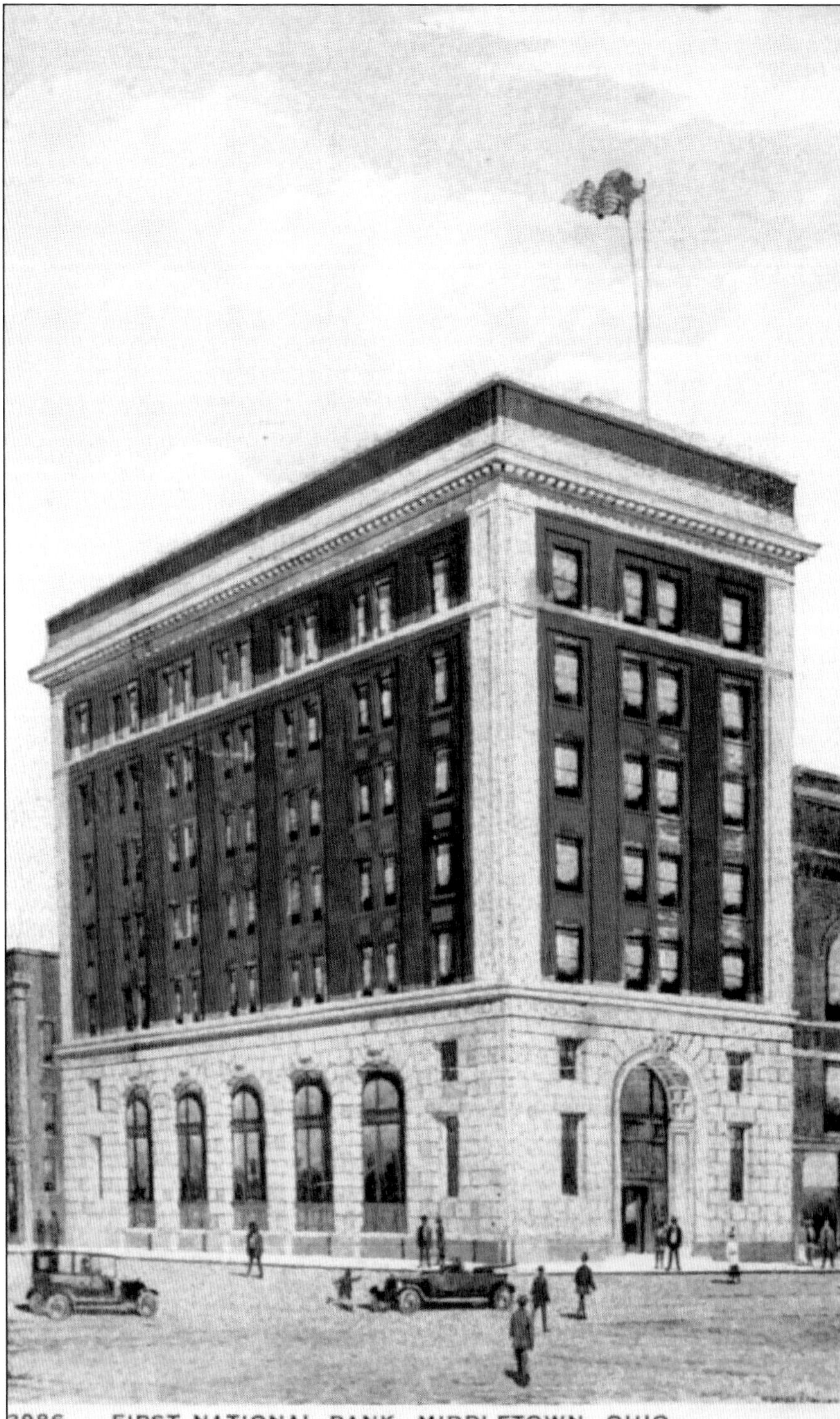

In 1919, the First National Bank and the Merchants National Bank merged. Shortly afterwards, plans for a new bank building were made. An unidentified artist made this drawing of how he thought the First National Bank building would look.

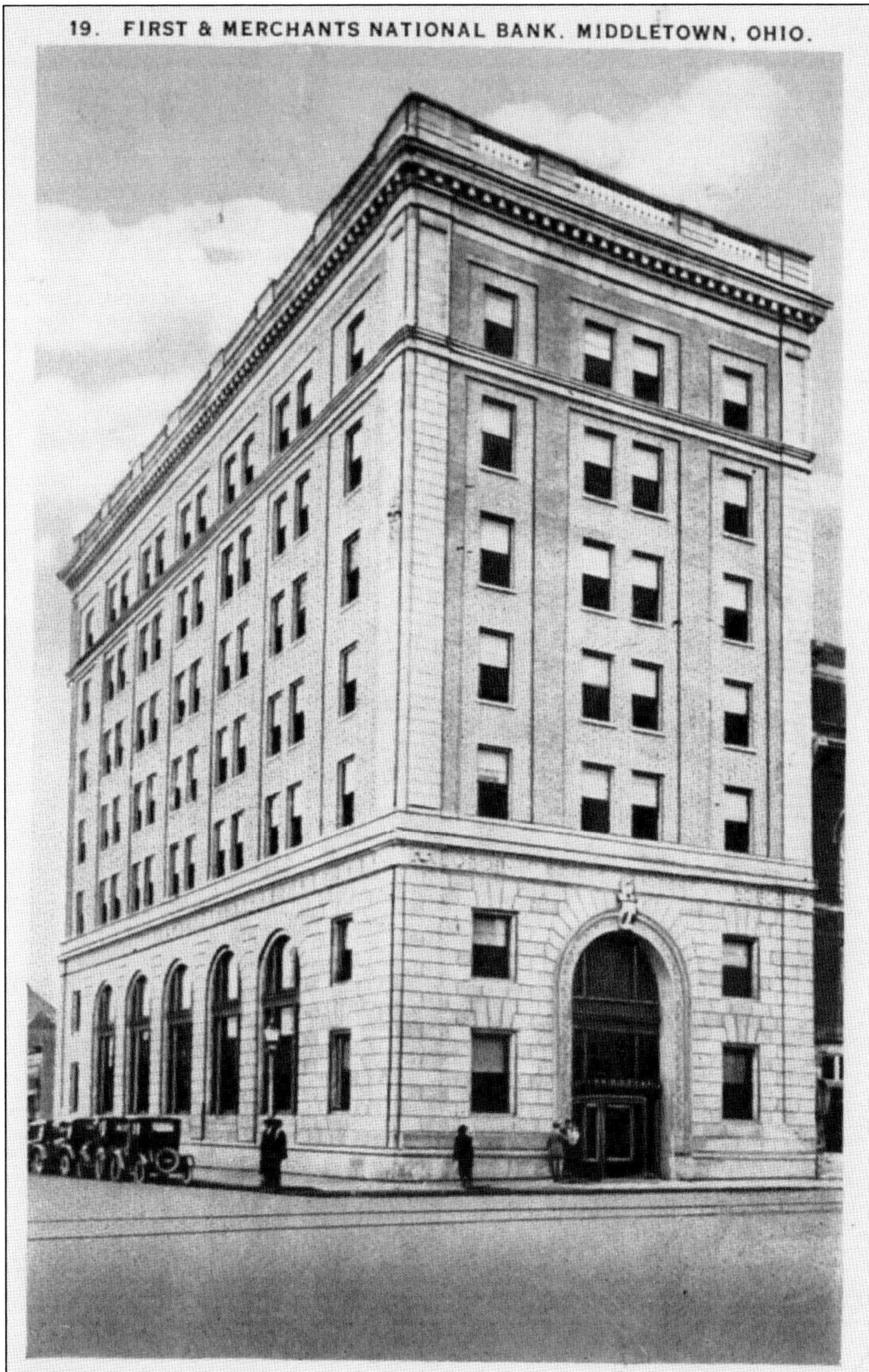

For a short time, the combined banks operated as the First & Merchants National Bank. The new building opened in June 1921 and provided space not only for banking but also for offices. It was not long until it was claimed to be "Middletown's Largest Bank."

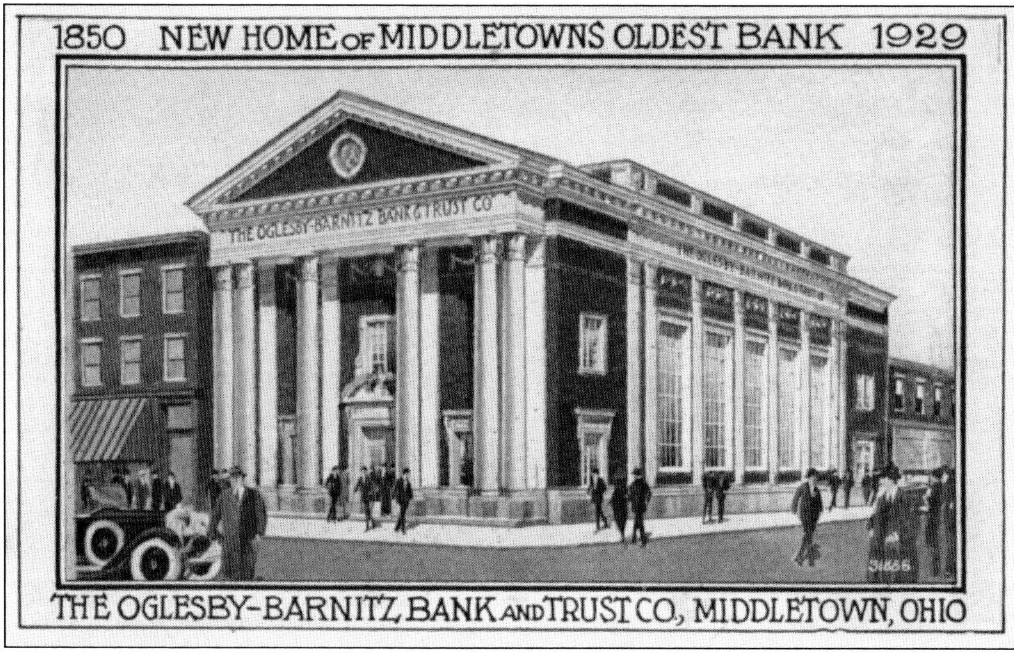

The first bank in town was the Oglesby-Barnitz Bank and Trust Company. It traced its history back to 1850, or earlier, when William B. Oglesby and George C. Barnitz provided a place for people to save their money. In 1929, the bank erected this building.

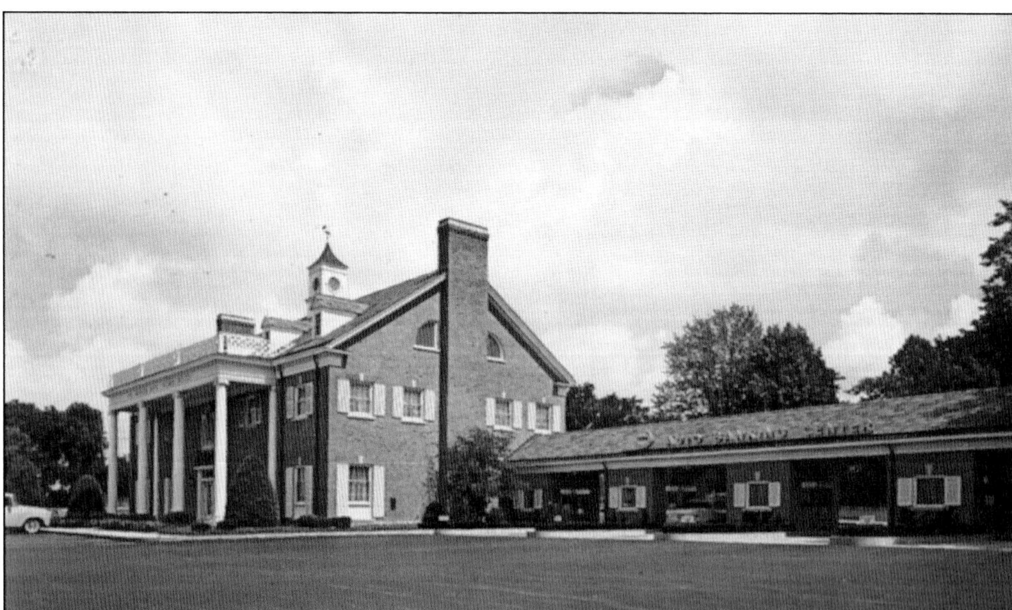

The Oglesby-Barnitz Bank and Trust Company was merged with other banks and took new names on several occasions. In 1957, when the bank built an office branch on Nelbar Street, it was known as Bank One. Today, it is a part of Chase Bank.

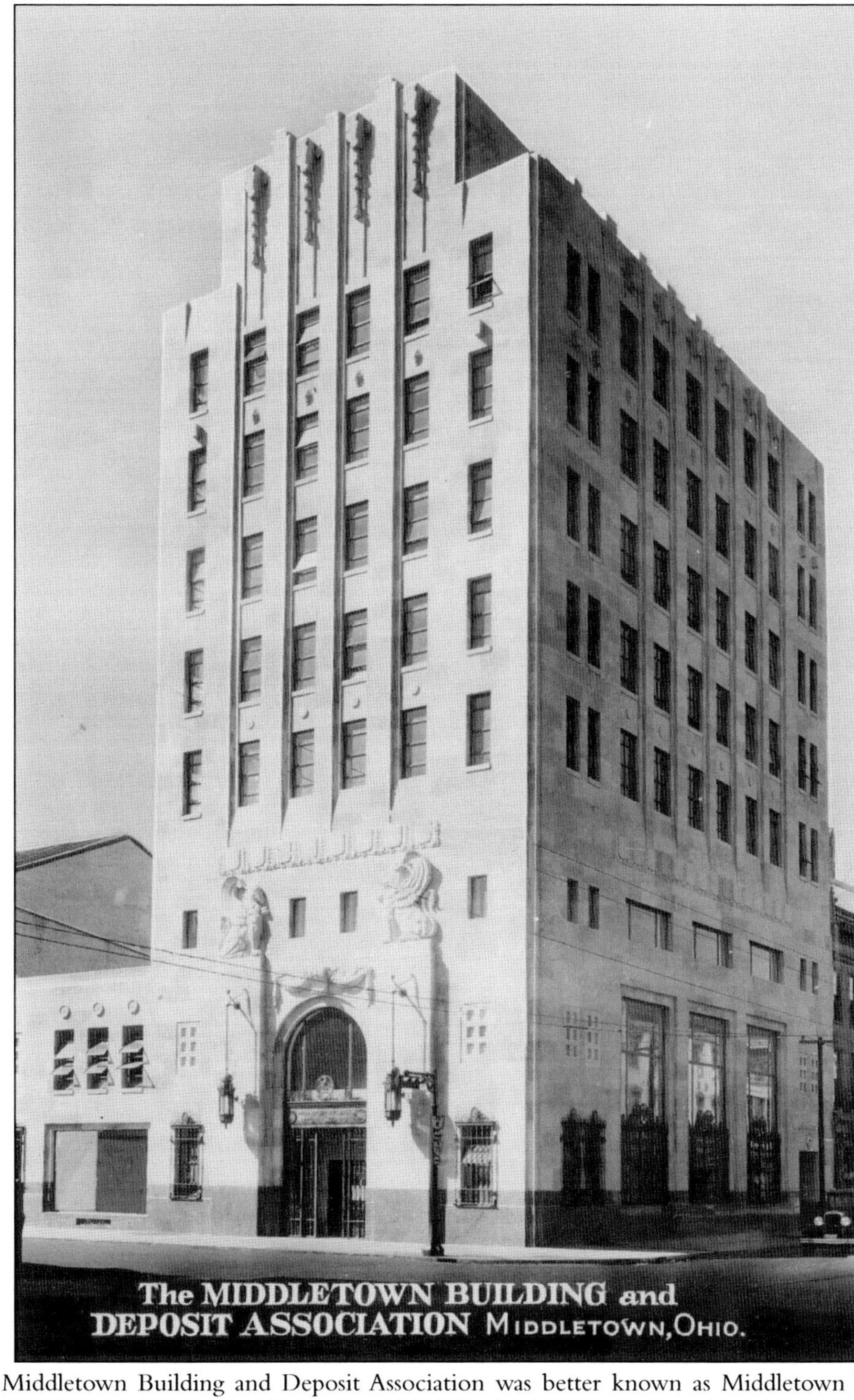

The Middletown Building and Deposit Association was better known as Middletown Federal Savings and Loan Association. They were one of the financial institutions that occupied three of the corners at Main Street and Central Avenue. The others were the First National Bank and the Oglesby-Barnitz Bank and Trust Company.

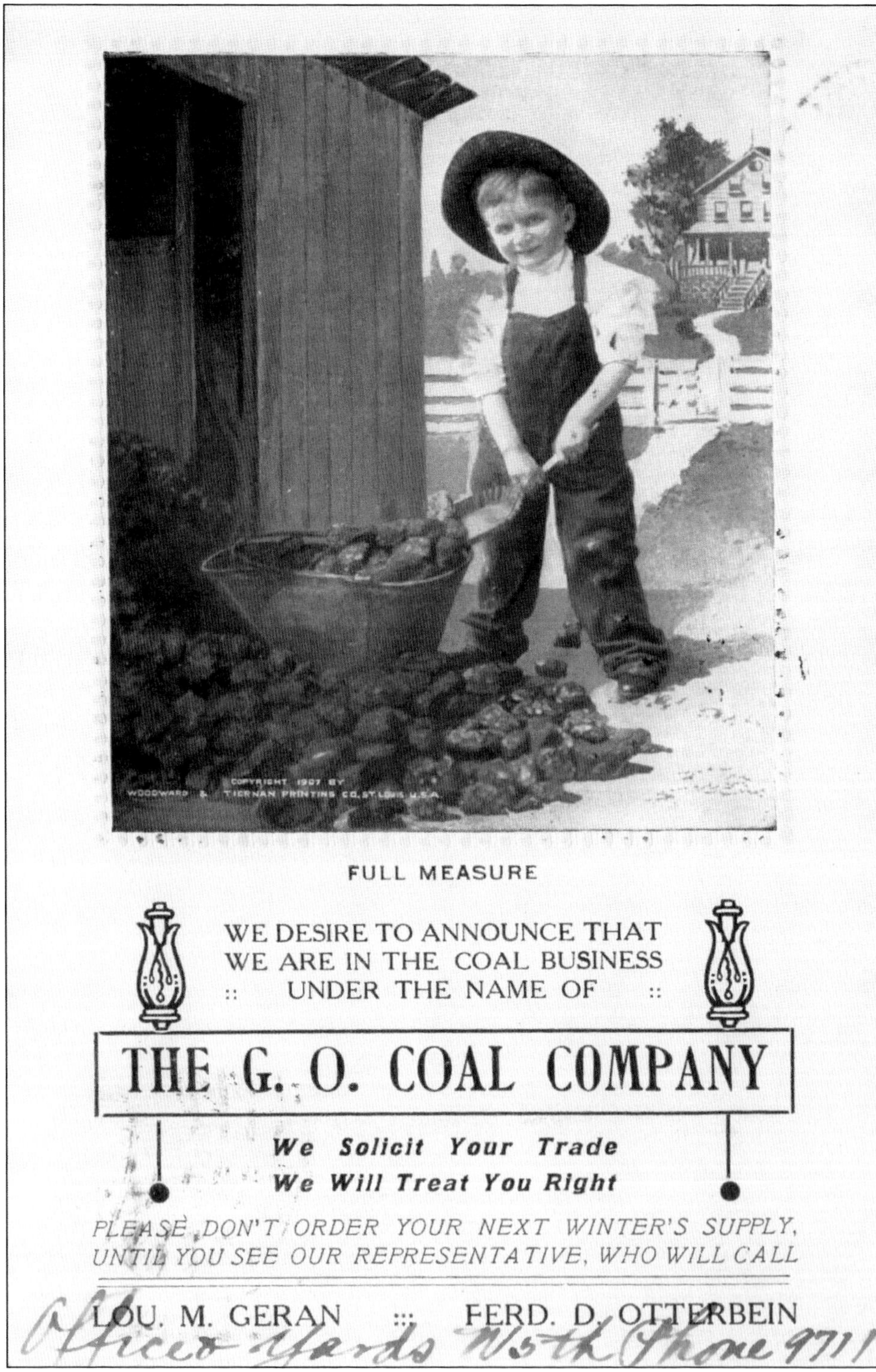

Postmarked April 13, 1910, this postcard advertised the G.O. Coal Company. At that time, coal was the chief means of heating a home, school, church, or business. The company was operated by Lou M. Geran and Ferdinand D. Otterbein.

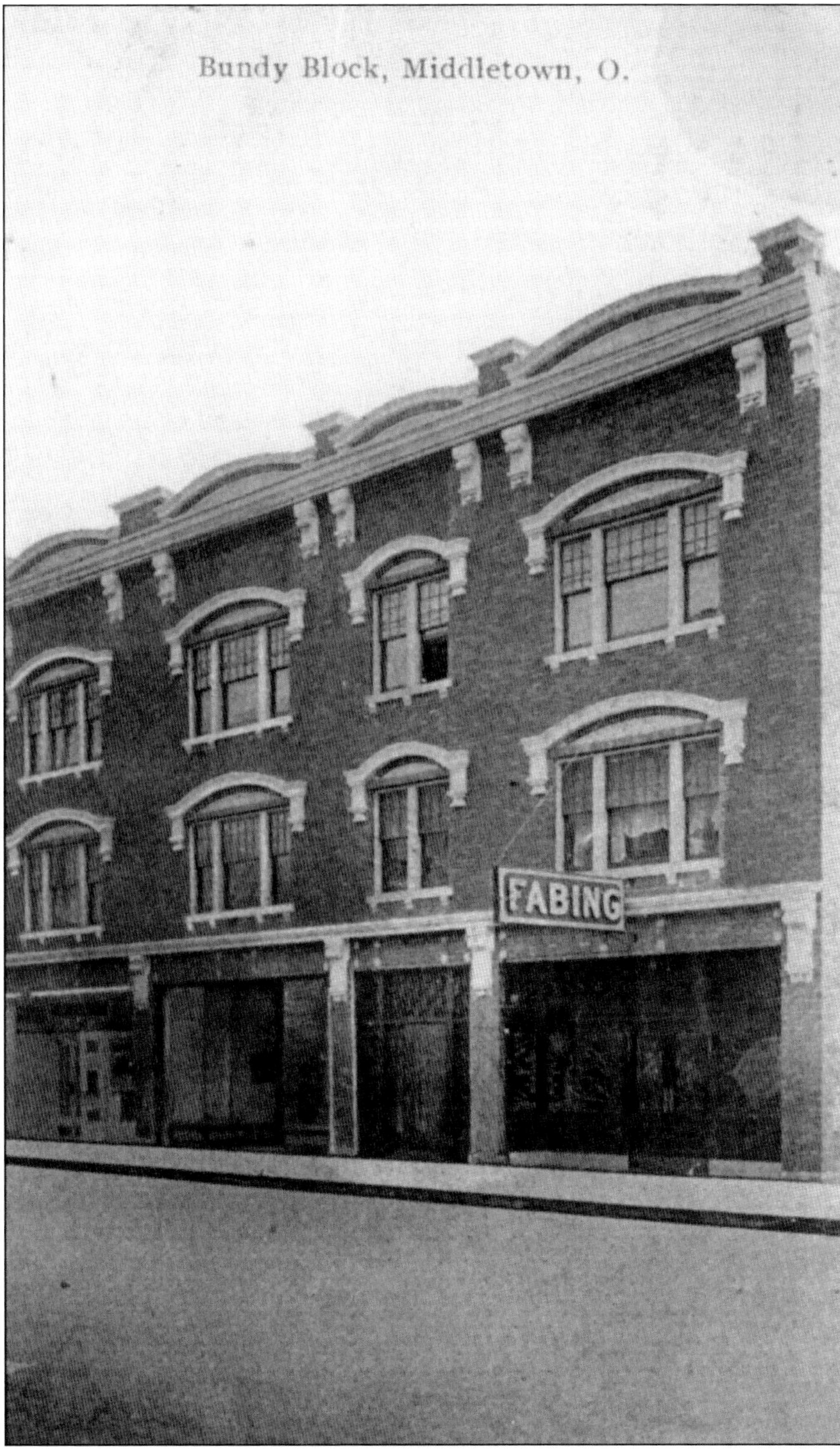

In 1910, Dr. D.B. Bundy purchased an industrial building on Third Street at the railroad tracks and converted the three-story building into apartments with storefronts on the first floor. In 1912, William E. Fabing operated a saloon in the building (714 East Third Street).

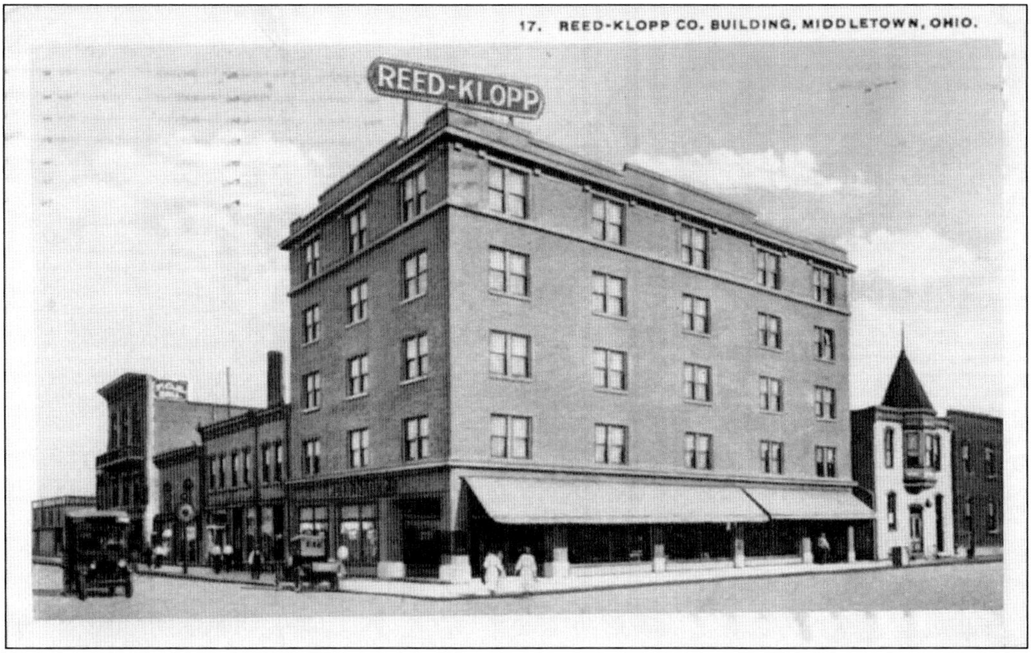

Starting in 1917, S.H. Reed and W.T. Klopp entered into business selling furniture. In August 1919, they moved into this new building located on Third and Canal Streets.

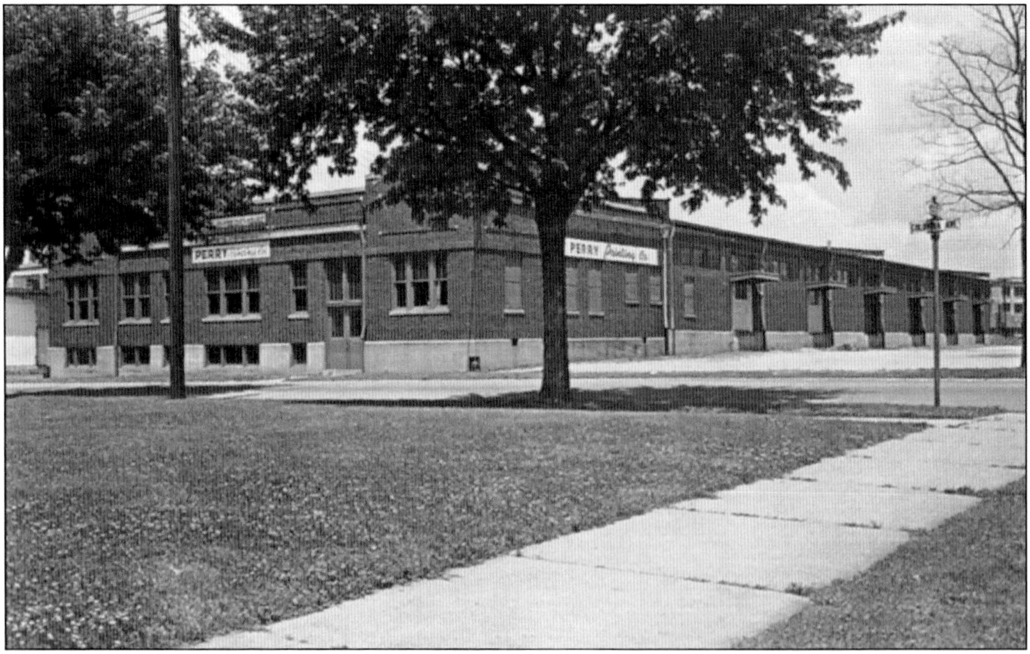

In 1961, the Perry Printing Company moved from Yankee Road to the freight house of the Big Four Railroad. The building was constructed in 1918 by the Big Four branch of the New York Central Railroad. Glenn Perry published several of the postcards that are in this collection. (Courtesy of Roger L. Miller.)

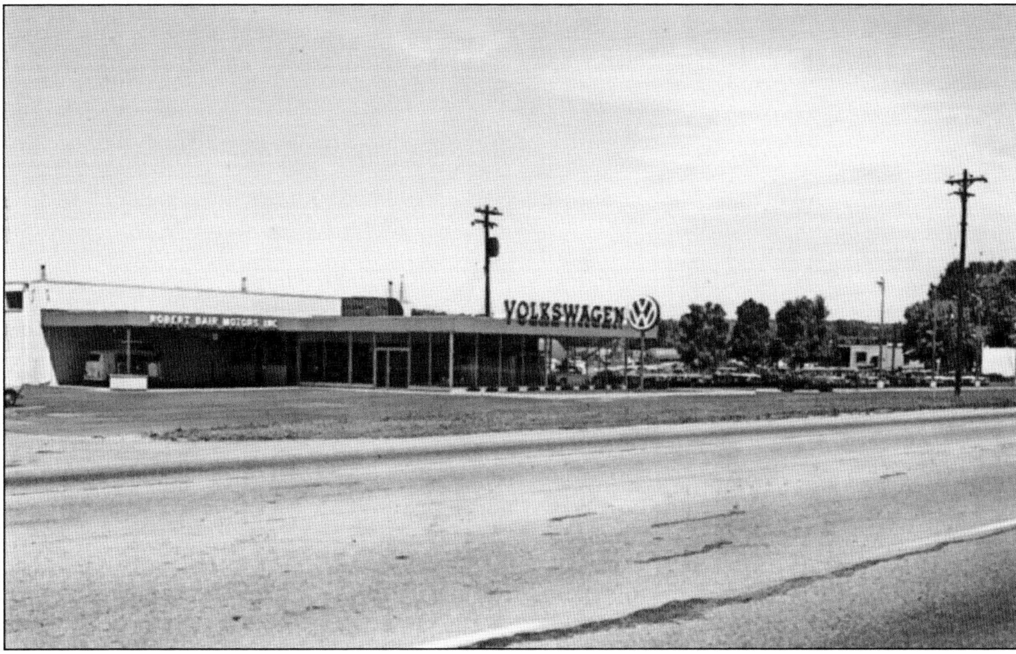

Robert Bair Motors was a Volkswagen dealer located just outside of Middletown in Madison Township's Poasttown.

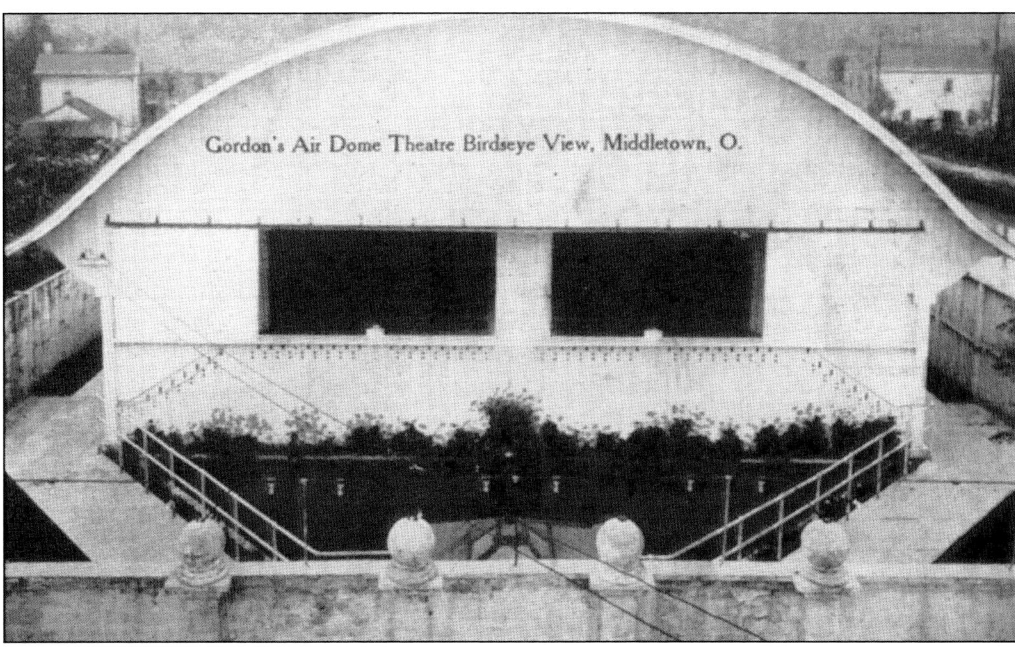

Located on Second Street (Manchester Avenue) at the Miami-Erie Canal, the Air Dome Theatre was operated by William Gordon. Later, he opened the Gordon Theater on Central Avenue, which was operated by his wife, Mayme, after his death.

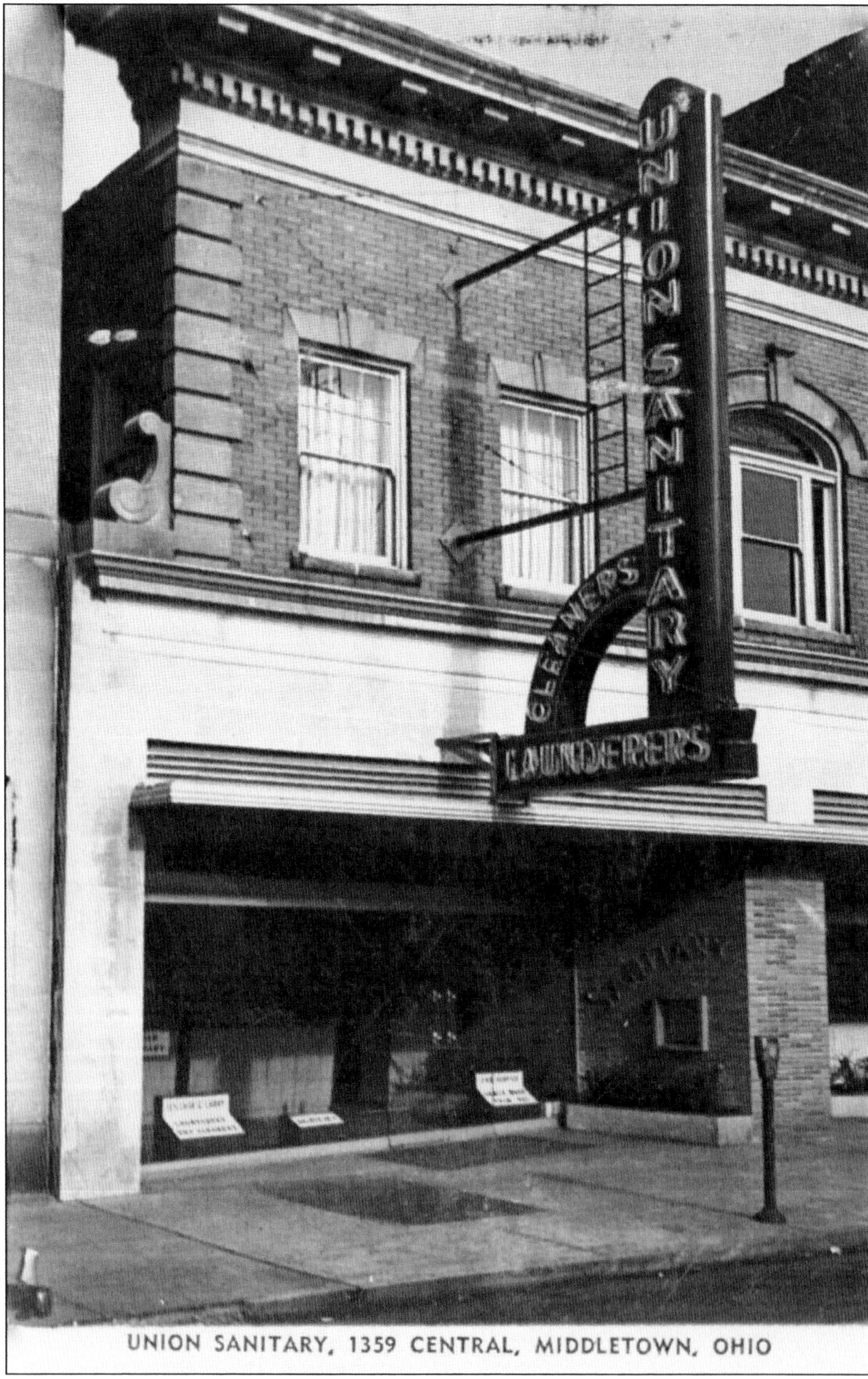

One of Middletown's many business enterprises was the Union Sanitary Cleaners-Launderers. By 1950, when this was postmarked, the company operated a store at 1359 Central Avenue and its dry cleaning plant on Park Street at Second Avenue.

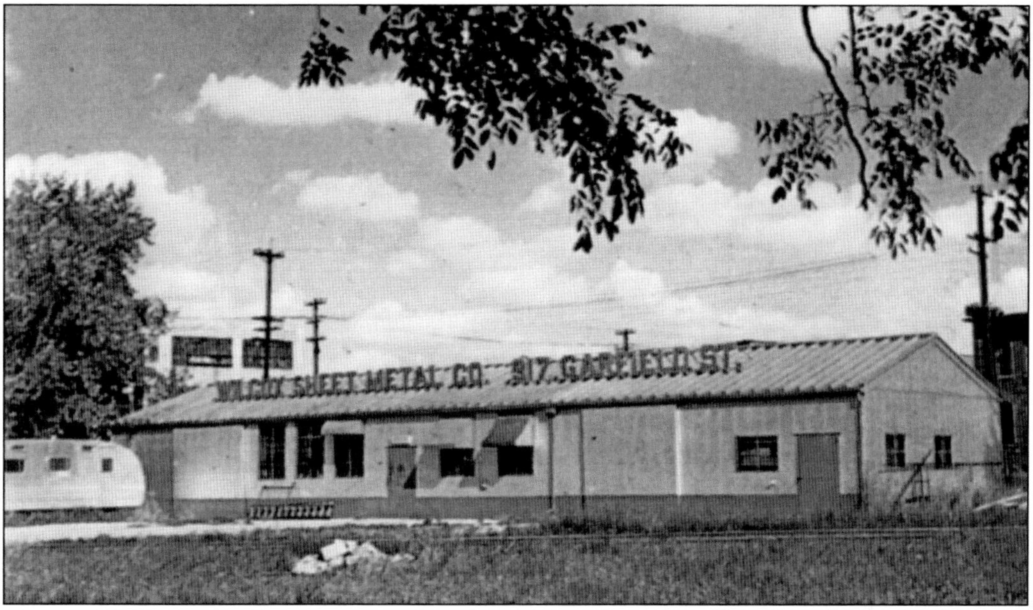

One of Armco's many products was Steelox building panels. They were used in industrial, business, and residential construction. This is the Wilcox Sheet Metal Company building, which was constructed of Steelox. It was manufactured by Armco Drainage & Metal Products, a division of the company.

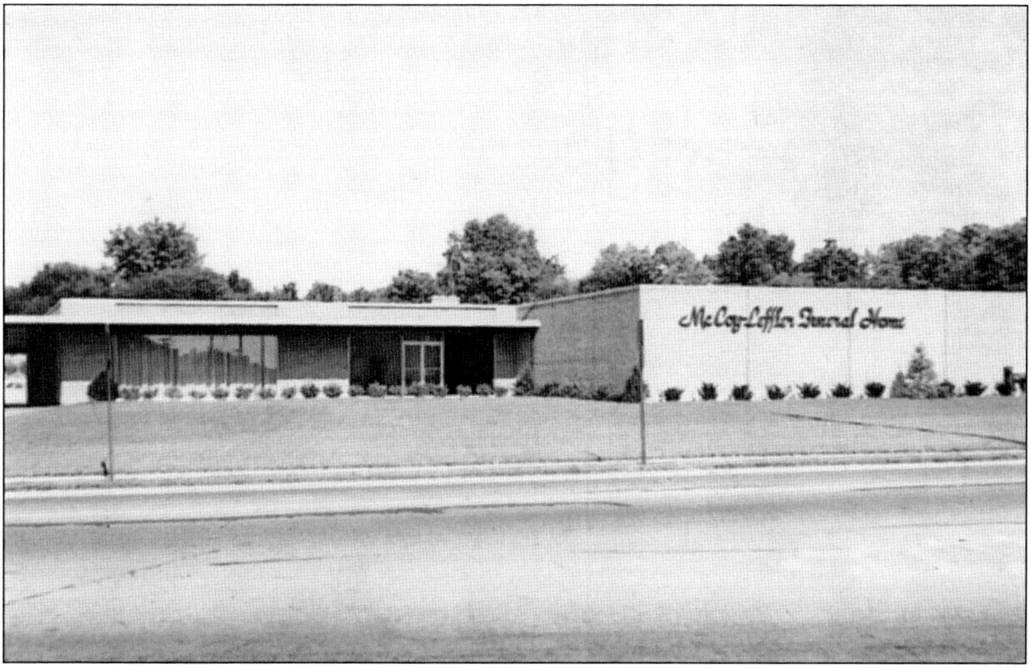

The two oldest continuously operating businesses in the city are funeral homes. Wilson, Schramm, Spaulding traces its history to 1839, while Breitenback McCoy-Leffler traces its history to 1849, when Godfrey Rathman began making furniture and added undertaking to the business.

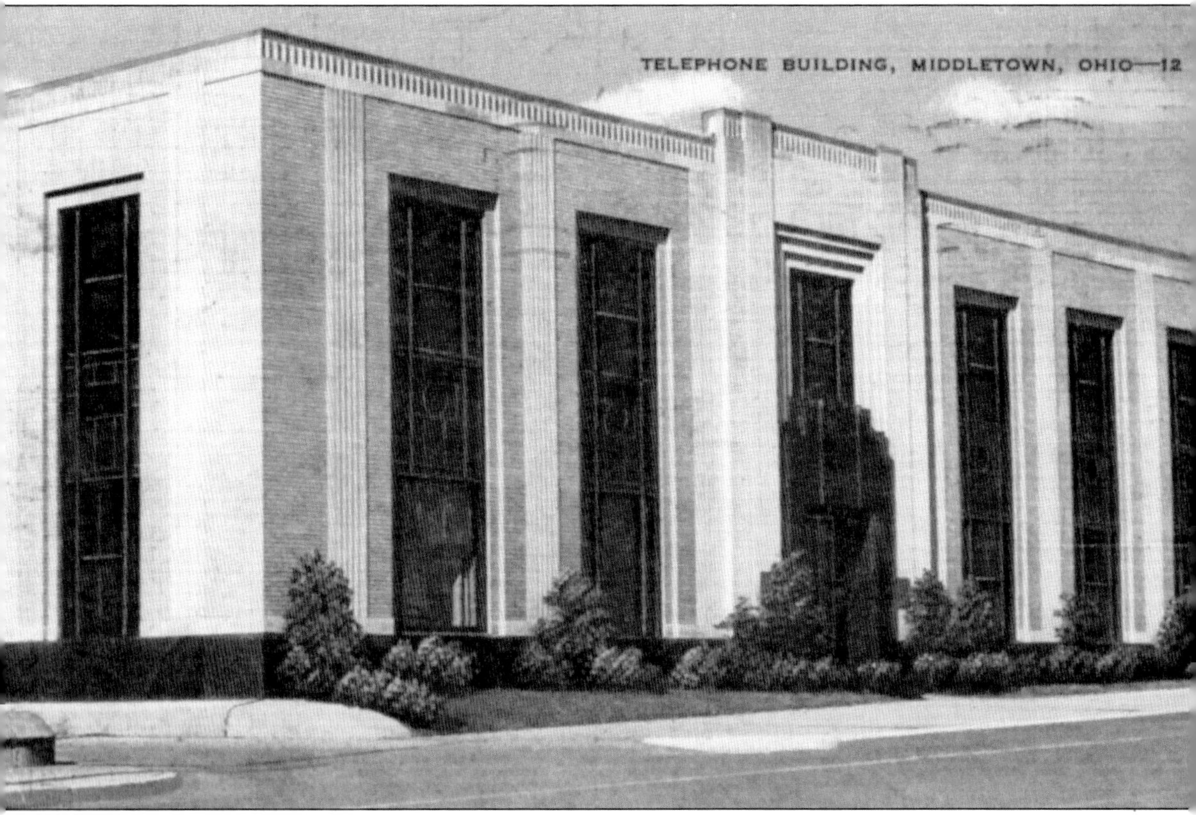

By 1881, Middletown had a telephone exchange started by Dr. Charles Bundy. In 1884, Bundy's concern became part of the Miami Telephone Company. Continual growth and additional mergers resulted in the need for this building that was erected by Ohio Bell.

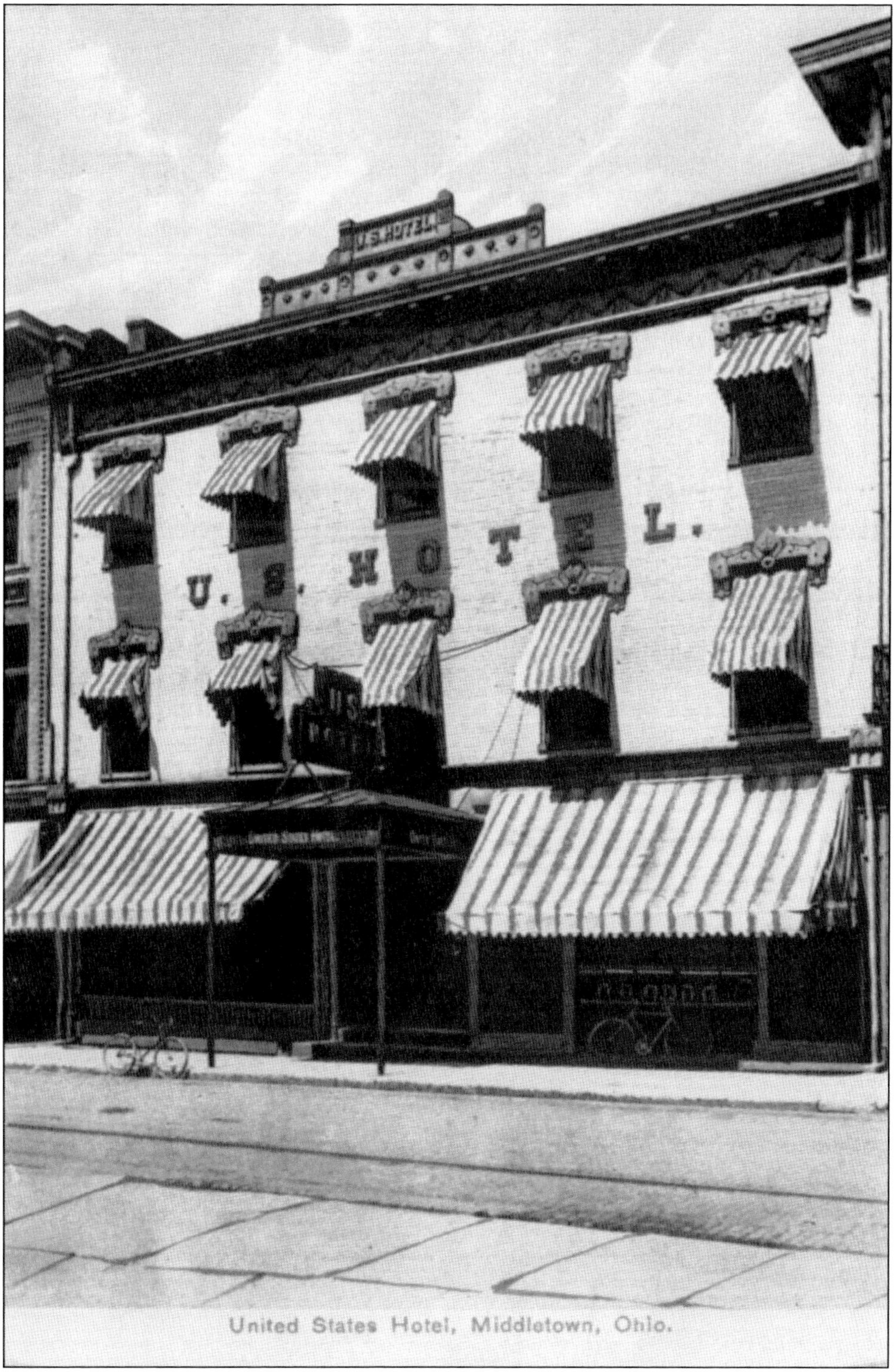

The oldest building in downtown Middletown is the old United States Hotel, which is better known as US Hotel. In 1831, it was constructed as a dwelling and coffeehouse. In 1845, it became a hotel, which has been added to on several occasions.

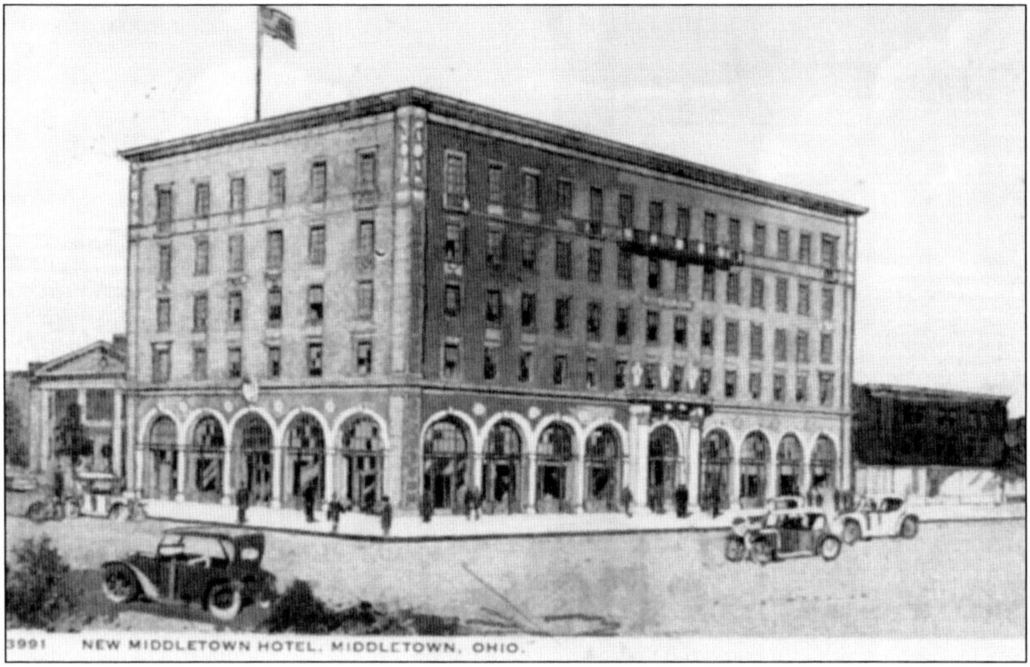

The Middletown Hotel Company was organized in November 1919 to construct a hotel on the corner of Manchester Avenue and Broad Street. The company sold $265,000 in stock to finance the project. Seen here is a drawing of what would be known as Hotel Manchester.

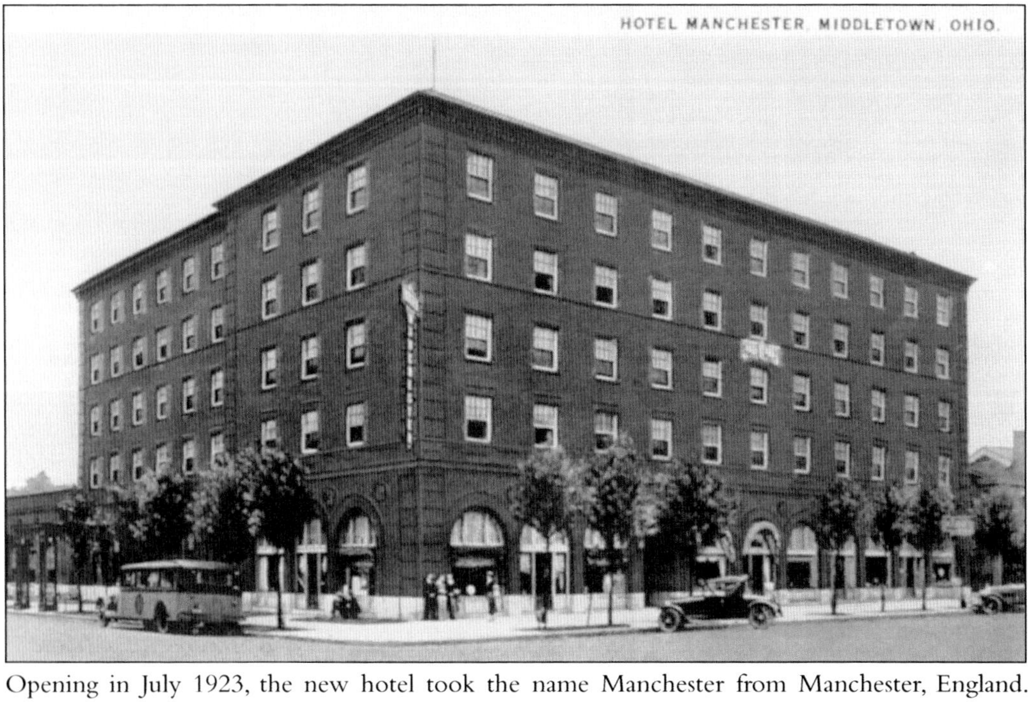

Opening in July 1923, the new hotel took the name Manchester from Manchester, England. Also, William Montagu, the ninth duke of Manchester, was well known in the area, for he had married Helena Zimmerman, daughter of Eugene Zimmerman. Eugene, a railroad financier and oil tycoon, became president of the Cincinnati, Hamilton & Dayton Railroad.

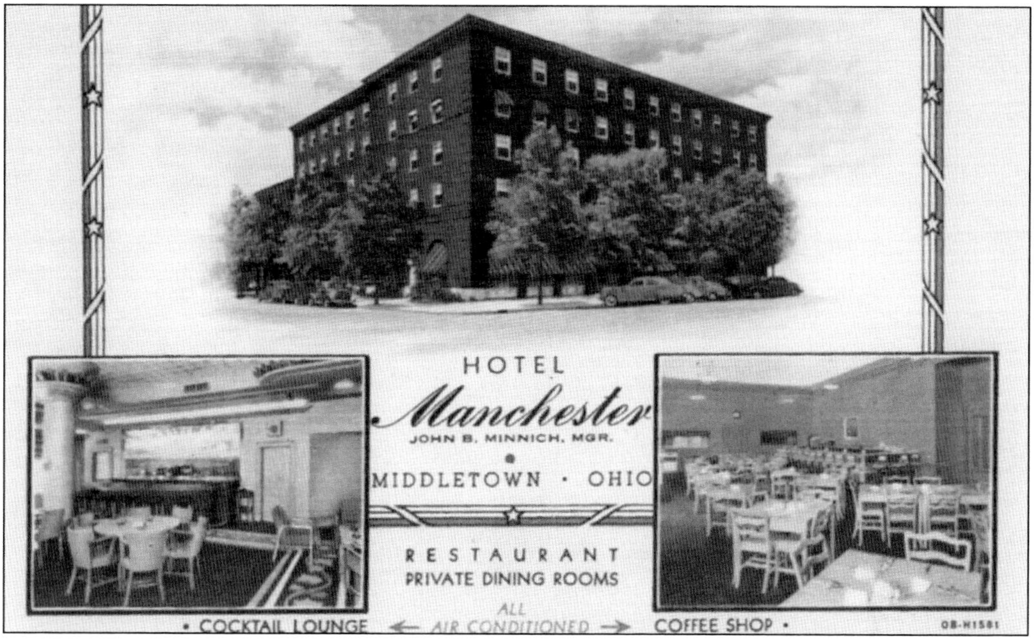

Formally opened to the public on October 29, 1922, the Hotel Manchester became an institution, dispensing hospitality to the people of Middletown and to visitors. The hotel provided fine dining and large banquet rooms.

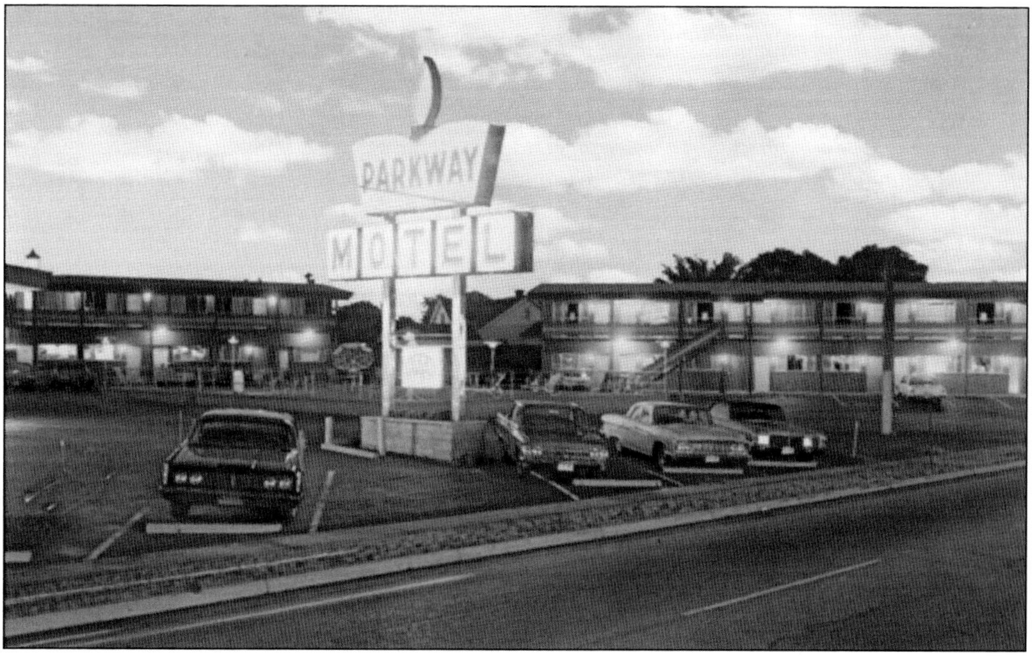

The Parkway Motel is one of the older motels in the city. It was owned by Dell Henderson. Located not far from State Route 4, it is on Verity Parkway, which is State Route 73, and is still very much used, especially for people who require longer stays than what other motels might provide.

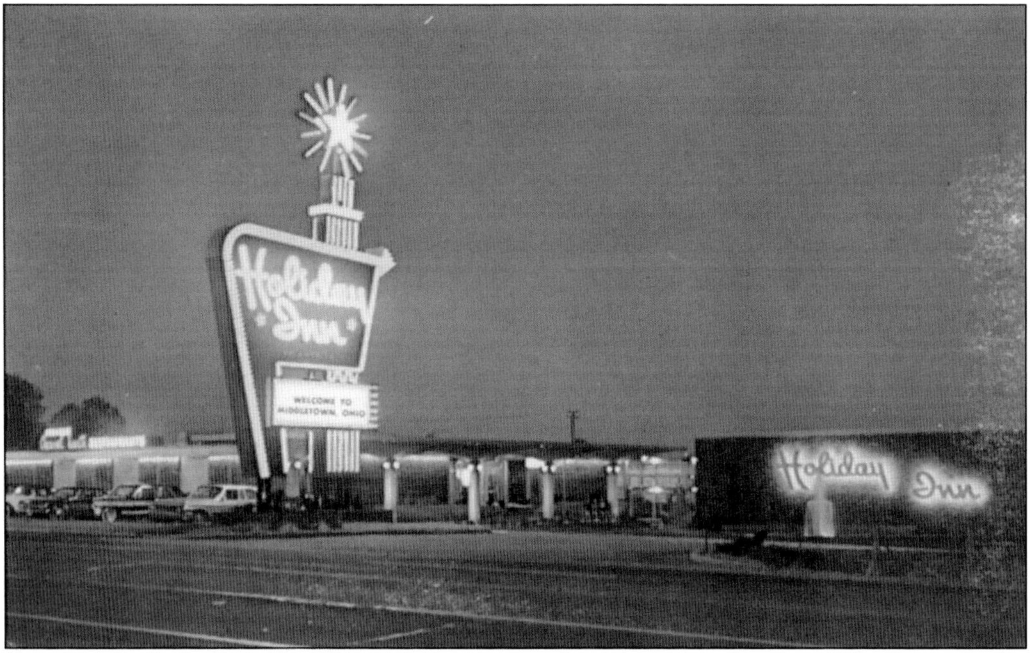

The Holiday Inn was the first of several motels that have opened at the State Route 122 interchange with Interstate 75. Interstate 75 is the main route from Southern Florida to Northern Michigan. It is a very busy route for moving truckloads, both north and south.

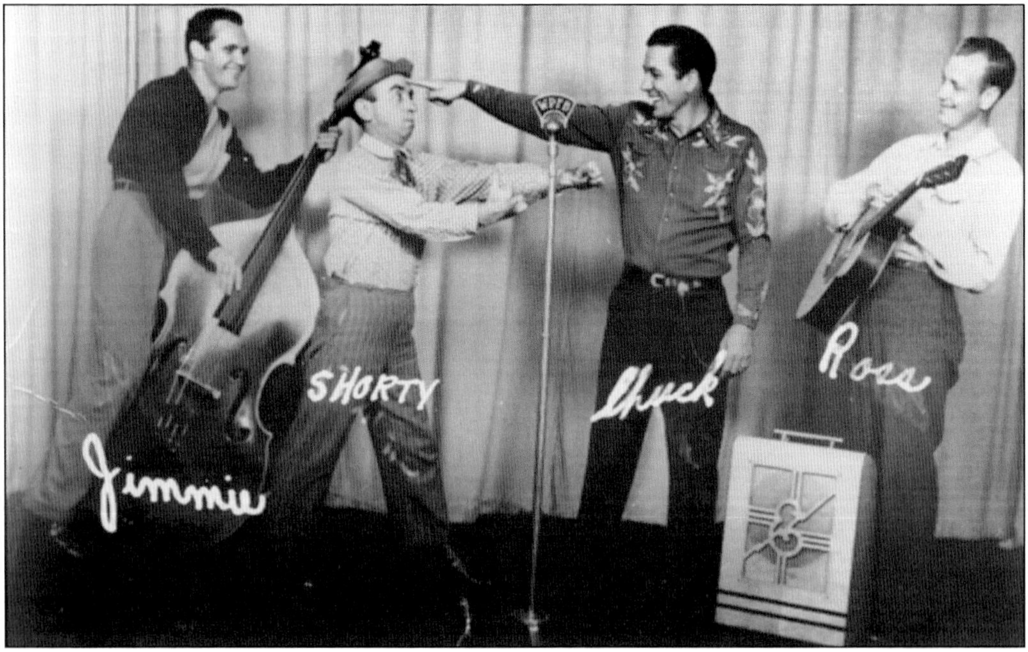

Middletown's radio station WPFB 9-10, "In the Middle of Your Dial," went on the air on September 1, 1947. Very soon after, it was a well-known bluegrass station, with live performers in its studios and onstage in the barn and tent located on the station's property. It is believed that Jimmie Skinner, Shorty Hobbs, and Charlie "Chuck" Swing are three of the people seen here, from left to right. (Courtesy of Roger L. Miller.)

Nine

Getting Around

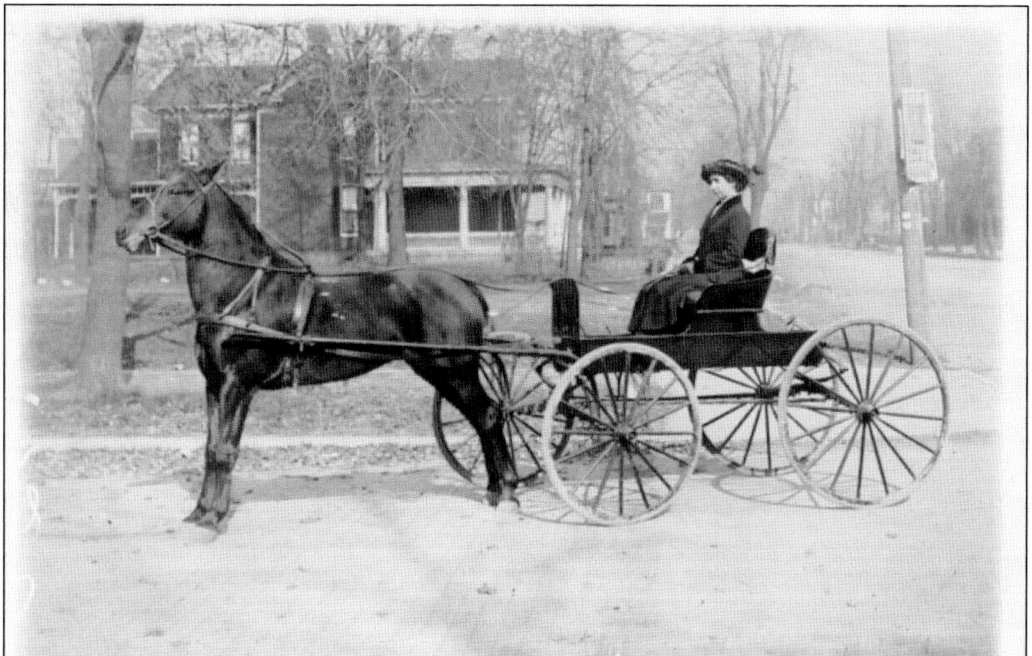

The young lady is taking a trip with her horse and buggy. The back of the card has 1912 written in pencil on it, and it is believed that the sign on the post is a playbill for the Sorg Opera House. (Courtesy of George C. Crout Collection, Middletown Public Library.)

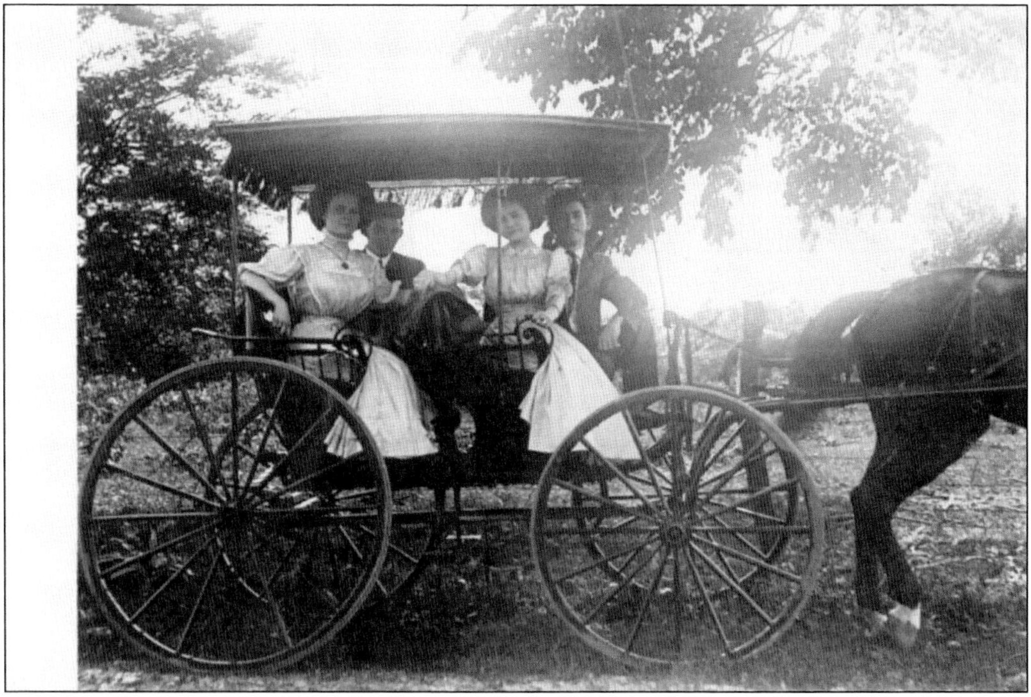

The surrey is ready to take the Fisher and Bayha families to church on a Sunday morning. Both families lived on South Sutphin Street. (Courtesy of Roger L. Miller.)

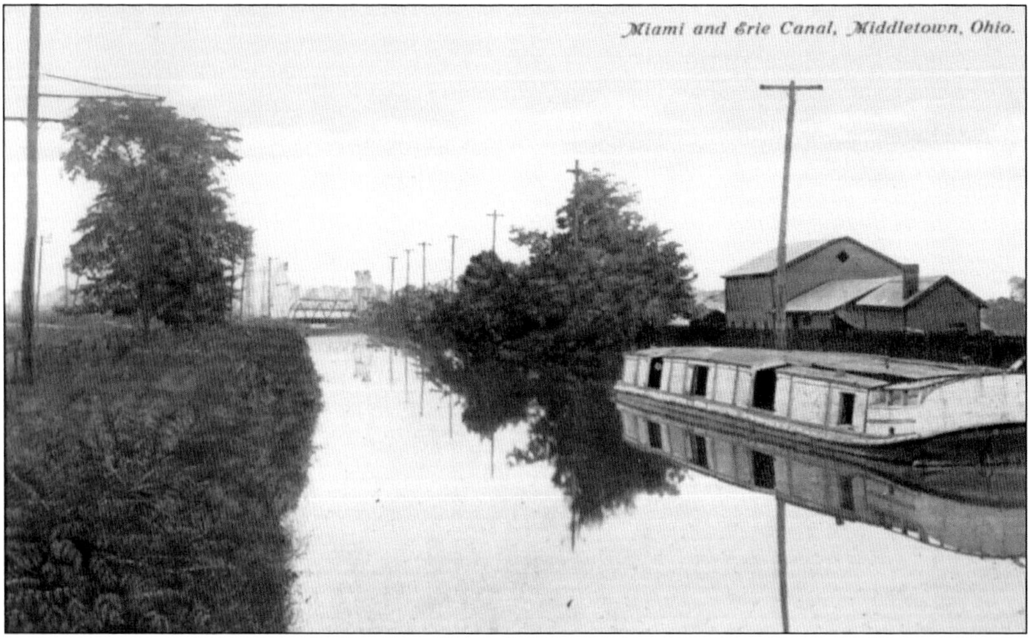

Not many postcards of the Miami-Erie Canal in use were made. In 1825, ground-breaking ceremonies for the start of construction of the canal were held in Middletown. The canal became an important part of the local economy, with the city becoming a port on the canal. Once the railroads came, the need of the canal for transportation decreased very quickly. (Courtesy of George C. Crout Collection, Middletown Public Library.)

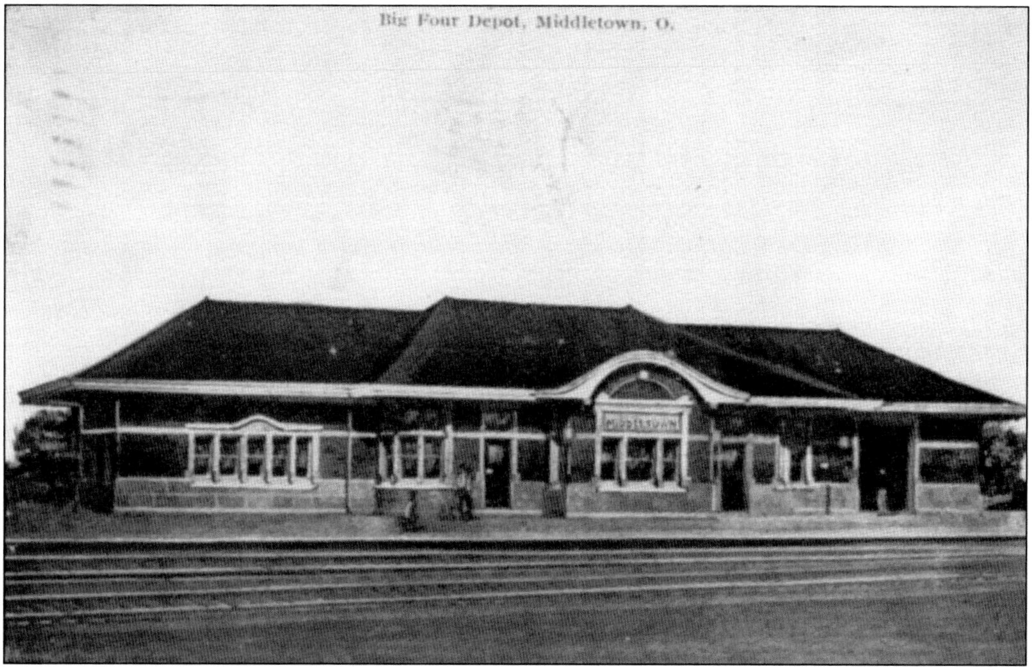

Several railroads have been constructed through Middletown. In 1871, the Cincinnati & Springfield Railroad was constructed. This depot was completed in 1909, when the line was part of the Big Four division of the New York Central Railroad.

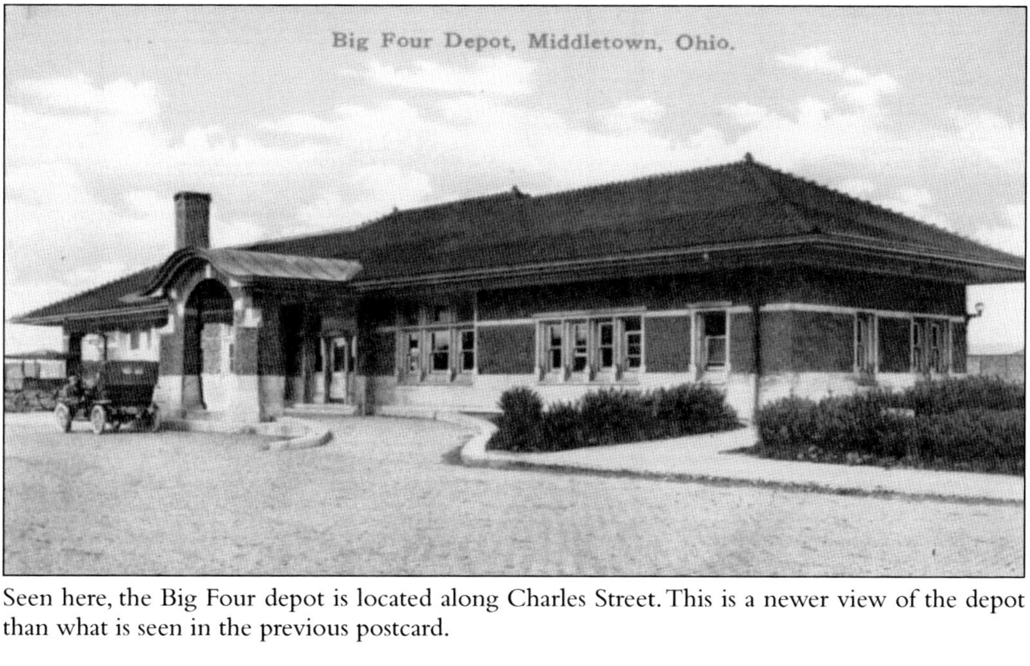

Seen here, the Big Four depot is located along Charles Street. This is a newer view of the depot than what is seen in the previous postcard.

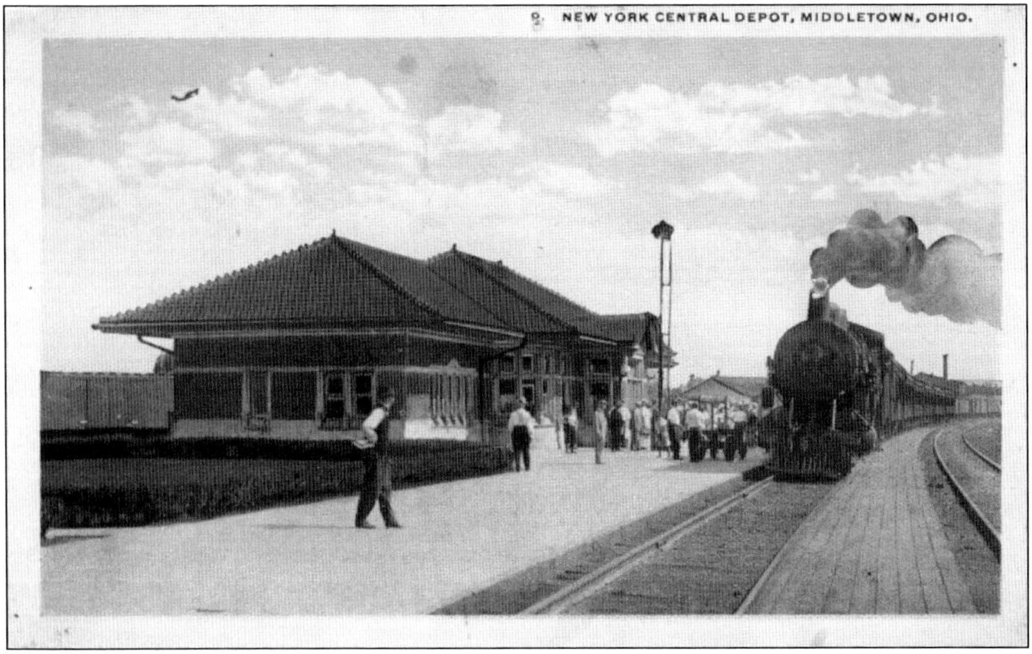

The New York Central Big Four division was not the first railroad in the area. In 1851, the Cincinnati, Hamilton & Dayton Railroad had come up the west side of the river. What became the New York Central arrived in Middletown in 1871.

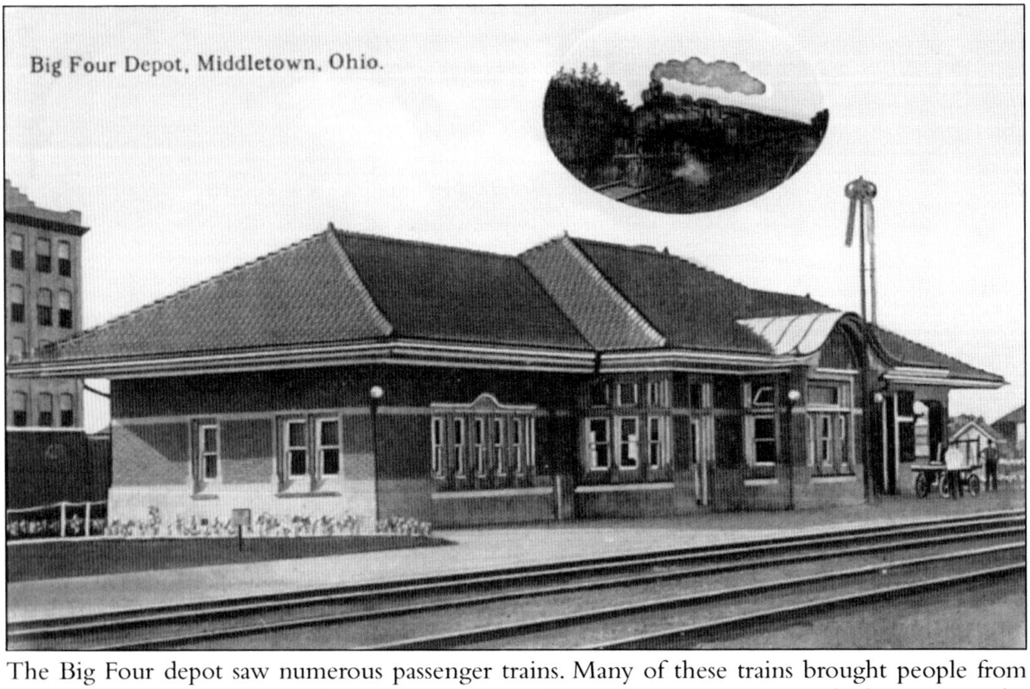

The Big Four depot saw numerous passenger trains. Many of these trains brought people from the South who were looking for work at the P. Lolliard Tobacco Company, which is seen in the background. When the conductor called out "Bull Durham," people on the train knew that they were in Middletown. Bull Durham was one of P. Lolliard's best-known products.

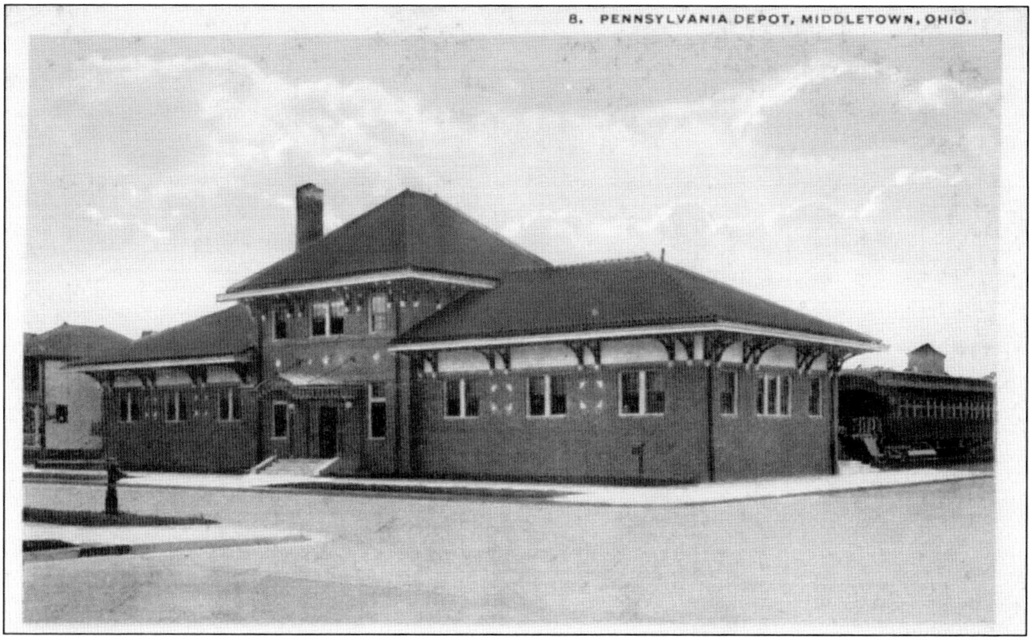

The Middletown & Cincinnati Railroad was an attempt by local businessmen to provide lower shipping rates than what the other railroads provided. It connected to a larger railroad system near Cincinnati and became part of the Pennsylvania Railroad. Its depot was located at First Avenue and Clinton Street.

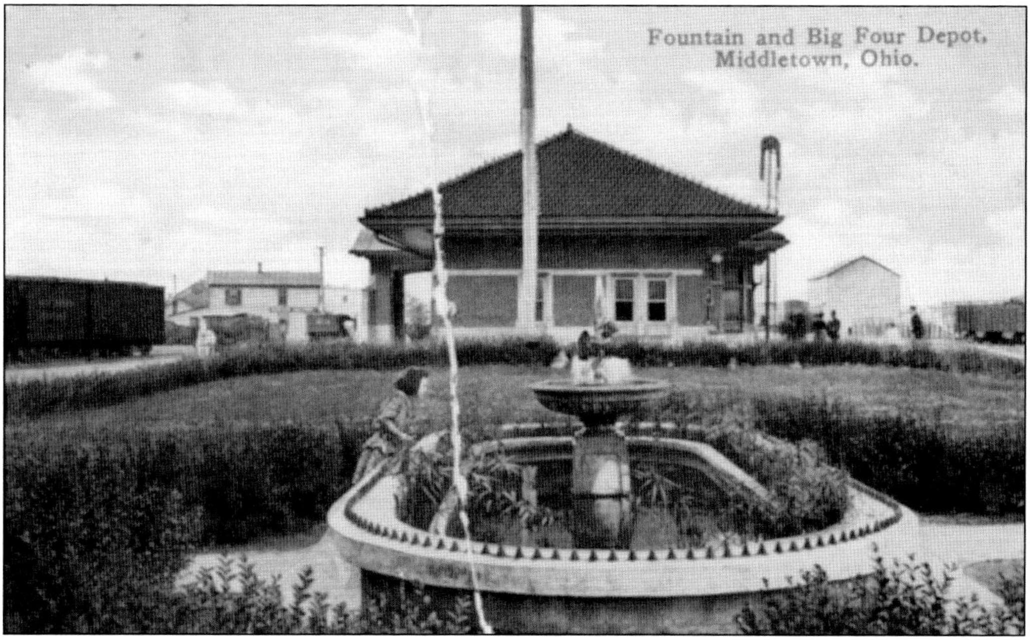

For many years, there was a small park with a pond and fountain on the south side of the Big Four depot.

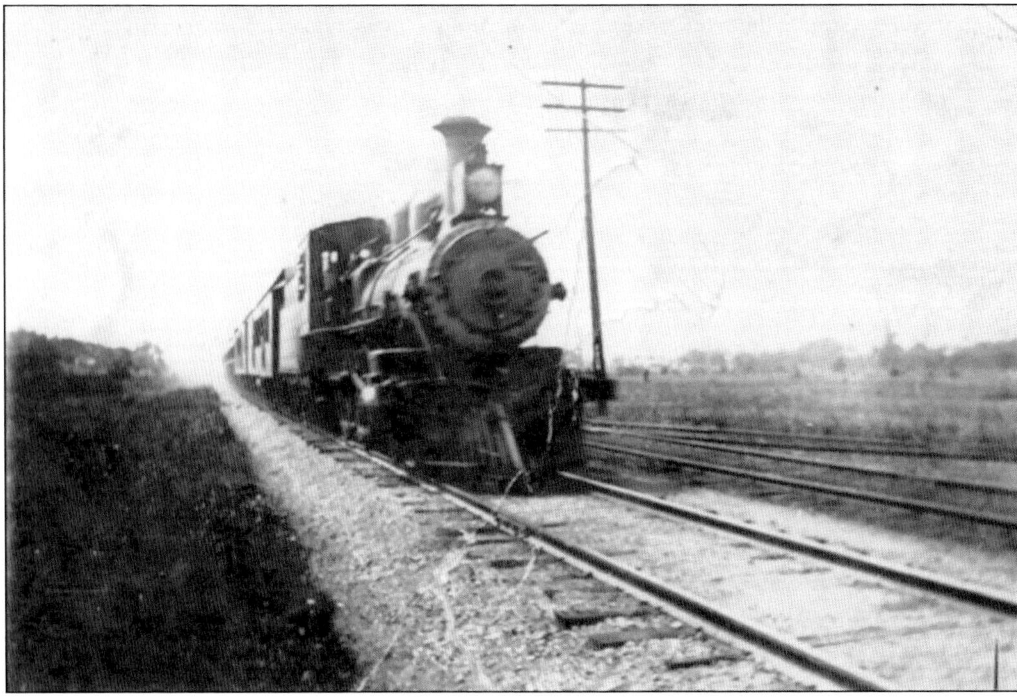

The Louisville, Cincinnati & Dayton Railroad never connected any of these cities. It only connected Hamilton to Middletown. The line was known as the "Long, Crooked, and Dirty." It did come to be important to Armco by connecting its Hamilton plant to its Middletown operations. (Courtesy of Roger L. Miller.)

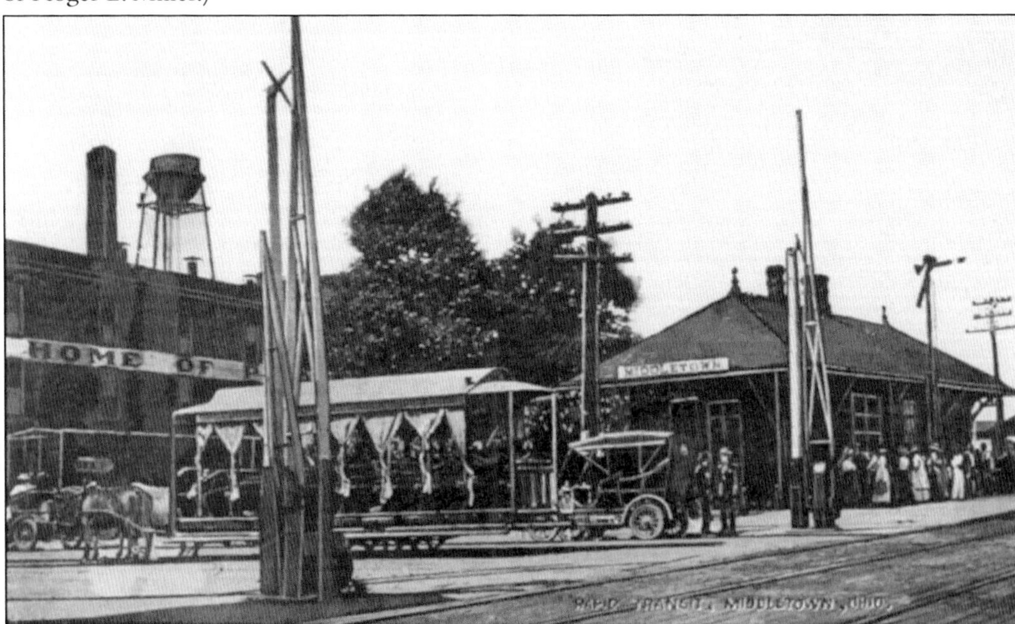

Here, Middletown's rapid transit was a horsecar. By way of Third Street (Central Avenue), it connected the Big Four depot to the Cincinnati, Hamilton & Dayton Railroad depot across the river. Seen here is the second of three different depots built by the Big Four.

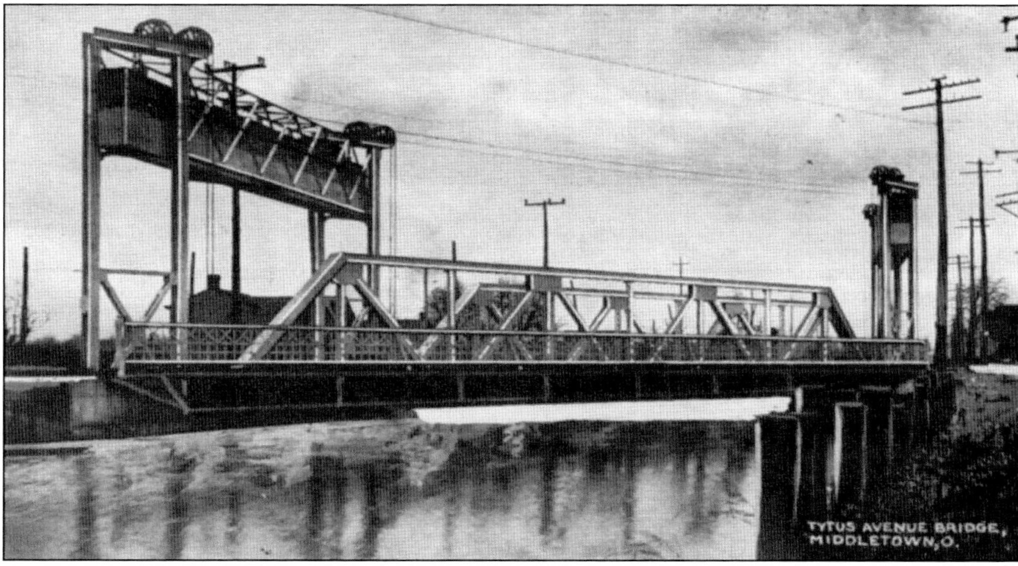

The Tytus Avenue Bridge over the Miami-Erie Canal was a lift bridge. Several streets in Middletown had such bridges at the canal. They replaced earlier humpback and swing bridges. Part of this bridge is over the hydraulic canal in Smith Park near the Canal Museum. (Courtesy of George C. Crout Collection, Middletown Public Library.)

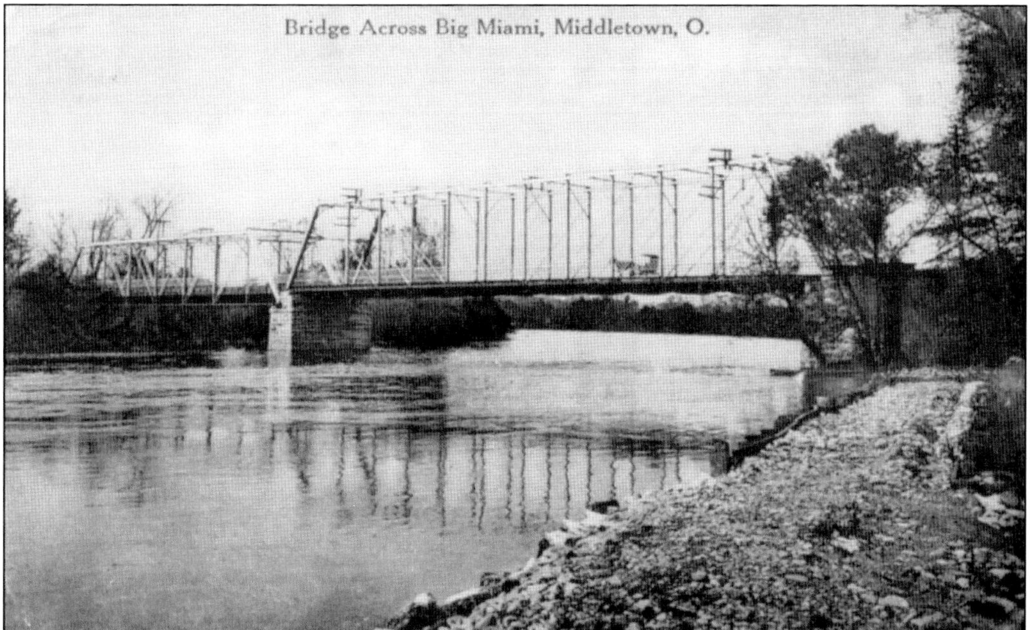

The March 1913 flood destroyed this bridge, which was between Middletown and West Middletown. When it was built, it replaced a wooden covered bridge.

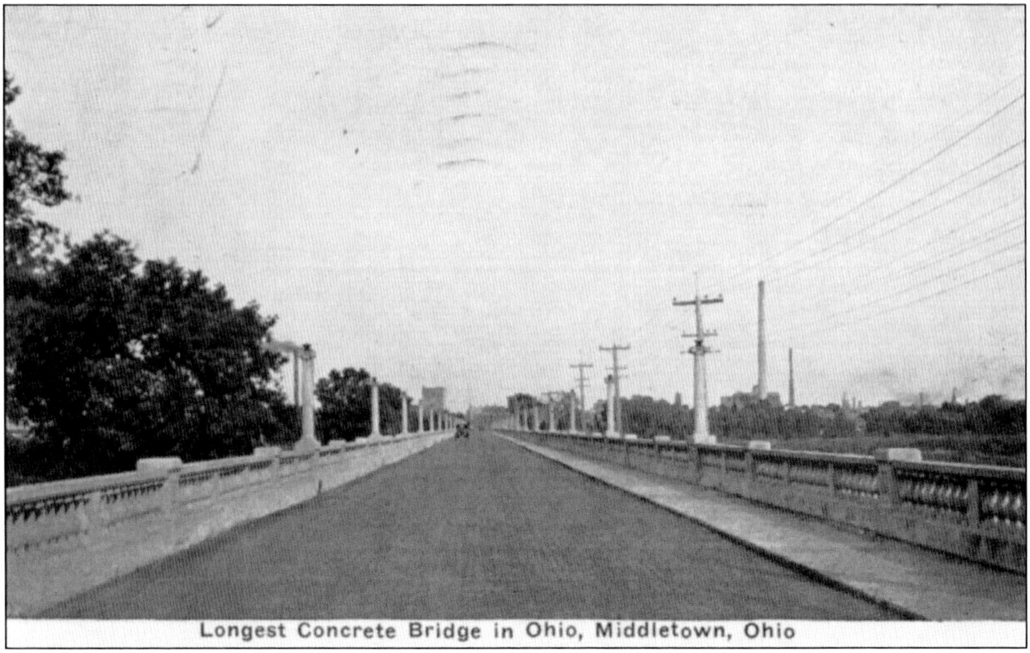

In 1915, when this bridge was completed, it was the longest concrete viaduct in Ohio. It replaced a temporary bridge that was placed here after the 1913 flood.

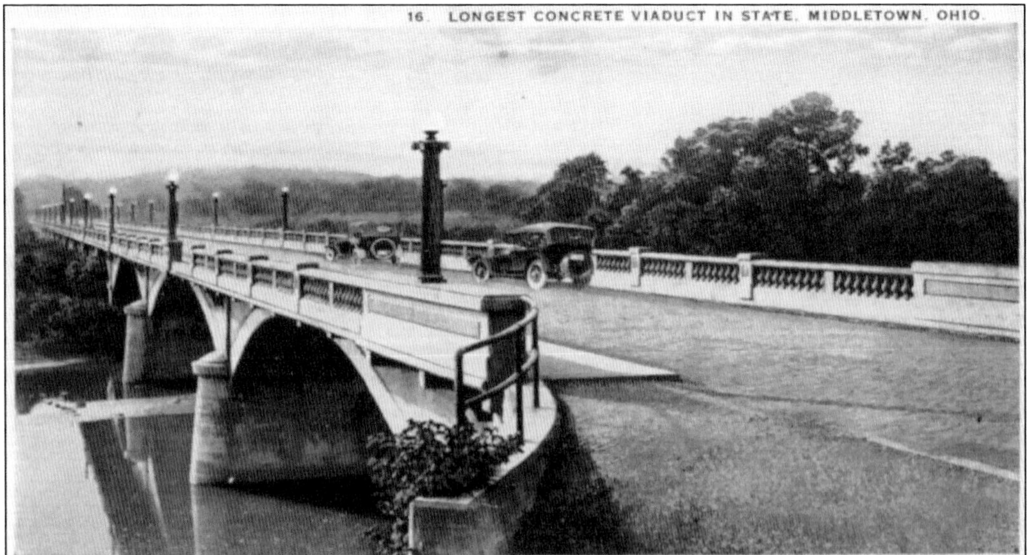

The viaduct did not hold up as well as the engineers originally thought it would. In 1948, it was replaced with a bridge that is still in use today.

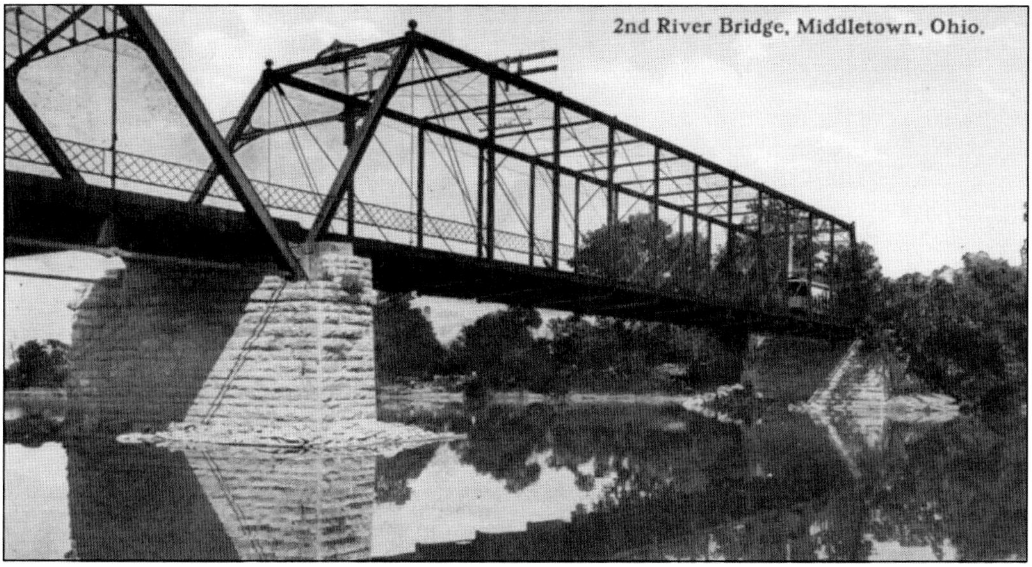

The 1913 flood not only took out this bridge but also the city's rapid-transit horsecar, which is in the process of crossing the bridge.

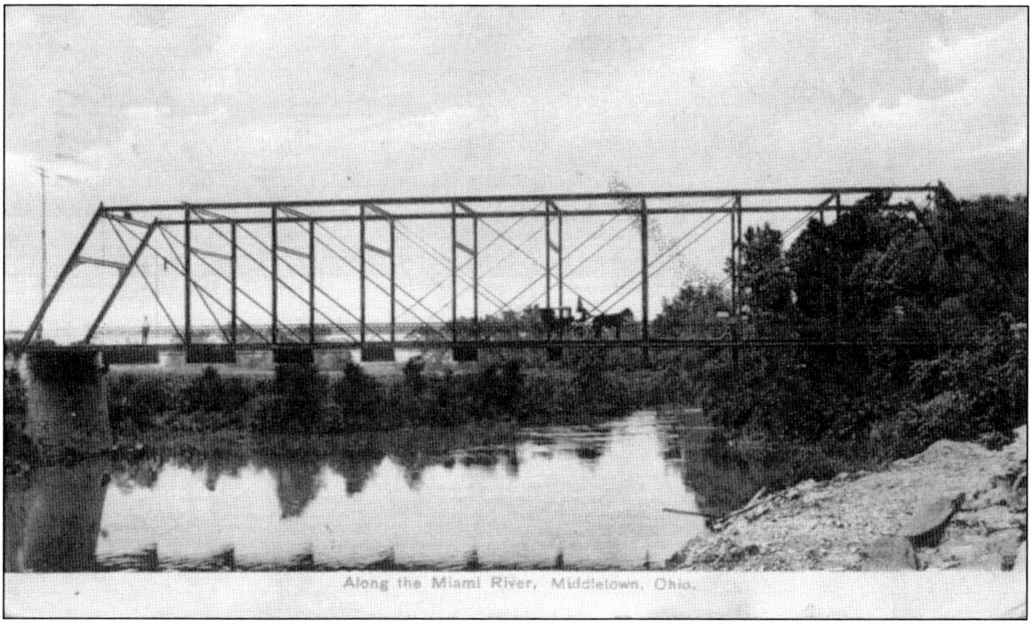

When the March 1913 flood hit the Miami River Valley, there was a bridge between Middletown and West Middletown, one north of town on the road to Poasttown and one south of town on the road to Trenton. The only one left standing was the one to Trenton.

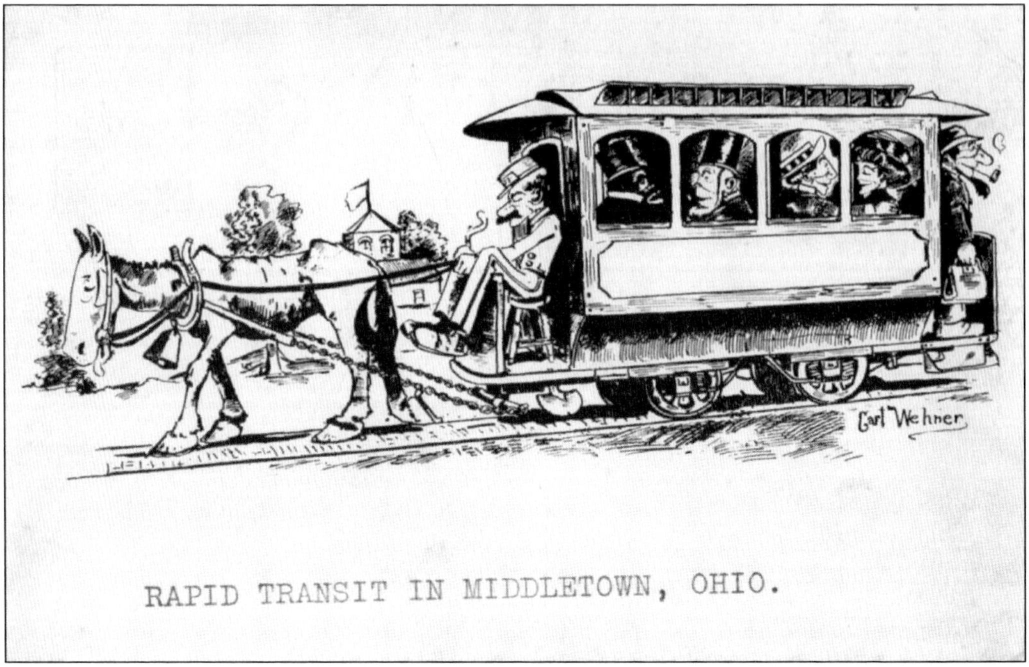

Middletown's rapid-transit service came to be a joke to other cities. The line ran east and west through downtown. Reportedly, this horsecar line was the last one to operate in the country.

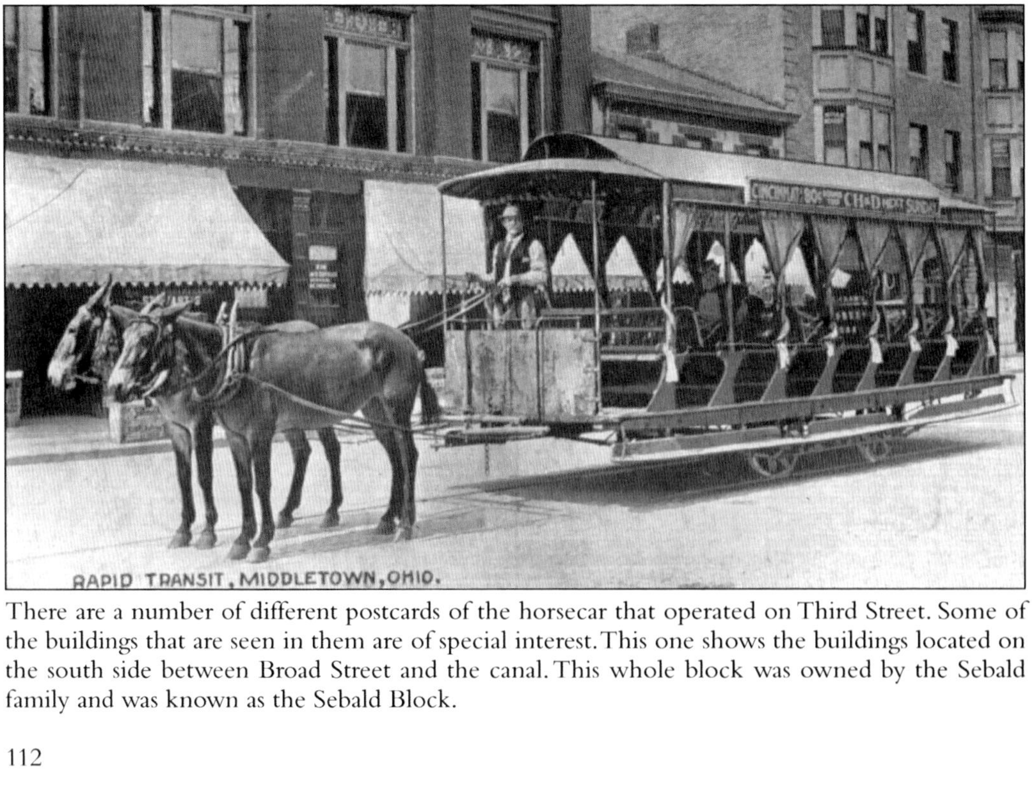

There are a number of different postcards of the horsecar that operated on Third Street. Some of the buildings that are seen in them are of special interest. This one shows the buildings located on the south side between Broad Street and the canal. This whole block was owned by the Sebald family and was known as the Sebald Block.

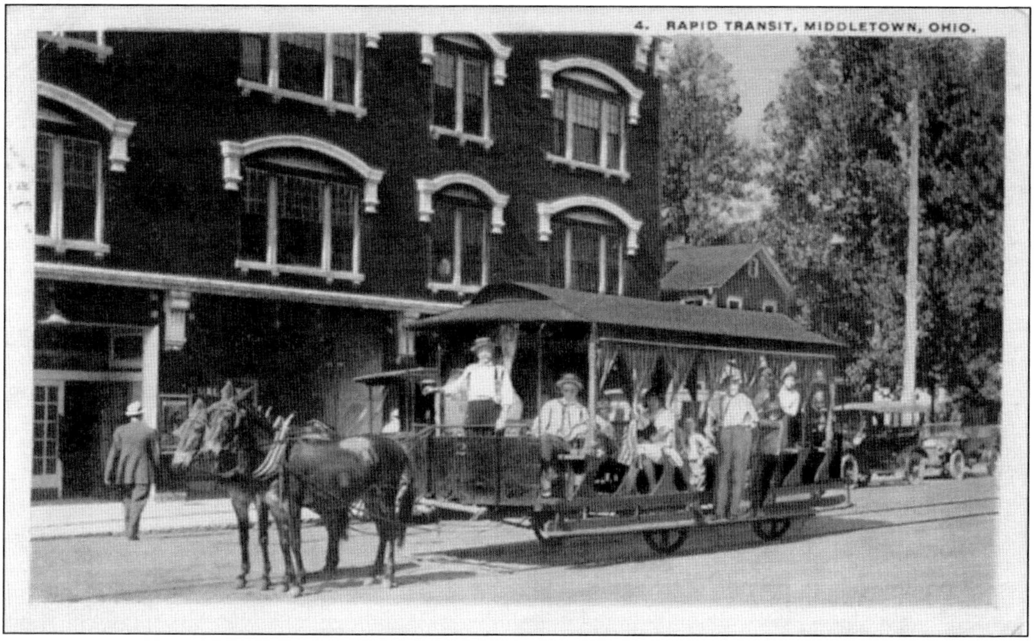

The horsecar line had a summer car, which was often pulled by mules. Mules were cheaper to operate than horses. Located at the Big Four Railroad tracks, the Bundy Apartment building is seen in the background. On the lower floor were storefronts and theaters.

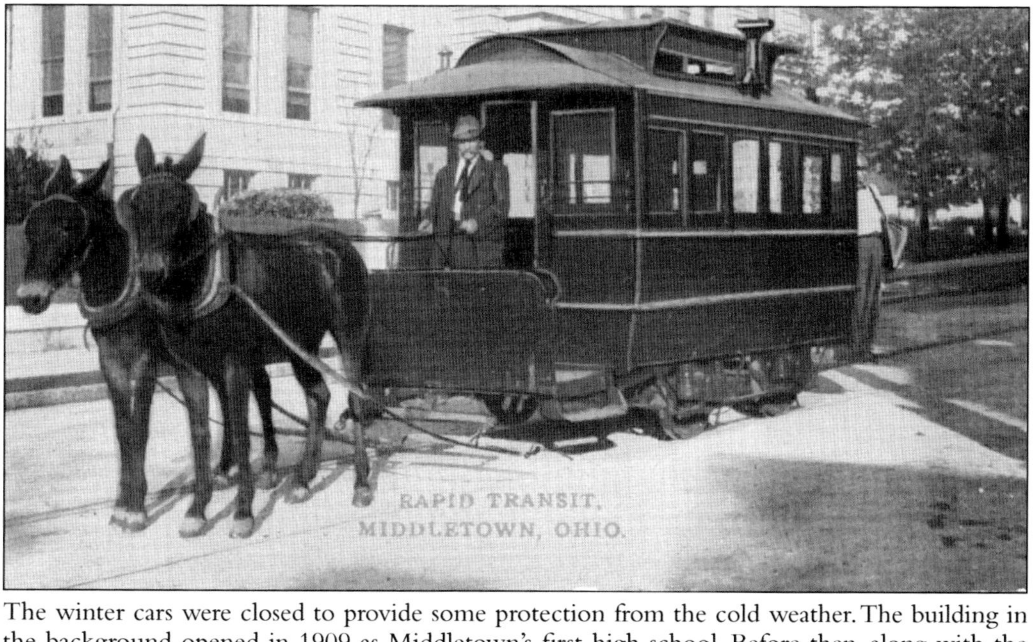

The winter cars were closed to provide some protection from the cold weather. The building in the background opened in 1909 as Middletown's first high school. Before then, along with the lower grades, the high school classes were held in South School. The building seen here later became Middletown City Building.

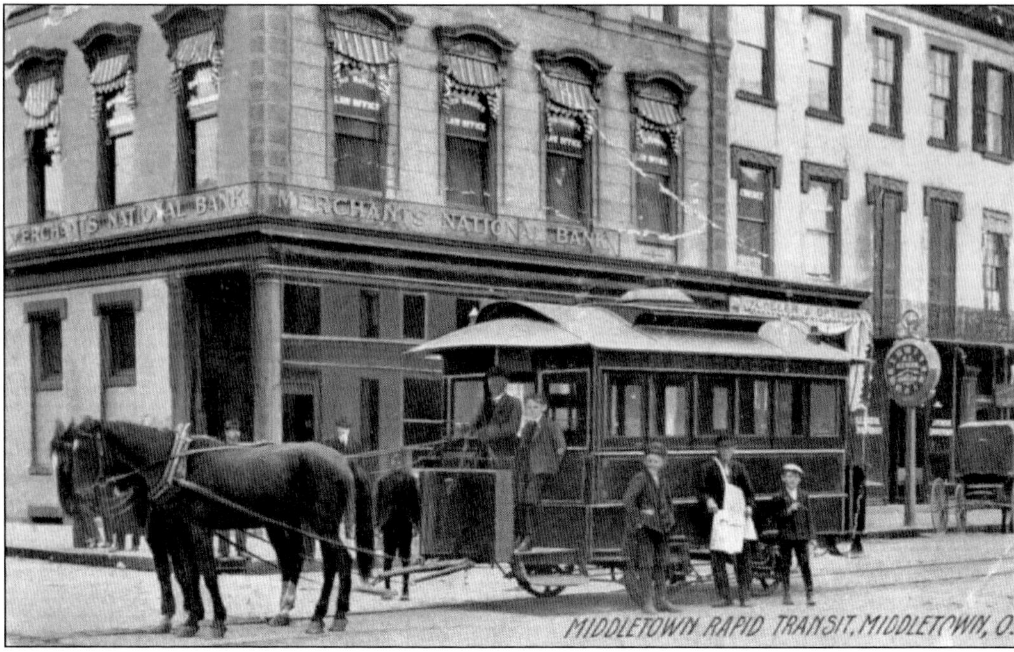

Going west, the horsecar is at the northeast corner of Third and Main Streets, the financial center of the town. Three of the corners contained banks, including this one with Merchants National Bank.

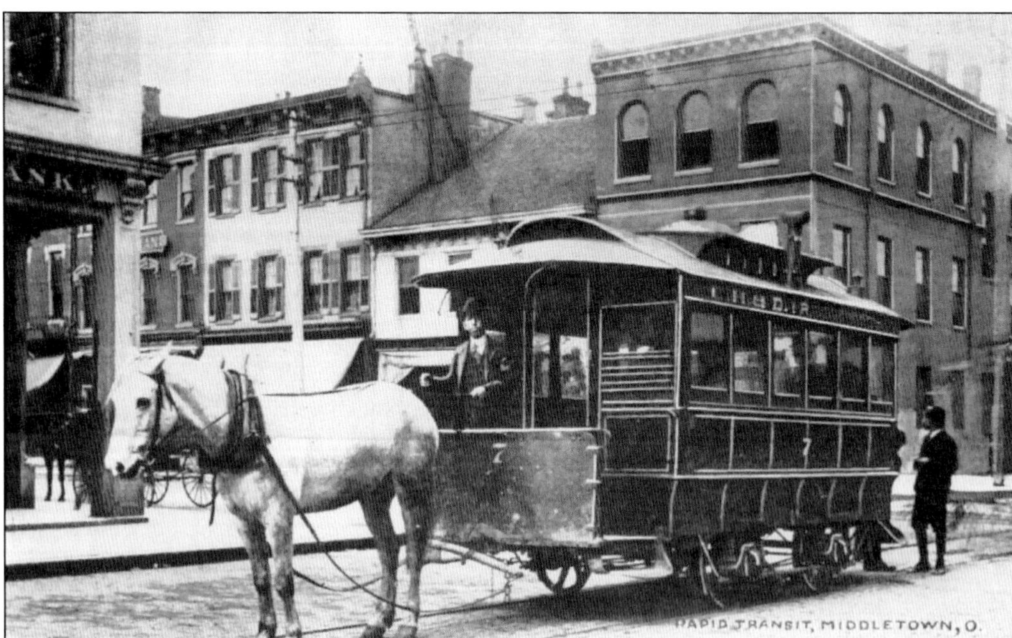

Here, the horsecar is at the same corner but going in the opposite direction. Two more banks can be seen: the First National Bank on the left corner and the Oglesby-Barnitz Bank and Trust Company on the right.

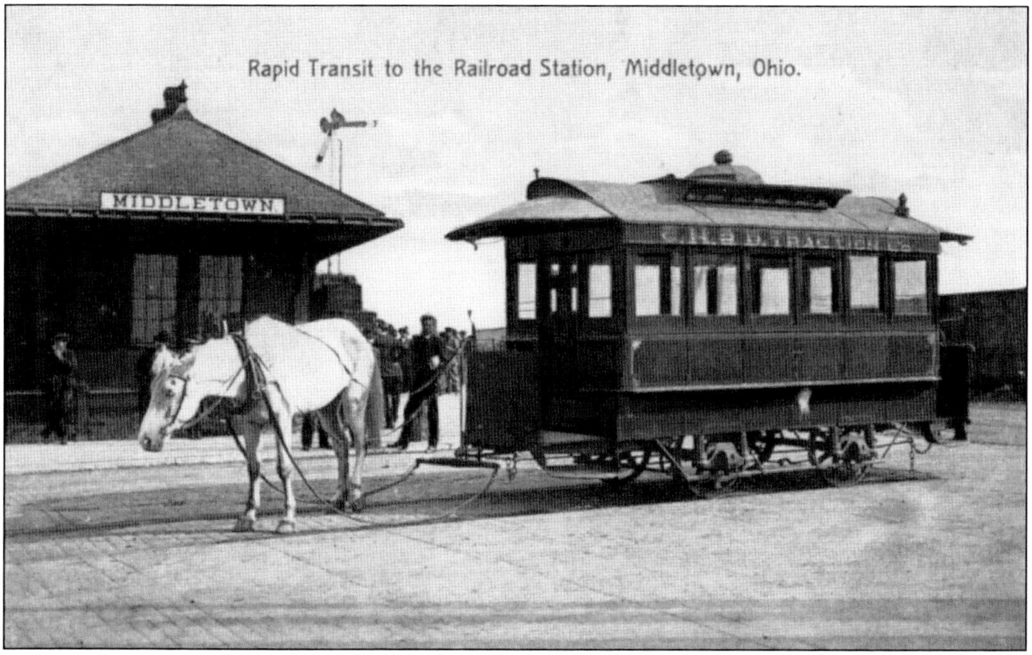

In 1851, the first railroad came up the Miami River Valley but was located across the river from Middletown. The stop was the Middletown station. When the railroad finally came to the city, it was on the east side of town. The horsecar went between the two stations.

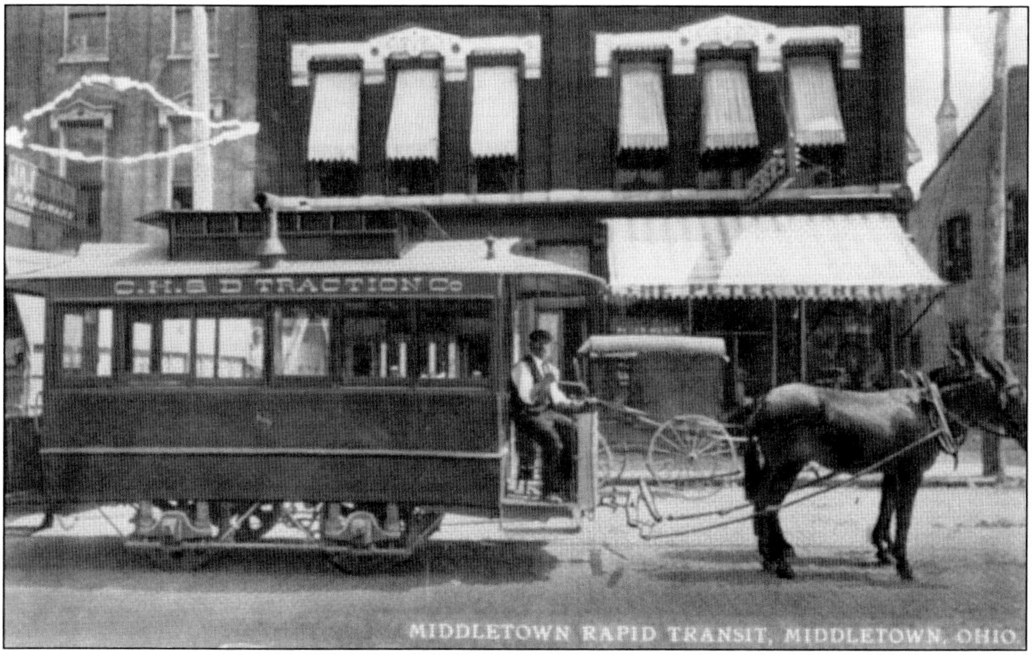

At one time, the village had its share of bars and cafés. Weber Café was one of the longest in operation. On the left is the J.A. Johnson Hardware Store.

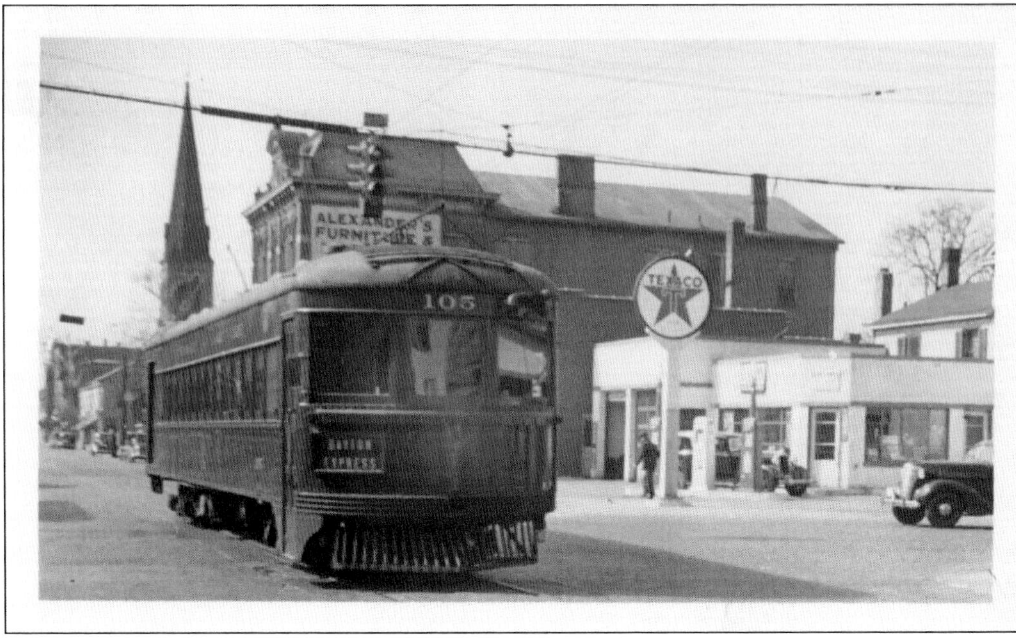

In 1897, an electric railroad line, called a traction line, came through Middletown. A later traction car is seen on Main Street in nearby Franklin. This car would have gone through Middletown on its way north. At this time, the route went from Cincinnati to Toledo, with branches going to other cities. (Courtesy of Roger L. Miller.)

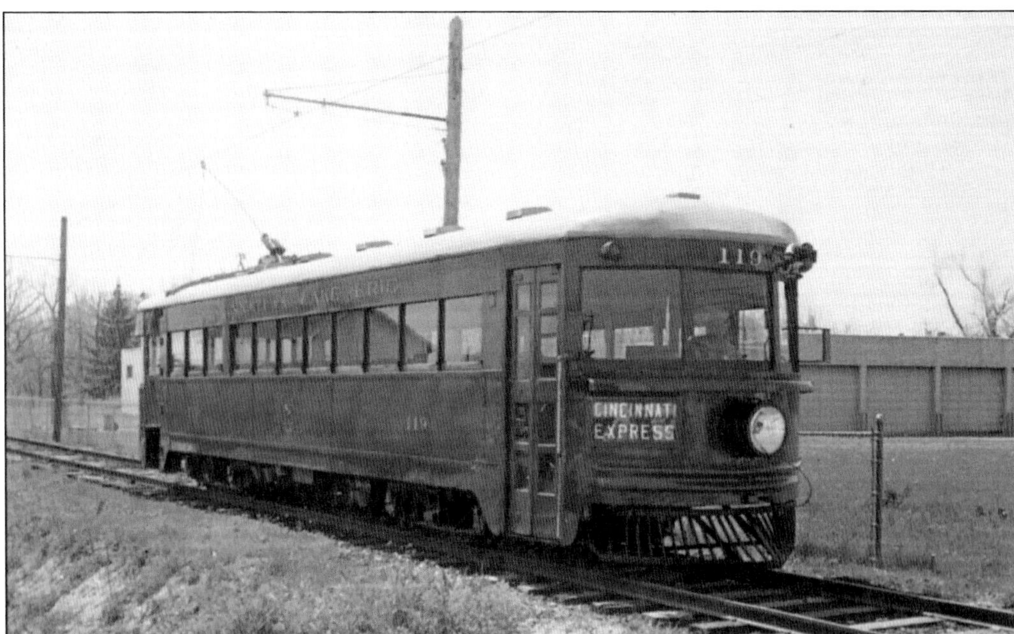

This *Red Devil* car was one of the last to operate on the traction system. In 1939, all service stopped in Middletown and was replaced with buses. (Courtesy of Roger L. Miller.)

Ten

THE LATER YEARS

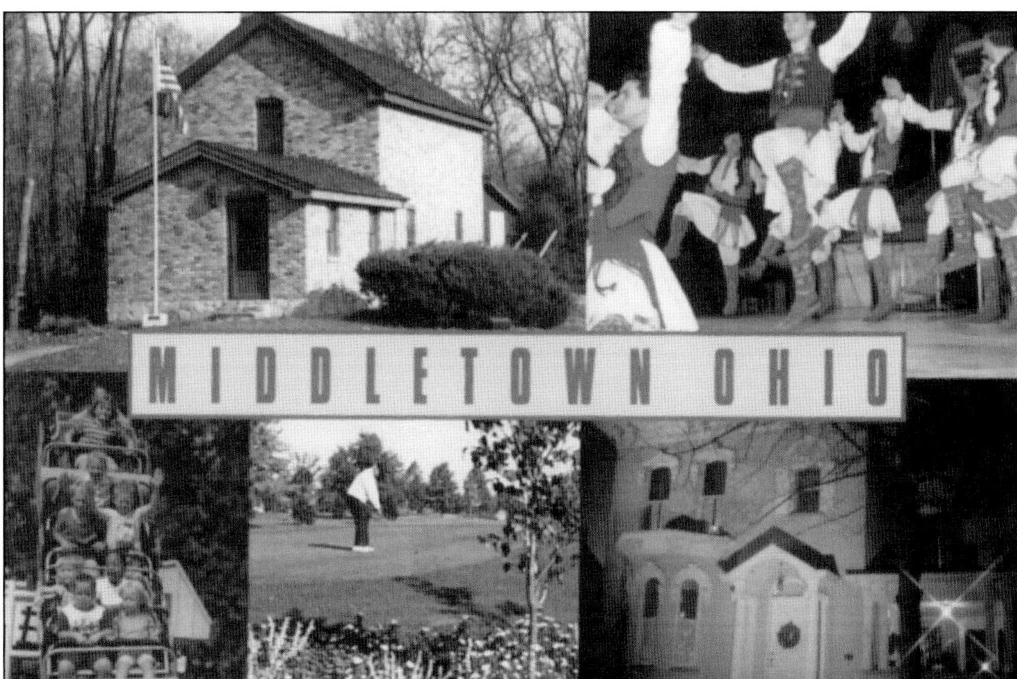

When this postcard was made, Middletown was about ready to enter the 21st century. Shown clockwise, starting at the top left, are the Canal Museum, Middfest International Celebration, historic South Main Street, Weatherwax Golf Course, and Americana Amusement Park.

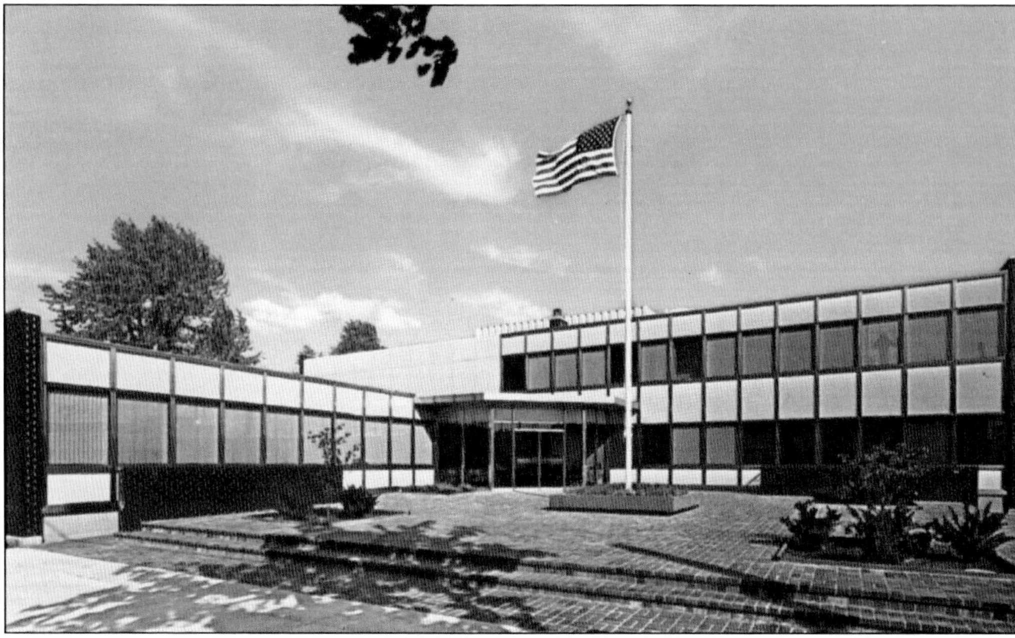

The Middletown Civic Association has been providing service to Middletown since 1923. This building was erected in 1957. Today, known as United Way, the organization assists many local civic and charitable groups. The organization has moved from this building, which is still being used. (Courtesy of Roger L. Miller.)

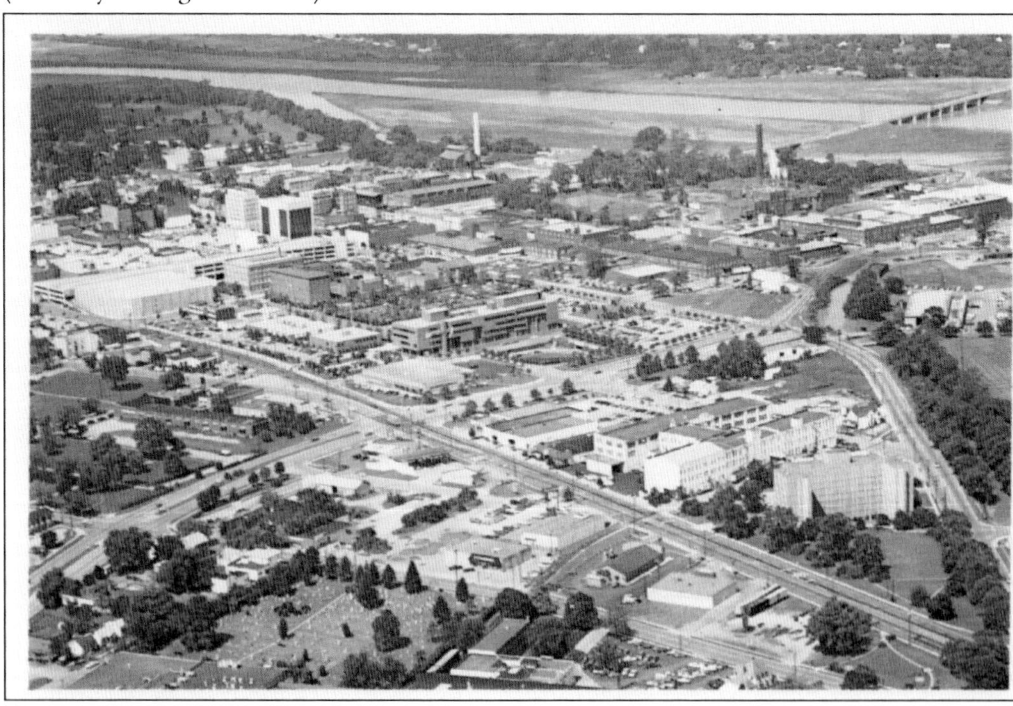

This 1974 aerial view shows much of the downtown area. The city building is in the center, while the old Sorg Paper Company comprises the buildings in the background. The older Sorg buildings are gone.

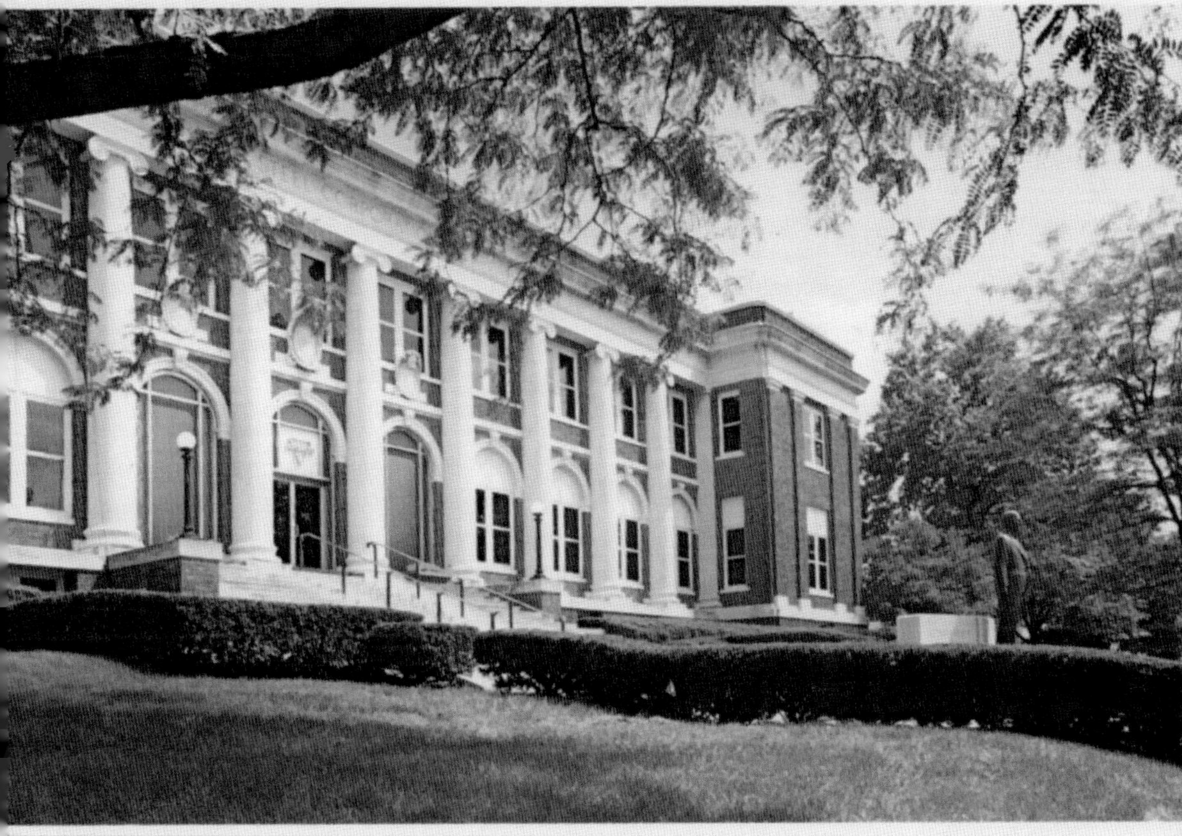

When this postcard was made, this building was the headquarters of Armco, Inc., a large multinational corporation. A statue of the founder of the company, George M. Verity, stands in front of the building. The statue has been moved to the campus of Miami University Middletown, and the general office has been torn down.

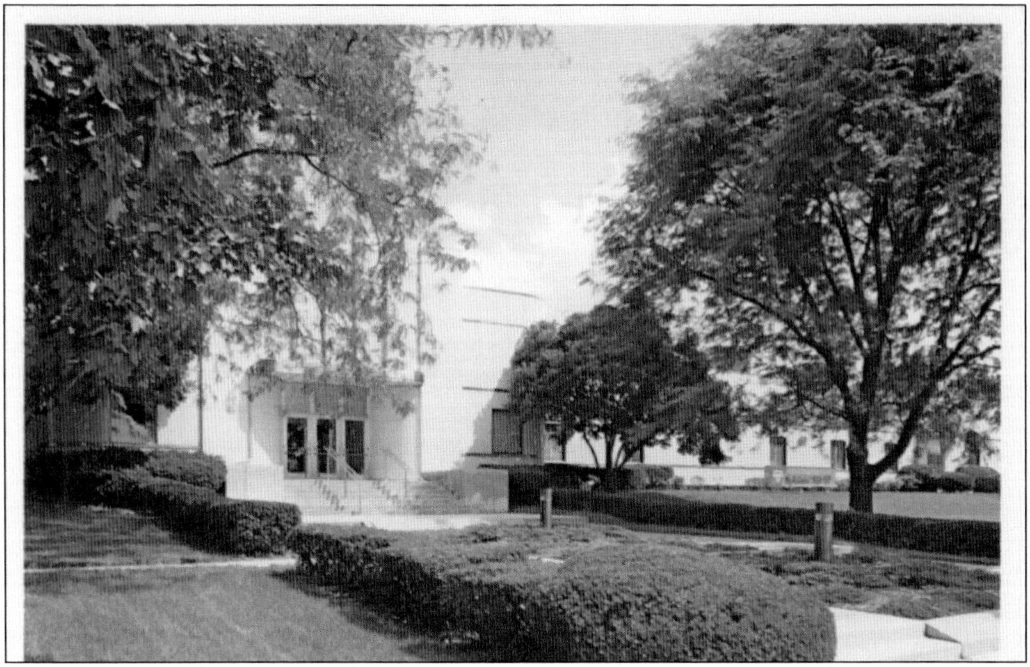

Armco always led the steel industry in research, setting up the nation's first independent research center in 1910. Constructed in 1937, this building was located next to the general office. Today, it is AK Steel's research center.

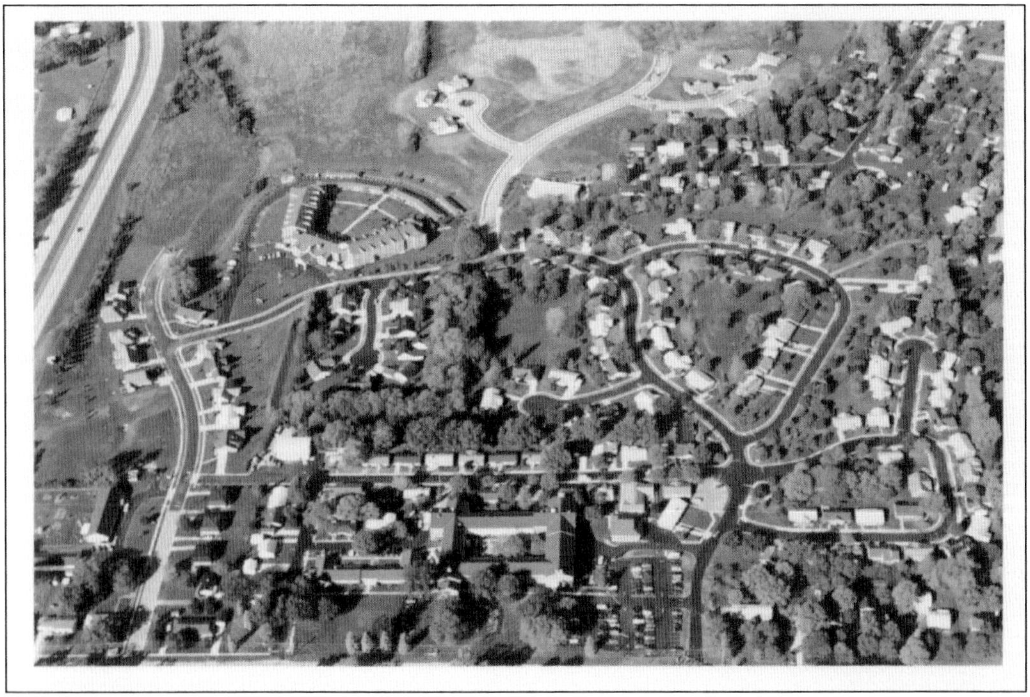

One of the authors of this book lives in a house that can be seen in this view of Mount Pleasant Retirement Community, which is in Monroe. Additional construction has been done in the area seen at the top. (Courtesy of Roger L. Miller.)

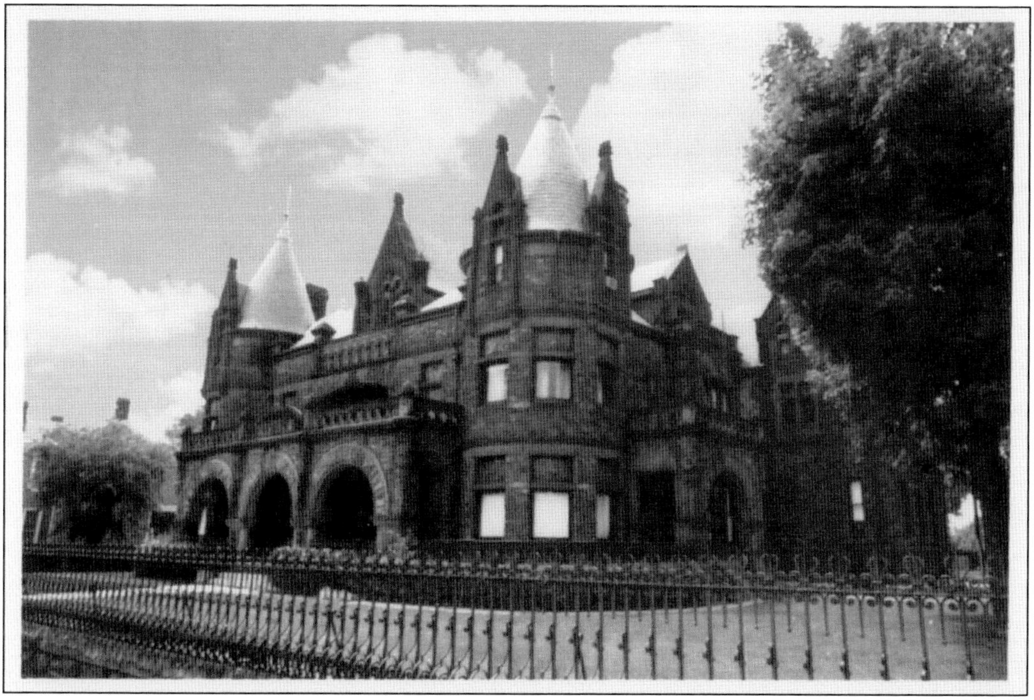

This house still dominates the South Main Street Historic District. It was erected by Paul J. Sorg, a multimillionaire who made his first money in the tobacco industry but invested in many other local businesses. Today, it is empty and up for sale.

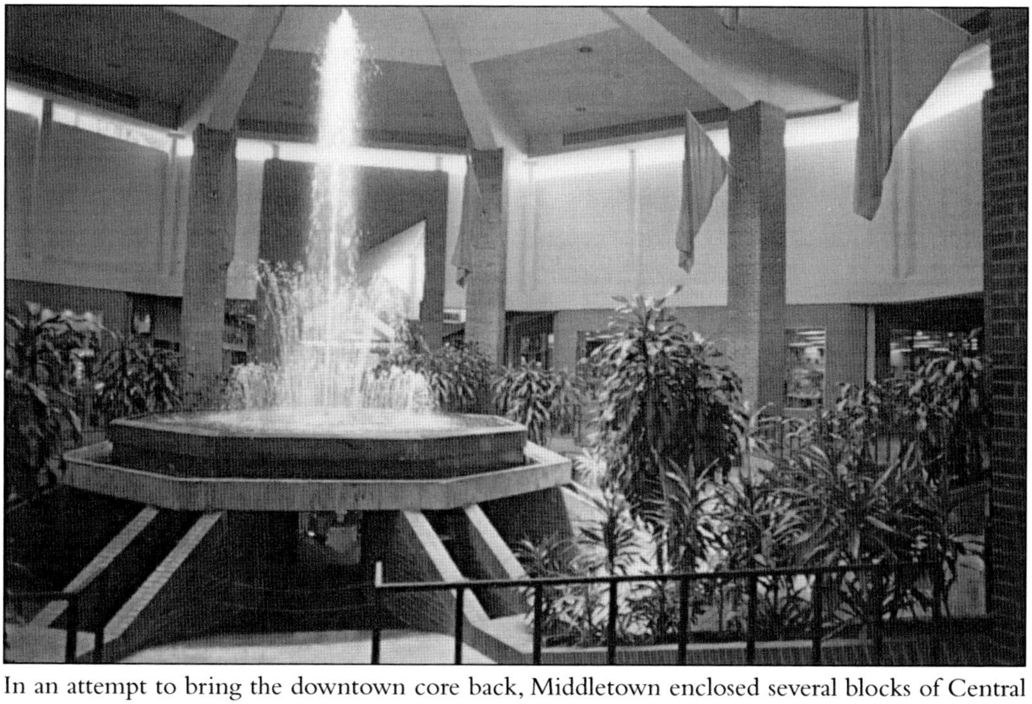

In an attempt to bring the downtown core back, Middletown enclosed several blocks of Central Avenue and Broad Street. Completed in 1974, the focal point of the City Centre Mart was this large fountain. The mart did not prove successful and has been torn down.

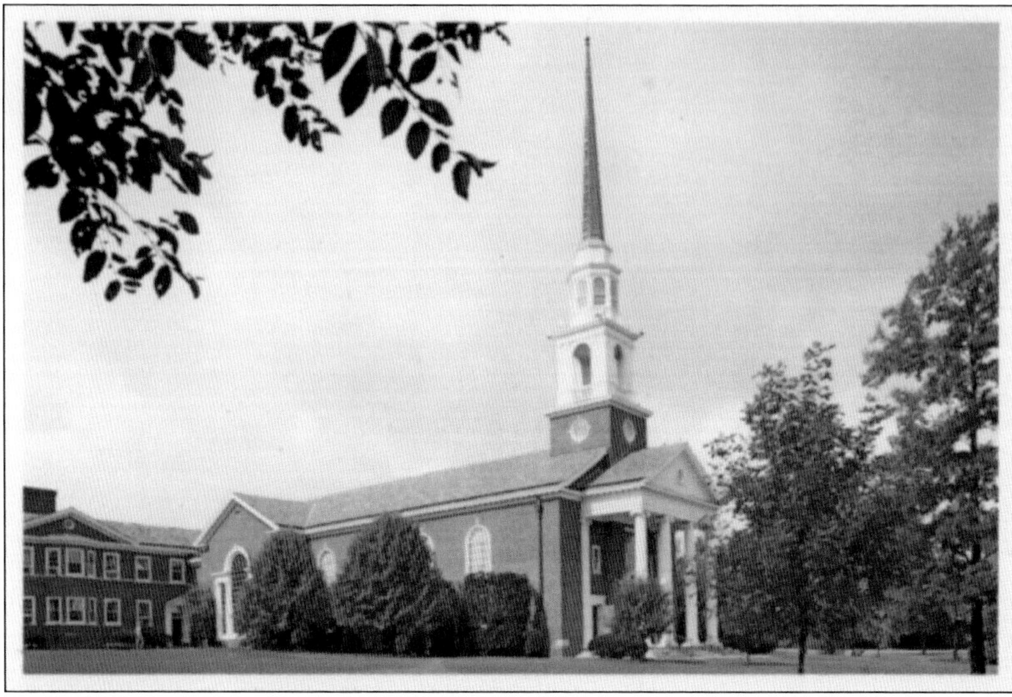

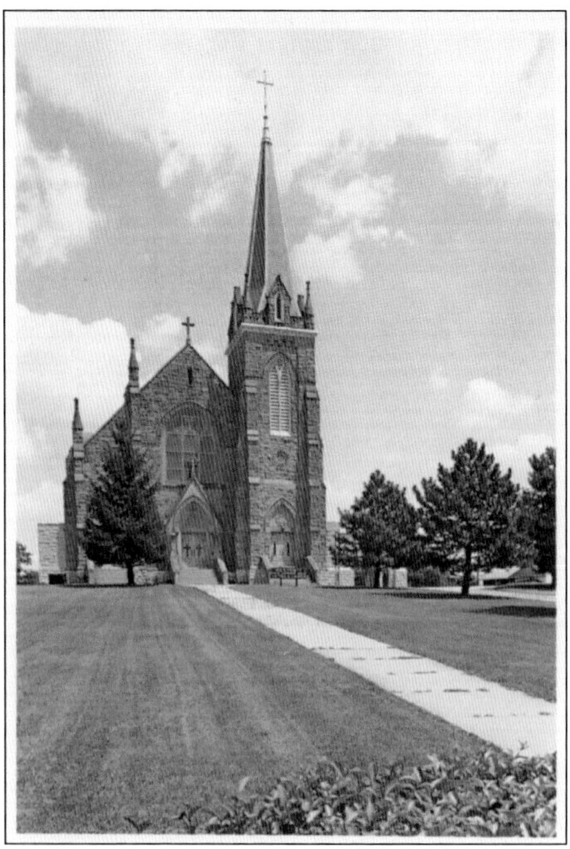

Middletown has many beautiful churches. Constructed in 1952, this is the First Presbyterian Church. Of lovely Colonial design, it is located on East Central Avenue.

Completed in 1899, this beautiful Gothic structure along Clark Street has become a landmark. It was built as Holy Trinity Catholic Church, the first Catholic congregation in Middletown. It overlooks a section of Middletown once known as Dublin, indicating the Irish ancestry of earlier settlers.

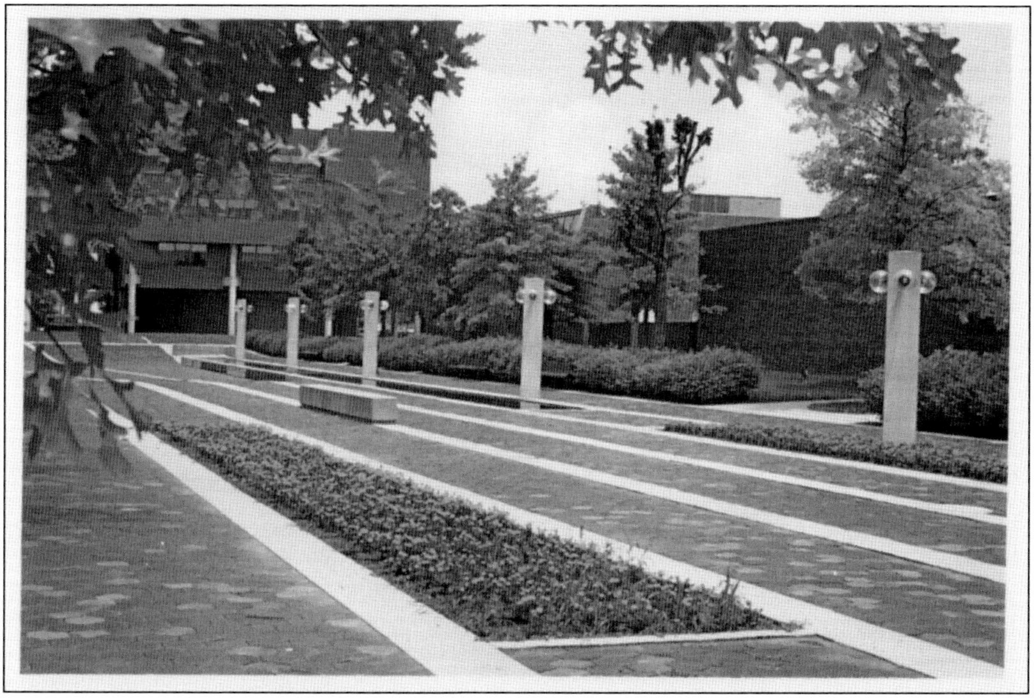

Now known as Donham Plaza, when this area was completed in 1977, it was the City Centre Plaza. The Middletown City Building anchors the plaza and serves as a center for citizens.

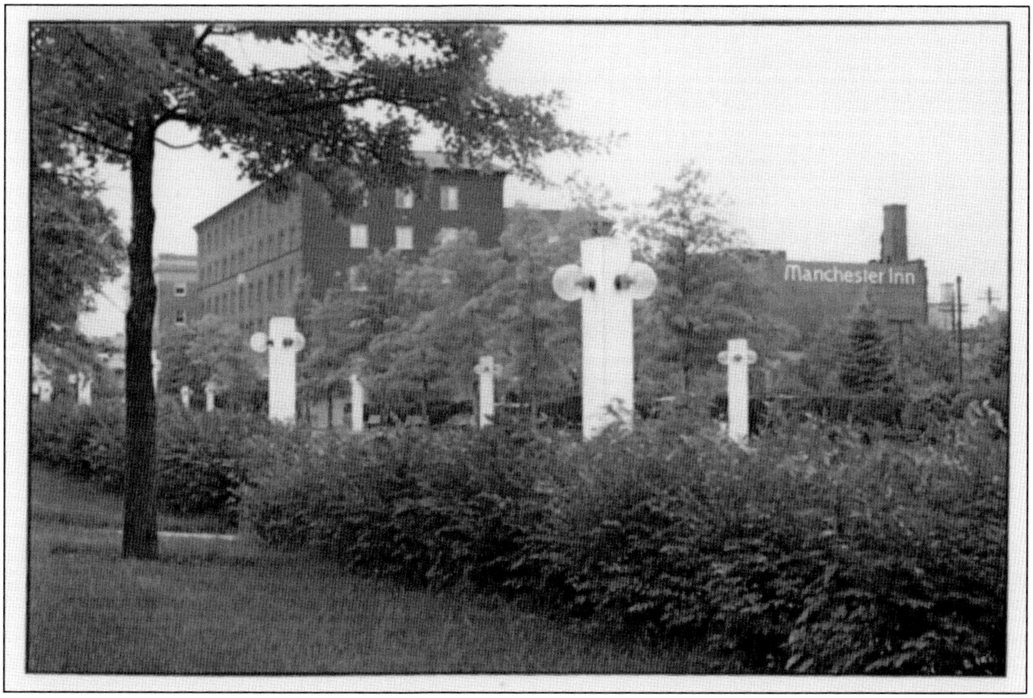

Built in 1922, the Manchester Inn was named in honor of England's duke of Manchester. It has been remodeled on several occasions and is located along Donham Plaza. It recently closed and is planned to become a branch of Cincinnati State Technical and Community College.

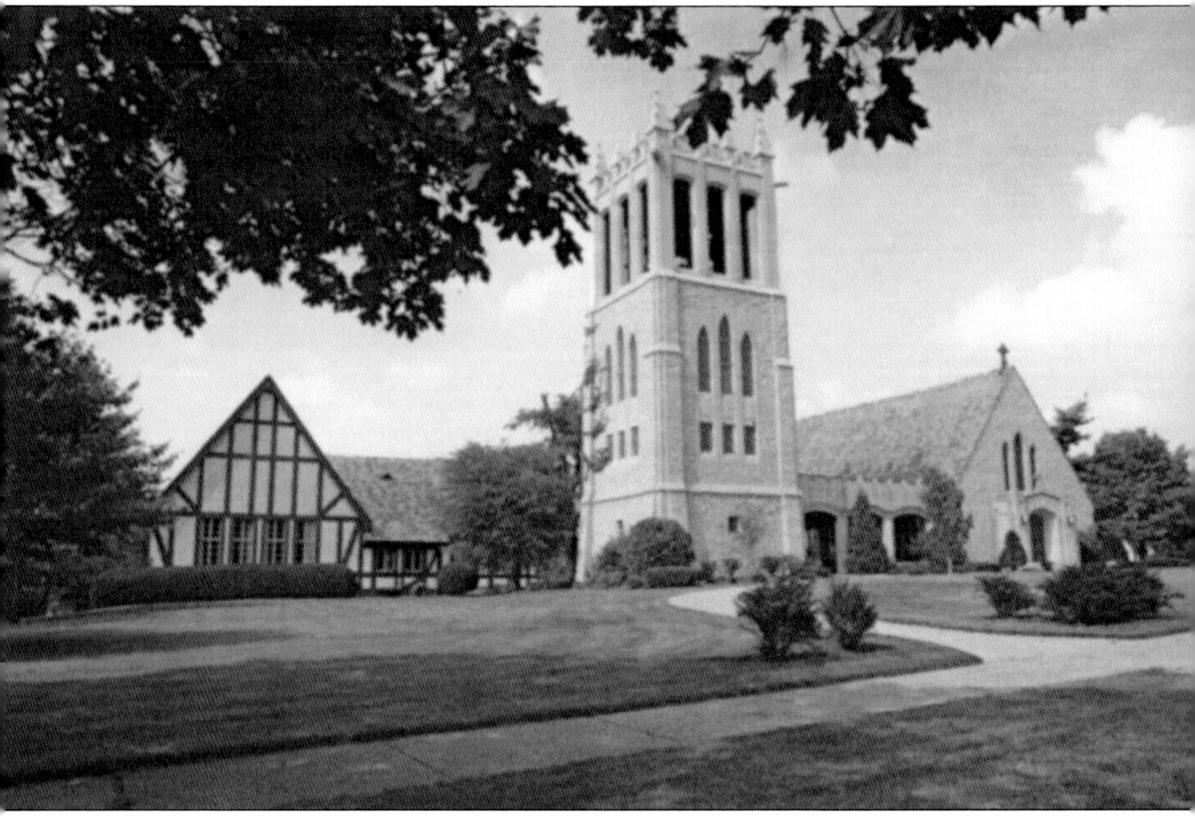

Dedicated in 1929, this beautiful English structure is home of the Episcopal Church of Ascension. Its name came about because it was founded on Ascension Day in 1868. In 1965, the bell tower was added.

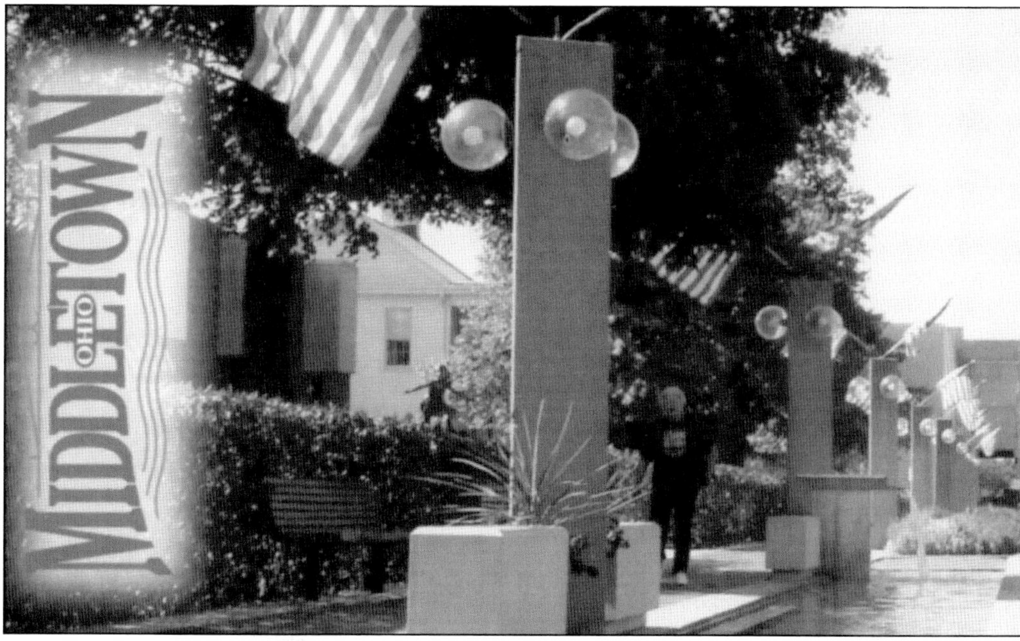

Named for longtime civic leader Bill Donham, the Donham Plaza is located downtown, next to the Middletown City Building and the Middletown Arts Center. It is the location of several yearly community events, including Middfest and the Christmas Balloon Glow. (Courtesy of Middletown Convention and Visitors Bureau.)

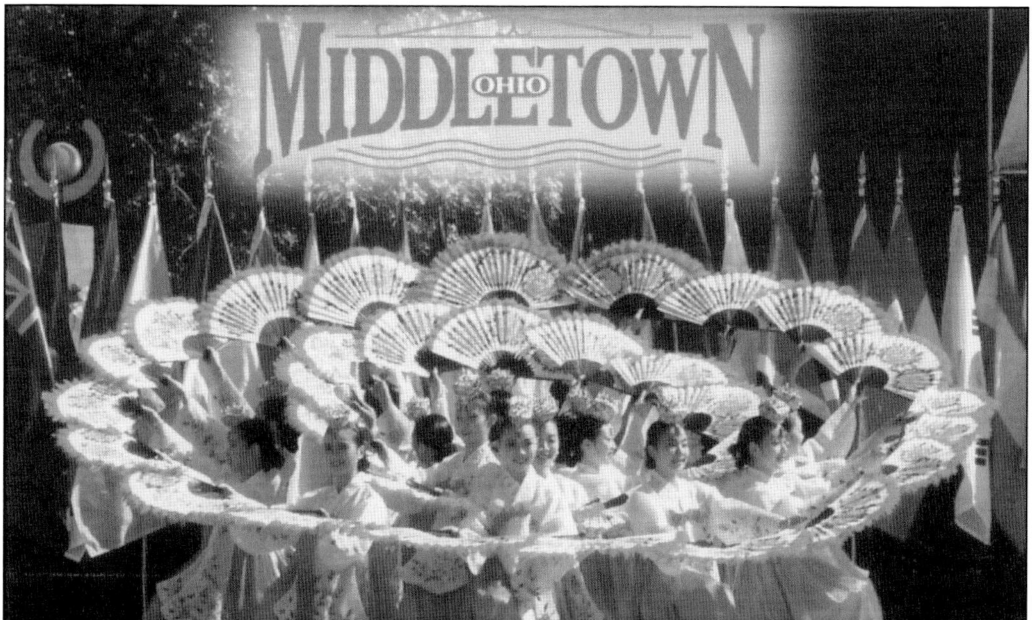

Middletown celebrates Middfest International on the first weekend in October. Each year, a different country's culture is celebrated. Activities and features include many food and craft booths, craft demonstrations, music, entertainment, and a children's area. Many of the activities are based upon the featured country. (Courtesy of Middletown Convention and Visitors Bureau.)

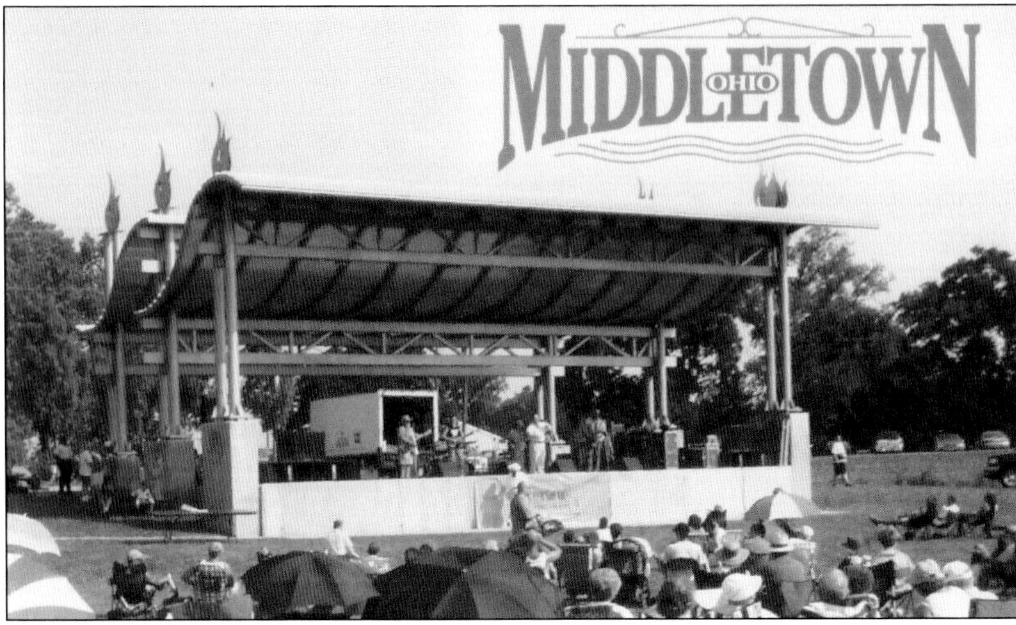

What is today's Bicentennial Commons came about as a result of the city's 200th anniversary in 1991. Features of the commons are engraved pavers that contain names of local citizens and a history timeline. The AK Steel Pavilion provides an outlet for musical performances and other activities. A paved trail along the river goes through the commons. (Courtesy of Middletown Convention and Visitors Bureau.)

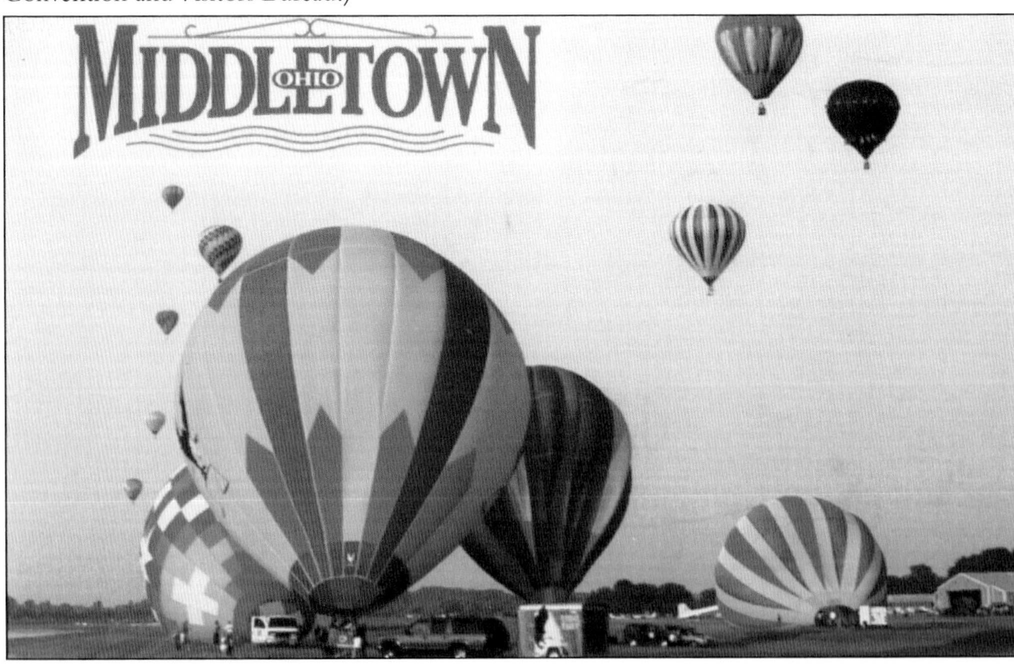

The Ohio Challenge Hot Air Balloon Festival is a yearly event held at Smith Park and the Middletown Airport. Weather permitting, balloons fly each morning and evening. Other activities include entertainment, balloon glows, arts and crafts, shopping, food, and events for children. (Courtesy of Middletown Convention and Visitors Bureau.)

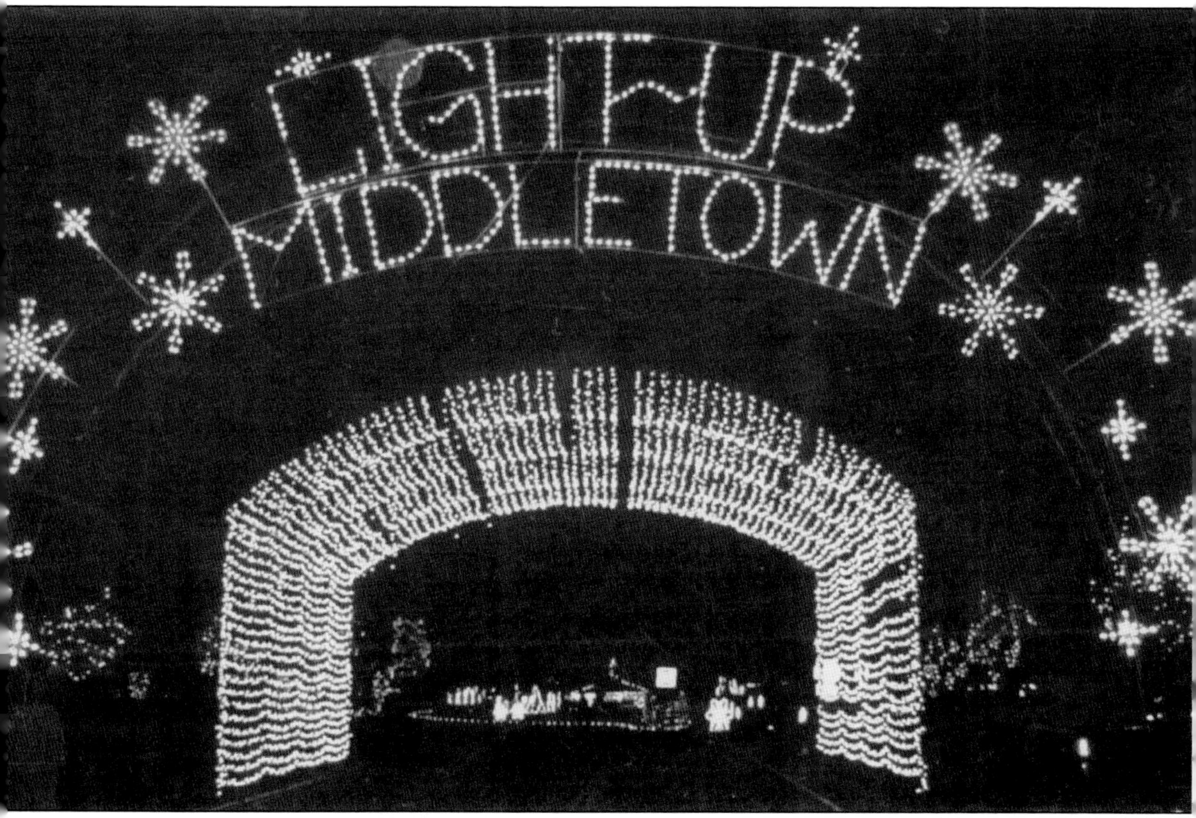

This is the end of the journey through Middletown by way of postcards. Light-Up Middletown is an annual celebration at the end of each year, but the idea of lighting up Middletown should be the collective thought for the future. (Courtesy of Middletown Convention and Visitors Bureau.)

www.arcadiapublishing.com

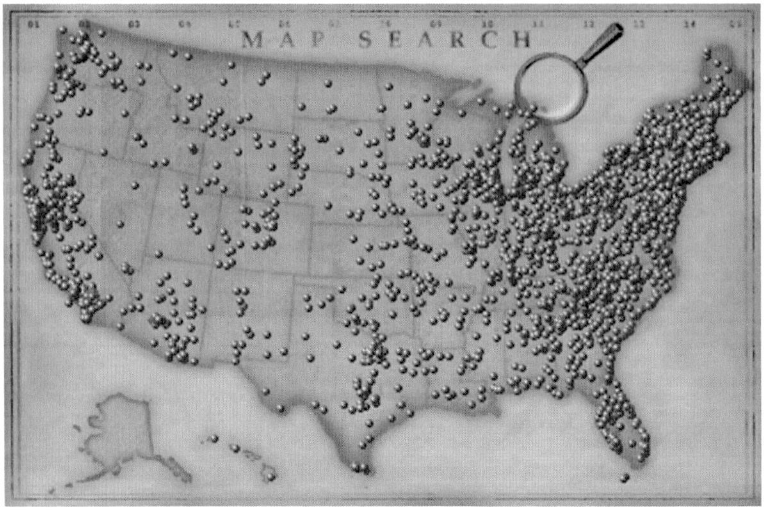

Discover books about the town where you grew up, the cities where your friends and families live, the town where your parents met, or even that retirement spot you've been dreaming about. Our Web site provides history lovers with exclusive deals, advanced notification about new titles, e-mail alerts of author events, and much more.

MADE IN THE USA

Arcadia Publishing, the leading local history publisher in the United States, is committed to making history accessible and meaningful through publishing books that celebrate and preserve the heritage of America's people and places. Consistent with our mission to preserve history on a local level, this book was printed in South Carolina on American-made paper and manufactured entirely in the United States.

This book carries the accredited Forest Stewardship Council (FSC) label and is printed on 100 percent FSC-certified paper. Products carrying the FSC label are independently certified to assure consumers that they come from forests that are managed to meet the social, economic, and ecological needs of present and future generations.

FSC
Mixed Sources
Product group from well-managed forests and other controlled sources

Cert no. SW-COC-001530
www.fsc.org

Find *Your* Place in History.